PREPARED:
READY TO ROLL

BOOK 1
WHY RESPONSIBLE PEOPLE ARE PREPARING

A Preparedness Manual By

SIG SWANSTROM

PLUS

A Novelette By

DAVID CRAWFORD

A *36*READY Preparedness Guide

Cover Photo

Lightning over Enchanted Rock State Park, located in the Texas
Hill Country near Fredericksburg. Image has not been
retouched except for segmenting and the elimination of aircraft
lights and stars which interfered with the cover text. The
exposure represents 100 seconds of intra-cloud lightning and
cloud-to-air flashes occurring in the same storm and location.

Photographer: Michael Tidwell
www.MichaelTidwellPhotography.com

LIBRARY OF CONGRESS CATALOGING IN PUBLICATION DATA
SWANSTROM, SIG
"Prepared: Ready to Roll"
Book-1 of 3 in the series of the same name
Also part of the publisher's series,
36READY Preparedness Guides
ISBN: 978-0692526682

Oxbridge Press

Oxford - Cambridge - Seattle
www.OxbridgePress.com
Copyright 2015 by SIG SWANSTROM
All rights reserved.
First Edition
+

Table of Contents

About Book-2 and -3 in this Series

PREPARED: Ready to Roll, Book-2

The focus of this book is *'what you need to know, and what you need to do, to be ready to roll'* in an evacuation (bug-out) situation. Included in Book-2 are the criteria for selecting a safe and viable retreat location, route selection for evacuation, maps, navigation, and communications. It also includes specific details on what you should include in your GO-Bag (Bug-Out Bag), and how to keep it small and lightweight.   Plus, selecting clothing and gear for your bug-out, emergency food options, methods of water purification, firearm selection, non-lethal self-defense options, and preparing for medical and dental emergencies during your evacuation. It even includes specifics on the often neglected area of essential personal records, and how to condense and encrypt them for safe transport. Publication Date: December 2015

PREPARED: Ready to Roll, Book-3

This last book in the series expands on setting-up a 'safe haven' retreat location. It includes criteria for selecting people to be part of your 'safe haven' community, as well as other vital details for successful community life. In it you will find an overview of retreat living basics, such as long-term food options, growing your own food, TransFarming and Aquaponics, do-it-yourself food storage, methods of water purification for small groups, safe storage of water, proactive medical preparations, group hygiene issues, and community health.   Often forgotten needs are also included, such as how to obtain helpful news updates during an emergency situation, along with primers which explain emergency-channel radio scanners, NOAA and S.A.M.E. multipurpose emergency radios, and the best 2-way radio communication options. It also includes information on how to help family and friends cope with an emergency situation, how to prepare for the increased violence which often accompanies it, gun selection for long-term self reliance, as well as how to address special problems such as solar storms and electromagnetic pulse (EMP) incidents. Publication Date: February 2016

Forward

My background as a police officer in the Los Angeles area during several riots and periods of social unrest, followed by serving as an international security consultant to Christian missionary organizations operating in war zones, was helpful for this writing project. However, it is the signs of the times and the looming potential for imminent disaster, combined with my personal experiences operating in post-disaster environments, which was used to goad me into writing this 3-book series. I hope you find it useful; I wrote it for you.

— — — — — — —

When my friend David Crawford sent me the following short story, I was delighted to see that it encapsulates the same riveting drama of his bestselling novel, *"Lights Out."* Frankly, I was disappointed when I was unable to convince him to turn it into a full length book. As you are about to discover, it's that good. You won't want the story to end.

I told David, "It's powerful!" "Don't' stop writing; make your novelette *'Ready to Roll'* the beginning of a full-blown novel!" But it wasn't to be. He is too busy, he explained, as he is involved with script revisions and the filming of a theatrical movie based on his novel, *'Lights Out.'*

A few months later he still felt the same way. So I asked him if I could use his story; he graciously agreed. Now that I have finished writing this book, I could not be more pleased to be able to include David's timely story, additionally so since it reminds us of the urgency we should feel toward the nonfiction 'how-to' topics which follow his fiction story.

Whether it be a naturally occurring disaster or one that is manmade, it has become increasingly likely that this generation

3

will face some sort of serious, major disaster. Therefore, thinking people need to apply renewed energy toward this subject. In this book you will find specifics on why a major disaster is likely, and what we can learn from current U.S. Government disaster preparations; measures which are quietly advancing, yet massive and unprecedented in scope.

Both the included novelette and the subsequent nonfiction chapters focus on preparing for various types of major disasters. This book includes a brief summary of the real-world problems we face, what we can expect from government, and what we need to personally do to prepare.

Diligently avoiding fear mongering as well as delusional optimism, the approach I used is hoping for the best, but getting ready for the opposite. It was written to help responsible people be responsible.

This volume series is intended to help: 1. Those who are not prepared but are thinking people; 2. Those who consider themselves prepared—but want to verify that they are *fully* prepared; and 3) For those who want a ready reference, a 'how to' and reliable 'reference guide' that covers a wide range of preparedness topics.

This first volume, Book-1, is the first in a three part series. It is designed to help you identify potential problems and to plan for evacuation, so that you can successfully escape the deadly effects of a serious natural disaster or a manmade emergency situation. It presents the case for being ready, outlines the scope of government preparations to help you formulate your own response, and walks you through what to do to make sure you are *fully* ready.

Continuing on these same themes, Book-2 covers the 'nuts and bolts' of what is needed for a successful bug-out. The series concludes with Book-3, which focuses on your bug-out destination; selecting and preparing a 'safe haven' retreat location.

By design, the format of this series makes it easy to move from one topic to another. Since each chapter is a self-contained unit, the Table of Contents of each book can be used to jump around to align with your priorities.

As you read David Crawford's "Ready to Roll (The Bug-out)," I encourage you to insert yourself into the fictional situation. This provides an important opportunity: The fiction story can be used to stimulate thinking and "What would I do?" reflection; whereas the nonfiction section can help you actually get ready.

The events and problems of the fiction story became the outline for the rest of the book, as well as the book series. It would be impossible to cover every aspect of preparedness, so I addressed the main issues which surfaced in the story, and then expanded it to include the foundational topics which are universal to any serious evacuation and relocation.

Please don't waste this opportunity. Many people talk about preparing or work around the edges of it. Yet few are physically equipped and mentally engaged. Most people are either totally unprepared or inadequately prepared. Don't fall into the trap of procrastination.

Hindsight is 20-20. After reading the fiction story, I encourage you to use the hindsight perspective to embrace your own situation and your potential bug-out problems. Honestly assess your own situation; then make notes, prioritize, and immediately begin implementation.

How can you improve your own readiness? What do you need to do to get ready for a quick, safe and successful bug-out? Don't just enjoy the fiction story, use it.

If you question whether all this is necessary, be sure to read the chapters on "Real-World vs. Normalcy Bias" and "Unprecedented Government Preparations are Underway." For most people the scope of U.S. Government preparations is startling. More to the point, these should help crystallize why we too need to get busy with our own contingency plans.

No one is 100% prepared.
We can all learn and improve.
Let's do it now, before it's too late.

Before you continue reading...

When you turn to the next page you will find David Crawford's powerful short story, 'Ready to Roll.' Amended to his story are footnotes with commentary. To avoid distractions which may ruin the story for you, I urge you...

DO NOT read the footnotes until after you have finished reading the entire story. Once you are done reading the story, then return to the beginning and read the footnotes.

As you reflect on the story, pay particular attention to the seemingly small decisions, as well as positive and negative factors which coalesced into watershed events.

In the nonfiction portion that follows David Crawford's novelette, you will find various on-topic helps and instructional materials which directly relate to themes in David's fiction story. These topics were selected to help you personally address those turning point 'bug-out' issues that all of us may face.

The fiction story illustrates the importance of the topic. The nonfiction portion focuses on identifying solutions.

Ready to Roll

By David Crawford

Author of the Bestselling Novel, 'Lights Out'

Joe woke up. An annoyingly cheerful series of beeps had roused him. He rolled over and looked at the clock. As he checked his phone, he noted that the red numbers of his alarm clock glowed 11:59 p.m. He'd been asleep less than two hours. It didn't happen often, but it still irritated him that one of his night owl friends was texting him at this hour.

The cryptic message from his friend Robert Townsend, read "Check your email." [1]

He normally slept through the night, but knew once he woke up like this, it would usually take a while before he could fall back to sleep. So he obediently got up to check his email. A message like this was unusual, doubly so as Townsend was not the type of person to send dramatic middle-of-the-night messages. As the owner of Joe's favorite coffee shop, he knew that Townsend would need to be at work in a few hours; therefore an additional oddity.

As one of an inner circle of friends, he and Townsend and a few others, had entered into an informal pact several years prior.

---

[1] Spoiler Alert: We urge you, do NOT read any of the footnotes until after you have finished reading the entire story.

Disastrous circumstances can obviously happen at any time. Therefore, make a pact with a small group of trusted friends and create a private Emergency Alert Network. To avoid bothersome use of the system, agree to only use it for developments that have the potential for imminent danger.

Since the world was becoming increasingly unstable, they had decided to immediately communicate with each other when they became aware of serious breaking news.[2]

As one who had not heard about the 9/11 terrorist attack until 3 hours after the event, Joe had welcomed this opportunity to guard against being caught unawares again. Yet, this private "emergency broadcast network" had only been utilized a couple times since he joined, so that prospect barely needled at the fringe of his consciousness.

Careful to not wake up his wife, Joe rolled out of bed and padded to the family room where the home computer was often left on. The dull hum of the fan and the clicking of the hard drive greeted him as he plopped down in the chair and switched-on the screen. As Joe logged into his personal gmail account, he started thinking about all the things he needed to accomplish today, and how he would regret this early morning email interruption.

Three messages down from the top, below two which promised "incredible sales," was the promised message from his friend Robert Townsend. The subject line read:

"FW: BREAKING RFN – TERRORIST ATTACK IMMINENT"

Joe laughed to himself. The tin-foil-hat brigade was always circulating messages like this when gas went up ten cents a gallon, or some other meaningless event happened that they somehow twisted into TEOTWAWKI [The End Of The World As We Know It]. Looking to find the name of the paranoid originator of the message, Joe was surprised to discover it was Ben Franklin. A fictitious name to be sure, but a nom de guerre he recognized.

Ben Franklin was a man that Joe admired. Though he had never met the man, he knew from his posts that he was no kook. Ben was a regular contributor to 36ReadyBlog, and was highly thought of for his insightful objectivity. Joe knew that he worked

---

[2] **Spoiler Alert: We urge you, do NOT read any of the footnotes until after you have finished reading the entire story.** // It is a huge advantage to set up an "Early Warning Network" (EWN) with a group of friends. The 'Text Messaging' feature on smart phones is ideal for implementing your private EWN. For more on this topic, read the chapter "Bug-Out Communications" in Book-2. If you have a smartphone, consider using an app such as "Group Tell" to quickly disseminate the same message to many people. Family and members of your personal evacuation group should also receive a phone call.

at a nuclear power plant, but didn't know what his exact job was. It seemed that he was one of the top men at the facility, but Ben had never been forthcoming about his title. He obviously used a false name to cloak his identity.

Joe nervously scrolled down to read the forwarded message. It read,

"I just got a call from my boss. There are confirmed reports that terrorists have bombs with nuclear material that they plan to detonate during rush hour in the morning. They found a dirty bomb in Boston about two hours ago and the guys they arrested told them there were a lot more of them. Estimates are that they are in ten or twelve major cities. It's possible that one or two of them could be full nuclear devices. Even if they are all just dirty bombs, the panic will be horrific. This is not a joke! My boss only found out because NRC called and told him to shut down the plant. If you are in a major city, get out now! The information I got is a little sketchy, but New York and DC are sure to get it. I don't know where else is going to be hit, but any big city will panic whether they get hit or not as soon as word gets out. This may not get picked up by the mainstream media for a bit, so maybe that will give us a few minutes head start to get out of town. I've got to go load up the truck. I plan to be out of here in ten minutes.[3] Good luck and God bless."

Joe's heart jumped into his throat. It was really happening. He always knew that it could, that's why he hung around in the survival forums and regularly scanned the alternative news websites. He just never expected that it would be this soon. He had first become interested in survival in 1999. He had stockpiled food and supplies for Y2K, but it had not happened. Since then his level of preparedness had fallen off some, but he still had a lot of things put back. He jumped up and ran into his bedroom.

"Linda, wake up. Wake up!"

"What?" his wife of twenty years moaned. "What do you want?"

---

[3] **Spoiler Alert: We urge you, do *NOT* read any of the footnotes until after you have finished reading the entire story**. // If you are prepared you will be ready to roll in 10-15 minutes. Practice loading up and time yourself. If you can't be on the road within fifteen minutes you need to make changes.

"We've got to get out of here! There are going to be some terrorist attacks and we've got to get out of the city!" he yelled.

"What are you talking about?" Linda asked while propping herself up on an elbow. "Did you have a nightmare?"

"I wish," he replied somewhat sarcastically. "No, this is for real. There are dirty bombs in several major cities. There could even be one here."

"How do you know?" she asked.

Joe quickly explained about the email message, and why he believed Ben Franklin.

"Maybe it's a joke," Linda suggested. "Maybe someone hacked his password and they're pulling a bad prank." She reached onto the nightstand and found the TV remote. She hit power and then tuned to CNN.

"He said it might not be on the news yet," Joe explained.

"It has to be if it's true," she answered quickly.

The talking head was droning on about the 40-point increase in the NASDAQ yesterday and how it signaled that the bulls were back in control.

"Think about it," he reasoned with her, "if the government told everyone, they would just panic. They're going to keep it under their hat as long as they can. Ben would not kid about something like this. We've got to get loaded and head to your parents' place," Joe said loudly.

"What if it's a joke or a mistake? We'll look like idiots to the neighbors and at our jobs."

"Who cares what people think? What if it's true?" Joe was almost screaming now.

Linda bristled. "Look Joe, you're being paranoid. CNN would know if something was going on and they would tell us about it." "Your friend," she said the last word with contempt as she folded her arms, "is wrong." [4]

---

[4] In regard to preparedness, rarely are both a husband and wife equally engaged. Yet, as typical as it is for one spouse to be more proactive, it's not enough for only one to be engaged.

"What are you guys screaming about?" Melissa, Joe and Linda's fourteen-year-old daughter asked from the door of their bedroom while rubbing her eyes.

"Your father is going off the deep end," Linda said.

As was too often the case, this would end up being a girls-against-the-boys argument, Joe thought. He took a deep breath and tried to calm down. "Look, maybe it is a mistake and maybe it's not. But, I'd rather be safe than sorry. Wouldn't you? We can go to your parents' house and if nothing happens by seven thirty we can all call in sick or something. We don't have to tell anyone anything."

Linda stared at him for several seconds while what he said sunk in.

"Alright," she said reluctantly, "but I'm not driving all the way up there and back and then cooking dinner tonight. When we get back, you're going for take-out or something."

"Okay," Joe agreed.

Linda threw back the covers and stood up. She looked at Melissa and spoke. "Go get dressed. But first, wake up your brother."

"Okay, Mom," the teenager answered. She turned and headed down the hall toward her brothers room. She opened the door and called his name.

"Andy. Andy, wake up! We're going to Grandma's and Grandpa's house."

Andy, seventeen and a slow riser, opened one eye and looked at his sister.

"Leave me alone. It's Wednesday, you dope. We have school in..." He looked at his clock, "...five hours? What are you waking me up for?"

"Mom told me to. Dad thinks the sky is falling or something and he wants to go to the farm."

If your spouse is unaware or unconcerned, ask them to read the chapters, "Real World vs. Normalcy Bias," and "Unprecedented Government Preparations are Underway." Better yet, read these chapters to them and then talk about it. Remember, preparedness isn't just about stockpiling supplies; it's about being physically and mentally ready. In each family and group of friends, all adults and teens need to be *ready*.

"Yeah, right!" Andy said as he pulled the covers over his head.

"Andy, get up now. Get dressed. I need your help," Joe said as he passed his son's room, threading a belt through his jeans.

Joe walked to the kitchen and tried to gather his thoughts. His in-laws lived 150 miles away in a remote rural area. Although they called their place a farm, it was only twenty acres. Originally, the house and barn had been the headquarters for a large family farm, but once the old farmer died, his kids had divided the place up and sold it off. Linda's parents had bought the farmhouse and the few acres that surrounded it when they had retired. The larger tracts had been sold or leased to local farmers that used them for crops or hay.[5]

All right, take care of the basics first, he thought. Water, food, and shelter are the most basic. For water there is the well at the farm. And, my generator will work the electric pump even if the power goes out. I just need to make sure we have enough gas to last for a while.[6]

So, we're okay for water. What about food, he thought as he opened the pantry. The shelves were almost bare.[7]

"Linda," he called, "is this all the food we have?"

Linda scurried into the kitchen looking flustered. "I was going to go to the store today," she said defensively.

---

[5] **Spoiler Alert: We urge you, do NOT read any of the footnotes until after you have finished reading the entire story.** // It's not enough to be prepared to flee "*from*" an unsafe location; we need to have a suitable place to evacuate "*to*" if we are to be safe. A location such as Joe's in-laws farm is important. For more about selecting a bug-out destination, read the chapter, *"Escape "From" vs. Escape "To"* in Book-2.

[6] The storage of fuel is dangerous if not done properly. For more on this topic, in the Appendix of Book-2, read *"Gas/Fuel Transport and Storage."*

[7] The 'just-in-time' approach to stocking the shelves of our grocery stores has trickled down to consumers. Few families have more than a few days of food in their panty. We need to get beyond this mentality and maintain at least 2-3 weeks of food at home. If this stockpile consists of the types of food normally eaten, it is a simple task to rotate the reserve supply to keep it fresh.

If you choose to remain at home rather than evacuate, it may not be important to have more than a two week supply of food. If grocery stores haven't reopened within a couple of weeks, hungry neighbors and gangs of thieves will be forcing their way into homes looking for food. Even if the homeowner is well armed, it will likely be impossible to remain secure in such an environment. This is one of the reasons that a 'safe haven' retreat is important.

"Where is all the food we had put back for Y2K?"

"We ate most of it. Some of it got so old that I threw it out. But you have that freeze-dried camping food and those MER's or whatever they're called."

"That's not enough. I only have two cases of MRE's. That's just six meals apiece. There might be enough of the Mountain House food to last a week or so, but what if we need to help out your parents or your brother's family? We had enough food put back to feed 10 people for three months and now we don't have anything."

"Well, after the millennium, you told me to use it up," she shot back.

"I told you to use it and replace it," he said pleadingly. "That way the food would be fresh."

"If that's what you wanted done then you should have done it. It was a pain in the ass to go through all those totes of food."

Joe realized that the argument was just wasting time. It didn't matter whose fault it was. They just had to fix it.

"You're right. I'm sorry," he said trying to calm her down.

Linda was surprised. He usually would have argued longer, even though she would have still won. She saw how scared he looked. Maybe there was more to this. Joe certainly thought so. Her hands fell from her hips as she began to feel bad that she had disappointed him. Not that she could admit it to him, but her tone softened significantly. "What can we do?"

"We have to get some more food. Look, I'm going to send you and Andy to the store. Buy as much dry and canned food as you can. Fill up the back of your SUV if you can. Melissa and I will stay here and load the truck." [8]

---

[8] Shopping when you should be bugging-out is a Catch-22 situation. If you don't have food and supplies, you will certainly need to get some. Yet, every minute of delay can literally be deadly. If you do find yourself in this lamentable situation, make a short list of items that are compact and lightweight—food that is mostly product not water, as is the case with most canned goods. Dry goods such as beans and rice may be uninteresting to eat but are high in protein and carbohydrates. Set a time limit for your shopping. For example, you might set a limit of 10-minutes in the store. Get in, and get out quick. Get on the road.

"It's almost three in the morning. The grocery store isn't open."

"But the Super Wal-Mart is," Joe said. "I know I don't like us going there, but that's our only option at this point." [9]

"Can't we just wait and see if your Internet buddy is right and buy food from the store close to my parent's place if we need it?"

"I'm afraid that if there is a big panic, the stores will get stripped quickly, even where your parents live."

"Well, how do you want me to pay?"

"Write a check."

"But, we don't have that much in the bank," she objected. "You don't get paid until Friday." [10]

"Look, we'll worry about that if nothing happens. Right now we just need to get what we have to have and get out of here. I want to save whatever credit we have on the cards for gas and other stuff. Do you think you could be back in thirty minutes?"

"We'll try. Come on, Andy, let's get going. I hope I don't see anyone I know without my makeup on."

Linda snatched up her purse and the mother and son were out the door.

"Alright, that takes care of food. Next is shelter," Joe said to no one. He looked at his daughter and smiled. "Grandma and Grandpa have plenty of room for all of us. Even for Uncle Larry and his kids. I better tell your Mom to call him."

Joe grabbed his cell phone and hit the speed dial for Linda's phone.

"Hello," she answered.

---

[9] If practical, leave home and begin your bug out; stop at a store that is along your evacuation route.

[10] If finances are tight, it may be difficult, but build-up a supply of cash to use in an emergency situation. If you can write a check, do it. If that doesn't work, use a credit card. Understand, if there are electrical power or banking problems, you will only be able to use cash. For your stash, small bills are best, mainly 10 and 20 dollar bills, as you may not be able to get change. When you are bugging-out, keep your cash in an under-clothing waist pouch. Out of sight, remove what you need before you approach the cash register, and put that cash in a front pocket. Keep the rest concealed.

"Hey, it's me. You think you should call Larry and your folks?"

"I don't think so. At least not yet. Remember how crazy Larry thought you were for buying all the Y2K stuff? He still makes fun of you. And, there is no sense waking Mom and Dad since they don't need to do anything. If it hits the news then I'll call Larry, okay?"

"Whatever you think," he said

"Okay, Bye."

"Bye," he said and hung up the phone.

"Alright," he said to Melissa, "the next priority is clothes and personal items. Let's get our GO-Bags." He knew that defense was really next on the list, but he needed to get Melissa on something. Besides, he thought, getting my guns out of the safe and into the car will be easy. I'll do that last. [11]

Joe walked to the hall closet with his daughter in tow. He opened the door and a ton of junk fell out around his feet.

"Damn it! I've told your brother a million times not to stuff things in here and then close the door."

He reached down and picked up the bag of golf clubs and kicked some of the smaller items out of the way.

"Here, set these in the corner for me, will you?"

"Sure, Dad," Melissa answered as she took the bag from her father.

Joe got down on his knees and started digging through the closet that was a catch all for his family. He pulled out three daypacks and then kept digging.

"I can't find your brother's GO-Bag."

---

[11] If your local government allows it, you should have a concealed handgun license. When it's time to bug-out, immediately arm yourself. Once the word gets out about the emergency, things may get dicey, so put on a waist holster and carry a concealed handgun as a first step in getting ready to bug-out. Put your other guns and ammo into your vehicle last, so that they will be more accessible.

"I think he emptied it and used the knapsack a couple of months ago, when he went camping with his friends," Melissa explained. [12]

"Great, these are supposed to be ready to go all the time," Joe spewed.

"Give me mine, Dad. I think I need to put some stuff back in it."

Joe handed his daughter her pack and gave her the look. It told her that he wasn't happy without him saying a word. She disappeared into her room and Joe could hear the dresser drawers opening and closing. He noticed that Linda's pack looked a little empty as well. He opened it and found that it only held a ratty pair of jeans and a couple of shirts with a few odds and ends.

Back when Joe had made everyone pack a GO-Bag, they had held enough clothes and toiletries to last at least three days. It seemed that everyone had raided their bag when they needed something and had not replenished them.

He opened his and found it was in pretty good shape. There was no underwear in it, Linda must have taken them out to replace some of his old ones, and his toothpaste had leaked. Fortunately, it was in a Ziploc bag so it didn't get on anything else.

"Melissa," he called.

"Yes, Dad." She answered, sticking her head out of her door.

"Hurry and finish repacking your GO-Bag. Then see if you can find your brother's and make sure he has enough clothes and stuff in it. You need to repack your mom's after that. I'll put it on our bed. Also, turn on the TV and listen to it. If they start talking about an attack, come get me right away. Don't let it slow you down, though."

"Okay, Pops."

---

[12] This knapsack is for emergency use, only. Your GO-Bag must always remain intact; don't ever 'borrow' things from it. If you seal your GO-Bag in a paper lawn-waste sack and store it the trunk of your vehicle, you are more likely to keep it complete, and it is with you when you need it. (A heavy-duty paper sack will keep your GO-Bag clean, but unlike a plastic sack it will not hold-in mold causing moisture.)

Joe grabbed his bag and took it to the bedroom. He threw the busted toothpaste away and got three pair of underwear out of his drawer and stuffed them in the pack. He wondered if they should take more clothes. [13]

"Melissa."

"I'm in here."

He found her in her brother's room, digging through his closet.

Listen, when you're finished with the bug out bags, come out to the garage and get a big duffle bag from me. I want you to get some more clothes for all of us and get all the stuff you can out of the bathroom closet, too. Got it?" [14]

"Yeah, Dad, I got it," she said as she nodded her head.

Okay, what's next, he asked himself.[15]   I better get the camping stuff in case the power does go out for a while. He headed out to the garage. At least this is organized, he thought as he looked at everything stacked neatly on shelves. He walked over and started pulling things down that he thought he might need and stacking them in the middle of the garage floor. He also grabbed the generator out from under his workbench and put it next to the pile.

---

[13] A GO-Bag is primarily for emergency food, water storage and purification supplies, and essential gear. In advance, it is best for one responsible adult to pack all the GO-Bags, equipping them with nearly identical gear. (Having the same gear makes training and practice simpler.) If desired, individual family members can add more gear to their GO-Bag knapsack. However, it is usually best to pack nonessential items in a separate bag. Remember, extra clothing is relatively unimportant in comparison to water, food, personal safety tools, medical kit, basic shelter and navigation aids. Durable, functional clothing should be stored in a separate bag and donned before bugging-out. This isn't a vacation.

[14] Don't waste time gathering unnecessary supplies. For packing, use soft sided bags as they can be compacted into available space better than luggage. Keep in mind, too, that if you end up walking, a duffle with shoulder straps, or a backpack, is much easier to carry than other types of bags. Wheeled bags or suitcases are not a good alternative. It is extremely fatiguing to roll a wheeled suitcase over uneven ground.

[15] Have a list of what you need to grab last minute, and keep this list with your GO-Bag. You will run out of space in your vehicle before you run out of things you'd like to bring. Make these decisions in advance.

What about gasoline, he thought.[16] He looked in the corner and saw two five-gallon cans. He picked them up. One was almost empty and he had no idea how old the gas was in the other. He could pour it out and refill them both on the way out of town, but ten gallons would not last long if they really needed the generator. He called Linda's phone.

"Hey, have Andy run over to the automotive department and get me six five-gallon gas cans, okay?"

"Alright," she answered.

"How much have you got done?"

"Not much, we just got here a minute ago."

"Does it seem like anyone knows anything?" he asked.

"No. The place is dead as a doornail."

"Good. Hurry as fast as you can, okay."

"I know!" she said.

He could almost see her rolling her eyes at him. "Okay, thanks," he said as he hung up.

"Your father wants you to go get six gas cans for him."

"Do you want me to go now?" Andy asked.

"No. Let's get the groceries first."

They each had a cart and were pushing them up and down each isle. Linda would point at things and tell Andy how many to get and he would load them onto the carts. When one of the carts was full, she told him to park it where it was and go get another. When all three carts were full, top and bottom, she decided that it was enough.

"Go grab one more cart and run over to automotive and get the gas cans. Make sure they are five-gallon."

"Yes, ma'am."

Andy took off to the front of the store and Linda tried to move two of the baskets at a time by pushing one and pulling the other. She could barely budge them. She gave up on the one she was trying to pull and concentrated on pushing just one. It was so heavy that she even had trouble getting it going. When she got it

---

[16] You need to bring with you enough fuel to get to your destination. In the appendix of Book-2, you will find more on *"Gas/Fuel Transport and Storage."*

20

to the main isle she went back for the other basket. She pushed it about halfway to the front where they had left the first full basket. She went back for the second basket and was pushing it when her phone rang again. It was Joe.

"What!" she answered.

"I'm sorry," Joe said, "but I need some propane for the Coleman stove and the lantern. Have Andy get about ten of the one-pound bottles. They should be in sporting goods."

"Alright. We're almost done here."

"Good. See you in a few minutes."

Joe looked at his watch. It said 2:40 a.m. He had hoped to be on the road by now, but as long as they got out before 4:00 a.m. they should be okay. Everything seemed to take longer than it should.[17] He wondered why Melissa had not come to get the duffle bag. He grabbed the duffle and walked into Andy's room where he found her looking at the TV while she was lazily stuffing clothes into his pack."

"Melissa!" he shouted. "I told you not to get distracted by the TV. You should have had that done fifteen minutes ago."

Melissa was very sensitive to being yelled at, especially by her father. Tears began to well up in her eyes. "But, Dad, I just found Andy's pack a few minutes ago. It was stuffed under his bed," she cried.

"Okay. I'm sorry I yelled. We just need to be ready to go by the time your mom and brother get home. You should have just gotten a trash bag or something when you couldn't find his pack right away."

"Okay, Dad," she said, sniffing and wiping an eye.

"Here's the duffle. Anything on the TV yet?"

"Not yet."

---

[17] Conduct a dry run now, to see what fits in your vehicle and how long it takes to pull everything together and get it loaded. In advance, set a time limit for everything that needs to be accomplished last minute. Store as much gear as possible in the same part of your home, so it's already in one place when it is time to load up. Don't rely on your memory; use a list or loading chart. A pre-loaded trailer may be ideal, but creating a simple chart to identify what goes where, can help you load your vehicle more quickly.

"Okay, Hon, let me know if you hear anything and try to go a little quicker, all right?" he pleaded.

"No problem."

Joe went back to the garage and pulled down some more camping stuff. That should do it. He spotted his chain saw and decided to take it too. If they had to stay until winter, a long shot he knew, but it was already fall, they could use it to cut firewood for the fireplaces. He put it and its accessories in the growing pile. He looked at it and couldn't think of anything else they might need. He opened the garage door to start loading his truck. He decided to back it in to make the job easier. Just as he was unlocking the door, Melissa called him.

"Dad, Dad, it's on TV," she yelled.

He rushed back into the garage and pulled the door down.[18] When he got in, he heard the TV in his room. He ran down and saw Melissa working on her mother's bag. She was quickly packing the bag from a pile of clothes on the bed. Her face looked older than it should have, Joe thought. He turned his attention to the television.

"…authorities to the highest level of alert. The Department of Homeland Security believes that the device found in Boston is the only one and that the terrorist are trying to cause a panic by alluding to others. However, the president has placed the military and FEMA on high alert and experts are searching other sites that might have a high probability of being a target. Authorities are urging all Americans to stay calm and stay in their homes. FEMA suggests that no one venture out until we have definitive word on where any other devices, if they even exist, might be. Moving from where you are might just put you in harms way. Authorities inform us that a dirty bomb is not immediately dangerous to anyone except in the small blast radius. It would take days of close exposure to absorb a lethal dose of radiation. If evacuation

---

[18] From this point forward, extra security precautions are critically important. Fear can transform an ordinarily honest person into a thief, or even provoke them to violent crime such as armed robbery. Similarly, those who are usually safe drivers may start driving erratically once panic overrides their common sense. Accidents caused by running red lights and other unsafe driving practices will be commonplace, so drive defensively. Be aware of your surroundings. Expect erratic behavior and irrational violence.

is needed, authorities will let the public know in plenty of time for a safe and controlled withdrawal from any dangerous area."

'Again, three men were arrested early this morning in Boston trying to plant a dirty bomb across the street from City Hall. A dirty bomb is an explosive device that has been laced with nuclear material. The arrest came about as the result of..."

Joe hit the mute button on the remote. He looked at the time. It was 3:30. He wondered where Linda and Andy were.

Linda had pushed her three carts, using her one at a time method, almost to the check out by the time Andy showed up with the gas cans. He helped her push all four carts into the only checkout line that was open and then ran back to get the propane. The cashier looked like she was only awake enough to be annoyed at the four basketfuls that she would have to scan and bag. Halfway through the second basket, Linda's phone rang.

"What," she said, irritated. She and Andy had been working feverously, and it seemed like just a few minutes had passed since Joe's last call.[19]

Joe was oblivious to her exasperation. "Is anything going on there? It just hit the TV."

Andy, who had needed to search for the location of the propane canisters, saw his mother go pale. She shook almost imperceptivity and her lips became tight. She didn't say anything.

"Mom, is that Dad?" Andy asked nonchalantly. "I need to talk to him."

Linda, wide eyed, handed the phone to her son.

"Dad, hey, we're checking out now." He paused. "No, everything is alright." There was another pause. "Yes, I understand. We will. Bye."

Andy hit the disconnect button and looked at the time on the display. He handed the phone back to his mother. "Dad says that we are behind schedule." He saw the clerk raise her eyebrows at what he said. "And, you know Dad. He always wants to leave at the crack of dawn."

---

[19] Activity expands to the time available. If you fail to set a time limit for each block of activity, your efforts will likely consume an excessive amount of time.

The clerk smiled and Andy wondered if her dad was really one of those crack of dawn dads. He knew that his wasn't. A minute later, a tall, thin, prematurely balding young man came up to the register. His nametag said 'Barry'. Linda assumed that it was the night manager.

"Kathy, we're closing in five minutes," he said.

"Why, Barry?"

Barry gave her a story about corporate calling and saying that the computers were going down for some unscheduled emergency maintenance. He announced over the intercom that the store had to close because of a computer problem and that all shoppers should bring their purchases to the checkouts. He also called all cashiers to report to their registers.

Linda had begun to compose herself and she figured that the computer problem story was just a cover that the manager had made up or was told to use in case of an emergency. The cashier finally finished scanning the merchandise and gave Linda a total. Linda wrote the check, knowing that there wasn't enough money in the account if their mortgage payment had cleared. She hoped she could get to the bank before this check cleared, and wondered if it would even make a difference. She and Andy loaded the carts back up with the bagged merchandise and pushed them toward the door. When they got there, two security guards were standing there with the keys hanging from the lock. The older man smiled weakly and reached to unlock the door.

"Could one of you help us with these?" she asked.

The two men looked at each other and the older one nodded once to the younger man. He grabbed a cart each from Linda and Andy and headed out the door as the other guard held it open.

It only took a few minutes to load the back of her Chevy Suburban with the bags. The guard shoved the four empty baskets together and pushed them toward the entrance. Linda noticed that there were quite a few cars rushing into the parking lot as she climbed behind the wheel. She started the vehicle and pulled out. As she drove by the store entrance, she saw several people banging on the door that she had just exited and a couple of them were yelling obscenities at the guards.[20]

She pulled back onto the street and saw that there was a significant amount of traffic for this time of night. Everyone seemed to be obeying the traffic laws except for maybe bending the speed limit a little. She found herself doing about ten miles an hour over as well. She pulled out her cell phone and handed it to Andy.

"Call your Uncle Larry," she instructed. "I think it's number seven on the speed dial."

Andy did as he was told. A minute later he spoke. "Uh, Uncle Larry, it's me, Andy." There was a brief pause. "Here, I think I better let my Mom tell you." He handed the phone back to his mother.

"Larry, hi. Listen, turn on CNN, there's some kind of terrorist attack going to take place."

"Where, when?" Larry asked groggily.

"I don't know. But Joe has us leaving for Mom and Dad's. Andy and I just left from the Wal-Mart with a bunch of groceries and stuff and they closed the store as we were leaving."

"Okay, I have the news on. Oh my God. I don't believe it," Larry said as he tried to catch his breath. "We'll meet you at Mom and Dad's, all right?"

"All right," Linda agreed.

"And Linda, tell Joe that I said he was right."

"I will," she said, not needing him to say about what. "I'll see you in a few hours."

"Thanks, Sis."

The line went dead as she pulled into their driveway. Joe was outside making some kind of weird gyrations with his hands. Linda rolled down the window.

---

[20] Many stores will close at the first hint of an emergency situation. They may reopen later, but since large chain stores such as Wal-Mart have been repeatedly victimized by flash mobs of looters, they often close until they are sure the situation is stable. If you encounter closed stores, drive to a small, independent (privately owned) 'mom 'n pop' store as these might still be open for business. Move quickly, but drive cautiously. If you find an open convenience store don't feel bad about buying everything you can, nor about the cost of the merchandise. This probably isn't the time to be cost conscious.

"What?" she asked.

"Back it in," her husband answered.

Linda backed the car out of the driveway and then backed it next to Joe's truck. Joe opened the back hatch. He pulled out the gas cans and placed them next to his truck. Linda and Andy came around to the back of the SUV.

"What do you want me to do?" she asked.

"Go inside and see if Melissa has all the GO-Bags and other supplies ready to go. Have her bring them out here and you see if we need to bring anything else with us." [21]

Linda went toward the house and Joe turned to Andy.

"Get a couple of those empty totes and start stacking these bags of groceries into them. Then we'll start loading the rest of the stuff."

"Okay, Dad," Andy answered as he walked into the garage.

Joe finished packing the rest of the gear he had assembled into the back of his truck. Then he placed the two old gas cans right next to the tailgate, followed by the six new ones. That done, he turned to his gun safe.

He opened the safe and pulled out all twenty-one of his firearms. He put most of them into rifle cases or pistol rugs and put them into the extended cab of his pickup. He kept four rifles and four handguns out. One of each, for each of them. He loaded the handguns from the ammo on his ammo shelf. Next, he loaded several magazines for each of the rifles. He had more magazines, but not more ammo. He had been meaning to buy more, but just never seemed to get around to it. Hopefully, he could find a gun store close to his in-law's house and buy or trade for some if they needed it. The little extra that was left for his

---

[21] Plastic bins and cardboard boxes waste a lot of space in a vehicle. If you need to divide up your supplies for travel on foot, medium size duffels with shoulder straps are easier to carry than boxes. If you find that you need to leave things behind but hope to return for them in the future, foliage-color bags are easier to hide. Waterproof bags are expensive, but they can provide added protection if you decide to bury some of your supplies. If the location of your stash might be forgotten or picked up later by a friend or family member, draw a diagram to help identify where your supplies are hidden.

other guns he put inside the truck. He put Linda's and Andy's guns in the SUV and his and Melissa's went into the truck.[22]

The girls brought out the GO-BAGs and the big duffle bag with the extra cloths. Linda also had another medium size bag that she handed to Joe.

"Here's everything else that I can think of," she said.

Joe nodded and loaded all six bags into the SUV, almost filling it to capacity. He looked at his watch. It read 4:32 a.m. Joe couldn't believe it. It had taken them over four hours to get ready to go. He looked up and down the street. There were a couple of houses with activity, but it looked like most of his neighbors were still unaware. If he had known any of them well, he would have knocked on their doors and told them. He really only knew the names of three or four of them. Even though they were more than an hour behind when Joe had wanted to leave, they were still ahead of 95% of the population if his neighborhood was any indication.

"Andy, you ride with your mother," he said. "Melissa, you're with me in the truck. Everyone has a rifle and a handgun. I don't think we'll need them, but just in case, I want to be ready if we run into any trouble. How much gas do you have in the SUV, Linda?"[23]

---

[22] It would have been much better if most of these guns were stored at their bug-out destination. Absent this foresight, you probably don't need a large number of guns. Firearms and ammunition are heavy and bulky to transport, so only bring what you will need.

When bugging-out by vehicle, each trained adult will ideally have a pistol which is carried in a holster and worn concealed, as well as an assault rifle or tactical shotgun, as these may be needed for more serious self-defense situations. These weapons should be kept out of view, but close at hand in case they are suddenly needed. Plus, each vehicle will ideally be equipped with one or two scoped hunting rifles, and perhaps a few special purpose guns (selected according to anticipated need).

From a logistics standpoint, it's best to be able to share ammunition, so there is a distinct advantage to having all handguns in the same caliber, all rifles in the same caliber, etc. From both a tactical and survival perspective, having more ammunition is far more important than having a quantity of extra guns. For more on the topic of firearms and ammunition, read the chapter, *"Firearm Selection for Emergency Situations"* in Book 2.

[23] Never let your vehicle's gas tank get below 1/2 full. This is not only important for a bug-out situation, it's also important for an emergency trip to the hospital, a nighttime run to aid a friend in need, etc.

"Just over a quarter," she replied sheepishly.

Joe had continually nagged her about filling up when she got down to half a tank. Unfortunately, Linda's indicator that she needed gas was the little light that came on at about one eighth of a tank. "Damn it," he said through clenched teeth. "That will barely get us to the next town. I was hoping to get at least halfway to the farm before we had to get fuel."

"Sorry," she mumbled.

"I know a station that leaves the pumps on for credit card purchases when they close. Maybe we can get there before they get mobbed. Let's get going. Stay right behind me, but if we get separated, use the radio."

Joe turned on one of the GMRS radios, looked at the channel display, and handed it to his son. He twisted the power knob, which also controlled the volume, on the second radio to find out that it was already in the on position.

"Shit!" he exclaimed. "Someone left this one on and the batteries are dead. Does anyone know where the AA batteries are?" [24]

"Melissa took the last ones for her Walkman," Andy said.

"Well, you used a bunch of them up in your portable DVD player," she countered.

"Are any of them still good?" Joe demanded.

Both children shook their heads sadly.

"Did you buy any batteries?" Joe asked Linda.

"Did you tell me to?" she shot back, happy that this, unlike the low fuel status in the SUV, was not her fault.

"We don't have any in the house?" Joe asked them all.

"I might know where a couple are," Andy volunteered.

"Go see if you can find them. Hurry."

---

[24] Extra batteries are one of the most important supplies. When possible, select radios and other electronics which use the same size battery. So you don't need to inventory as many. Redundancy is important. Not only do you need extra batteries, you also need extra radios, flashlights, etc. See the chapters on *"Bug-Out Communication,"* and *"GO-Bag: List of Supplies to Include"* in Book 2.

Andy nodded his head and ran into the house. Joe rechecked the gear in the back of his truck to make sure nothing was where it could blow out.[25] He glanced again at his watch. He walked around both of the vehicles and noticed a low tire on the front of the SUV. Well, he thought, how can I expect her to keep air in the tires when she won't even keep gas in the tank? He would air it up at the station.

Where was Andy? Joe walked to the door and stuck his head in. "Andy, did you find them?"

"No, not yet. They weren't in the junk drawer. I think maybe I saw them in one of the desk drawers."

"Come on. We've got to go."

Andy raced past his father and got in his assigned vehicle. Joe quickly locked the house door and tripped the switch on the automatic garage door. He walked up next to Linda's car and motioned for her to roll down the window.

"Just try to stay right behind me.[26] Maybe we can find somewhere to get some batteries."

She nodded he head and started he car. Joe got in the truck, cranked it, and put it into gear. He glanced at the time on the radio as he turned onto the street. 4:49 a.m. He was exasperated that it had taken this long. Ben Franklin had said that he was leaving in ten minutes. He was probably already at his bug out location. Next time I'll make sure I'm ready to go that quickly, Joe promised himself.[27]

---

[25] If you can, use a tarp to conceal what you are transporting. If you look well equipped, you will be a target for theft or armed robbery.

[26] It may be a good idea to caravan with your spouse in a separate vehicle, but it's far safer to caravan with additional vehicles that belong to friends traveling to your same destination. Don't take risks with your driving. It is not important to remain literally bumper-to-bumper together with the other members of your group.

The front seat passenger in each vehicle should keep their eyes on the other vehicles in your group. Use 2-way radios to stay in contact. (For more on radios, in Book 2, read the chapter "Bug-Out Communications.") The driver should concentrate exclusively on driving. Note: Do not depend on mobile phones for communications. In an emergency situation there is a high probability that cellular phone systems will not be operational.

[27] Do it right the first time. We need to be prepared for what may become a life-or-death situation. Don't risk it; prepare now.

There was a little more traffic than he would have expected, but it was moving well. When he entered the Crosstown Expressway, it looked like rush hour. There was a lot of horn honking and finger gesturing, but not much more than there usually was at five o'clock on Friday afternoons. At least they were moving, not as fast as Joe had hoped, but it wasn't too bad. Joe worked his way over to the left lane and made sure with each lane change that Linda was behind him. He calculated that at the speed they were moving, they would be at the gas station he wanted to fill up at in twenty minutes.

Along the way, every open gas station had a line of cars. Even the ones that were closed had cars at the pumps. Joe figured that those drivers believed it was quicker to wait for the station to open than to get in one of the long gas lines.

As they drove, the traffic got heavier and heavier. It took almost forty minutes to get to the gas station he had in mind. It was a few blocks off of the access road. Joe only knew about it because he had needed fishing bait one time and a local had sent him here. As they pulled into the lot, there was a car at every pump. Some had another behind them. Compared to the other stations, this was a dream though. Since only a few of the outside lights and none of the inside ones were on, most people probably thought the pumps were off, too. Joe waved Linda behind a car at one pump and he pulled up behind another.

Linda didn't have to wait too long before she was able to pull up to her pump. Andy jumped out, swiped the credit card that she had given him, and began to pump gas into the Suburban.

Joe was behind a Ford F350 truck. Once that driver finished filling his tank, he switched the pump nozzle to a second tank. So Joe reached into the bed of his truck and pulled out one of the 5-gallon Scepter[28] gas cans he intended to fill. Joe was anxious to get back on the road.

A minute later, a car pulled out from one of the other pumps and the car behind it did not move. Joe looked and could see no one in the vehicle. He put his truck in gear and pulled in next to the pump. Swiping his credit card, he was pumping gas seconds later.

---

[28] For details on the U.S. military Scepter gas can, read the section *"Gas/Fuel Transport and Storage"* in Book-2.

"Hey, I was next!" A man shouted, startling Joe and making him turn.

The younger man was coming from behind the store. He was quite a bit taller than Joe and appeared to have a bad attitude. Joe wasn't sure if it was just because of the situation or if it was normal for him.

"I'm sorry. There was no one in your car and I didn't know where you were. I'll be done in just a minute," Joe said.

"I had to go take a leak," the man said as if it were Joe's fault that his bladder had filled. He sat on the hood of his car and stared at Joe's truck. The pump soon kicked off as Joe already had more than half a tank when he pulled in to the station. He reached in the back and started pulling out the jerry cans.

"Oh, no," the young man said as he jumped off his hood and clenched his fists. "You're not gonna fill those up too." He took a step toward Joe.

"It'll just take another minute or two."

"You're moving that truck now or I'm moving it for you!"

He stepped to the back of his car and lifted the hatch. When he reappeared from the back he had a tire iron in his hand. Joe had no idea what the man meant to do with the bent metal weapon, but he didn't want to find out. He reached in through the open door of his truck and pulled out his Kimber 1911 pistol. The man, seeing the .45 caliber weapon and the almost half inch hole of the muzzle, seemed to shrink in size. He quickly backed up.

"Sorry, Mister, I don't want no trouble," he told Joe.

Joe prayed that the man couldn't see his hand shaking. "I...I...I think you better get in your car until I leave."

"Okay, okay man, relax. Don't shoot me. I'll get in the car." He did as he said.

Joe stuck the pistol in his waistband[29] and stood where he could watch the little car and its occupant. He looked over at his wife's SUV. Andy was hanging up the hose, oblivious to what had just happened. Joe didn't trust the guy to stay in his car.

"Andy," Joe called. Pointing to the grass verge, he said, "tell your mom to pull over there, and you come help me."

Andy did as he was told. "Finish filling those cans, while I watch this guy," his father told him.

"What happened?"

"I'll tell you later, just fill the cans as fast as you can."

Joe thought to get Melissa to help Andy with the pump nozzle, so that Andy could lift the filled gas cans into the back of the pickup. He looked into his truck to talk to Melissa and saw that her eyes were already riveted on him. His daughter's eyes were the size of manhole covers.

"Melissa," he said. "Melissa! MELISSA!"

She jumped as finally heard her name. "What?"

"Get out here and help Andy put the gas into the cans, so that your brother can cap them and lift them into the truck as soon as they are filled."

"Dad, you pulled a gun on that guy!"

"I know," Joe said as he glanced in the direction of the tire iron brandisher. "He acted like he wanted to hurt us, so I had no choice. Now get out here and help your brother so that we can get out of here."

Melissa opened her door and scurried around to the back of the pickup. Joe carefully watched and made sure that the man could see he was guarding his children, with the Kimber ready.

---

[29] A self-defense handgun needs to be on your person, not just in your car. If you need it you may not have time to get into your car to get it. Plus, you may lose sight of your assailant if you need to look for a gun in your vehicle's glove box or center console. Moreover, you need to carry your handgun in a holster, not in a pocket or the waistband of your pants. Sticking a gun in your waistband may work on television, but in real life, guns tend to fall out when running or at the worst possible moment. A gun carried concealed in a holster is readily available when you need it, and you don't lose the element of surprise as with open carry. Moreover, you can choose to expose a concealed, holstered gun, which is an intermediate step between having an invisible gun and having one in your hand. This is an important distinction if a police officer gets involved.

Joe counted the thuds as Andy swung the now full jugs onto the tailgate and pushed them into the truck's bed. It seemed to take forever for his children to finish. Finally, he heard the tailgate shut and Andy spoke.

"All done, Dad."

"Good. Load back up and let's get the hell out of here."

A moment later, they were on the street and headed back to the Interstate. Joe grabbed his cell phone and dialed 9-1-1. He figured that he better call the police before the jerk with the tire iron did. All he got in three tries was a busy signal.[30]

The traffic seemed to have doubled or tripled while they were buying fuel. Joe wondered if they should try to find another route, but he didn't really know any others. He decided to go ahead and get on the freeway and then look for another route once they got out of town if the traffic got any worse. Linda was not able to get on right behind him, but there was only a car between them. Joe had no problem seeing her.

Traffic would move along at 45 or 50 miles per hour for a ways and then slow to a crawl for a few minutes. Joe couldn't see any reason for the disparity in speed, but he reckoned that there must be a reason. He hoped that the further they got out of town the better things would be. Joe mentally kicked himself again for taking so long to leave. Well, he thought, if I hadn't been awakened by the beep of the text message, we'd still all be in bed right now. At least he could take some comfort in that.

His musing reminded him to check his truck's radio for news updates. As he turned the radio on, he told Melissa to use her phone to check for news updates on the Internet.

---

[30] Even if you only brandished your gun and didn't fire it, it is important to immediately report the incident to the police. The person who calls first will set the tone for the police response. This is also true for the use of pepper spray, brandishing a baseball bat, or any other weapon. In a disaster situation you may be unable to get through the jammed phone lines to reach a police dispatcher, but your phone will have nevertheless registered your attempt. This may prove to be important later, if the police arrive on the scene. This simple phone call, or at least the attempted call, may spell the difference between a responding officer filing a report rather than arresting you. In the early hours and days of a disaster, police officers may make frivolous arrests to defuse volatile situations, calm public fears or restore order.

The channel he liked played oldies, but a man's voice came over the speakers.

"…is urging everyone to stay at home. Please keep the streets clear so that emergency personnel can respond. Also, the 9-1-1 Emergency system is being overwhelmed with calls. Please, only call 9-1-1 if you have true medical, police, or fire emergency. 9-1-1 is not an information service. Operators there cannot give you any information. Your best source of information is to stay here with us at KNAA Golden Oldies.'

"Officials in Washington believe that the device found in Boston was the only one and that the terrorists' plan was to start a nationwide panic. Local authorities assure us that there is no indication that any nuclear material is in our city. They have stated that even if the threats of twelve devices are true, it is not likely that we would be in the top twelve cities selected. The mayor is asking for everyone to cooperate. He asks that all schools and businesses close for the day and that only critical personnel report to work. The State Department of Transportation is urging everyone to stay at home. Please keep the street clear so…"

Joe turned the radio off. "Well, we don't have to worry about work and school now, do we sweetheart?," he whispered to himself.

If she heard it, Melissa ignored the rhetorical question. "Dad would you have really shot that guy?"

Joe glanced at her, and then was quiet for a long moment. "I was pretty sure that he would back off if I just showed him the pistol. I know I wouldn't have shot him for hitting the truck with the tire iron, but if he had tried to hurt you, or Mom or Andy or me, I'm pretty sure I would have pulled the trigger. Would that bother you?"

"Yes and no."

"Me, too," Joe said thoughtfully. "Thank God it didn't come to that."[31]

The traffic continued to slow. It still moved okay at times, but the time they spent just creeping was increasing. Joe looked at the clock. 6:03 a.m. is what it read. Almost an hour and fifteen minutes since they left the house, yet they had only gone 18 miles. It was obvious to Joe that traffic was getting worse, not better. He had to get off of the interstate.

"Honey," he said to Melissa, "if you've not learned any new news on the Internet, maybe you'd get the map out of the glove box. Do you know how to read a map?"

"Of course, Dad. We learned last year in Geography. But why not use the map app on my phone?"

"Great idea, but let's use both. Reach in the glove box and pull out the State map. Find where we are."

Melissa opened the box and found the map. She unfolded it and Joe saw her looking over the whole map again and again. He thought that, by now, she should have at least narrowed down where they were to half of the map.

"Having trouble?" he asked.

"This isn't like the maps we use at school. This one has so many roads on it, I can't find anything. Let me try the map app on my phone."

A minute later she said, "It not working. A few minutes ago I was able to check the news on the Internet, but now it's not working at all. I can't even get on the Internet." [32]

---

[31] For travel on foot during a catastrophic event, in urban areas it is usually best to have a concealed pistol carried on your person, and a collapsible rifle that fits inside your GO-Bag. Plus, 2-4 extra high-capacity magazines for each, all preloaded with self-defense ammunition. Each situation is different, but the open carry of a gun in an urban area can be problematic, even after a disaster when lawlessness is rampant. Open carry is sometimes prudent because you can react faster, while on other occasions it may make you a target, so carefully evaluate the situation before choosing which is best. Since the 2nd Amendment of the Constitution gives you the right to carry a gun, you may feel that local laws are the least of your concerns during a calamitous situation. Regardless, it is still a factor to be considered.

Also, if the combined weight of a GO-Bag, plus a pistol, rifle, and extra ammunition is too much for an individual, opt for the one weapon which provides the most strategic advantage. Every gun-trained adult should have a permit to carry a concealed weapon and be armed with at least one firearm.

"Then use the paper map, and look for our city. It's in the southeastern part of the State. It should be in the lower right hand corner."

Melissa looked for a few more seconds. "Got it."

"Now find where your grandpa and grandma live. It should be toward the top center."

"I found it," she said.

"That's great. Now, come back to where we are and follow the Interstate north until you get to where it intersects with Highway 59." Joe knew they were only five or six miles from the intersection. He hoped that he could turn west and then find another route north that would not be so clogged.[33]

"Okay, I've got it."

"Follow 59 west and see if there is a road or highway that intersects it and goes up close to your grandparents' place."

After a few minutes of tracing roads with her finger, Melissa spoke again. "I found one. It's just a thin line but it runs almost right to the farm. It's SH 983. You have to go about this far on 59 to get to it." She held her fingers about four inches apart.

"How far is that?" Joe asked.

"About this far," she said holding her fingers up for him to see again.

"I need to know how many miles that is. Look at the legend and see if it says how many miles to the inch."

Melissa folded the map over and studied the legend. "It says one inch equals 12.3 miles, Dad."

---

[32] During disasters, it's not unusual for the cellular phone system to become overloaded due to increased demand. If the incident involves civil unrest, or is an event such as a terrorist incident, the government will shut down the telephone system. They do this to make it more difficult for insurgents to communicate with each other, so don't rely exclusively on mobile phones for communication. For more on this topic, read the chapter, *"Bug-Out Communications"* in Book 2.

[33] Make sure that everyone in your group knows how to read a street map, and also a topographic map. Keep both types of maps in your vehicles, as well as in your GO-Bags. Also, even if your vehicle has an electronic compass or GPS, keep a standard compass with each GO-Bag, and teach everyone how to use their compass with their maps.

Fifty miles, Joe figured. That wasn't too bad. His in-laws were forty miles west of the interstate, so this should only be about 10 miles out of the way. If the traffic was moving any faster at all, they could make that up easily.

"Great job, honey. We're going to take your route." [34]

Melissa beamed.

Joe looked to his right and could see the sky turning pink. He looked in the rear view mirror and saw that now there were two cars between him and Linda. There were more and more cars trying to shoehorn themselves onto the expressway at every entrance. Joe looked at his watch and figured it would take another twenty or thirty minutes to reach Highway 59 at this rate. He prayed that the traffic on Hwy 59 would be better.

A few miles up the road he decided that he had better start getting over so that he could exit. He looked behind him. Linda was three cars behind. It was starting to get light now, so she should have no problem seeing him change lanes. He put on his blinker and hoped that someone would let him over. Everyone on the road seemed so intent on getting out of town that no one would give him room to move right. He finally had to force his way over and ignore the response of horns and middle digits. He watched in the rearview and saw that Linda was able to find a generous soul to let her over.

He repeated the maneuver and now was in the correct lane. Linda was not as lucky this time. No one wanted to let her over and she was about to pull the same rude stunt that Joe had.

"I don't know why your father is getting over," she huffed. "The left lanes are moving better."

Andy, determined to help his mom, rolled down his window and looked at the drivers on his side, pointing his intentions to change lanes. The on comers just ignored him like he wasn't even there.

---

[34] The selection of a route is a critically important decision. If you can't stop the car to personally confirm the decision, use your phone or 2-way radio to contact the other vehicle(s) and ask them to accomplish the same task. If their recommendation is different, converse using your 2-way radios, and discuss the matter with them. You don't just want a viable route; you want the best possible route. For more on this topic, in Book-2, read the chapter, *"Maps and Navigation."*

Joe was getting worried. He was getting very close to the exit for 59. He tried to wave at Linda to come on up and he would let he over. She didn't see him as she was spending more time looking back than forward. In addition, with a few cars getting off at the exit, Joe's lane was now moving faster than Linda's. Since Linda was ignoring him, he decided that he would go ahead and take the exit. That would force her to get over. Joe appreciated the fact that she was a very cautious driver, but in this situation she was just going to have to be a little more aggressive.

Andy was still looking for space to get over. When the right lane moved some, the driver he was looking at seemed distracted and he didn't move. This created an opening and Andy told his mother to go. Just as she cut the wheel and mashed on the accelerator, the driver saw that traffic was moving and he gunned his pickup. The sickening crunch of metal was the result of the two vehicles trying to occupy one space.

Joe saw the collision in his mirror.

"Shit, shit, shit!" he said under his breath, hoping that Melissa wouldn't hear.

He pulled the truck over to the shoulder and put it in Park.

"Stay in the truck," he told his daughter.

Joe got out and loped back to the accident. Behind the bonded vehicles, traffic in both lanes had come to a halt. Only the left lane was moving and the rubberneckers wanting to see what had happened tremendously slowed it. The driver of the pickup was out of his car and surveying the damage. Joe, breathing hard, stopped next to him. Linda started to get out, but Joe signaled for her to stay in the car.

"You okay?" he asked the man.

"Yeah. I think so."

"Sorry about this."

"Why?" the man asked. "You didn't do anything. I appreciate you stopping."

"That's my wife in the Suburban," Joe explained.

"Oh," the man said in a tightlipped manor.

"We could call the cops, but it will probably take them a long time to get here," Joe said as he looked at the impact site. The truck looked to have almost no damage. The bumper might be a little bent, and it was probably scratched up some. Overall, it could have been much worse. Joe saw that the truck's bumper was one of those heavy-duty steel pipe jobs and it had done its job of protecting the front of the truck quite well. The bumper had hit the front wheel of the SUV. There was a little sheet metal damage, but it didn't look too severe.

"Naw," the man drawled, "I just want to get out of town. I don't think my truck is hurt. Just give me your name and address and your insurance info and we'll settle this later."

"Sounds good," Joe agreed.

They quickly exchanged names and the man got back in his truck, backed up a little, and went around the SUV.

Joe motioned for Linda to get going as well. Cars on both sides of her were creeping past. She started the engine, put the car in drive, and mashed the gas pedal. The SUV didn't want to move at first. She pressed the gas further and the big vehicle lurched forward with a horrible squeal. Joe looked back at the noise and could see that the front wheels were pointed in different directions. He held up a hand to stop Linda. He jogged back up to the front of her car while cursing their luck. He looked under the vehicle and could see that one of the tie rods was broken. They wouldn't be taking the Suburban any further.

"The steering for one of the tires is broken," Joe explained to Linda when he got to her window. "I'll stop the traffic. Try to get it off of the road."

Linda nodded tersely. Joe stepped into the lane she needed to cross and held a hand up, becoming a human barricade. Tires screeched and horns blared, but the traffic stopped. Linda herded the beast with a wounded leg over behind Joe's truck. It sat catty cornered, half on the shoulder, half on the grass.

"Can you fix it?" she asked when Joe came off of the expressway.

"Not unless you have an extra tie rod."

"What are we going to do?"

"We'll just have to leave it here and go in the truck. I think we can stack most of the stuff in here on top of the stuff in the truck. You and Andy start bringing me everything."

Joe climbed in the bed, removed the tarp, and quickly stacked the cargo from the SUV as best he could. He covered it all with the tarp and added rope in addition to the ratchet tie-down straps he had used previously. [35] Then, they locked the damaged vehicle and they all climbed into the cab of the truck. It was crowded in the back for the kids since they had to share the space with the guns and ammo, but it worked. Still young and a bit clueless, Melissa started to whine about it some, but Andy shut her up. Joe was thankful that his son was grasping the seriousness of their situation.

"Look, it's just for a couple of hours. You'll just have to make due, okay?" Joe said, trying to pacify his increasingly cranky daughter.

The sun had been up for some time, but Joe could still see the ball of fire in his rearview mirror as he rocketed west on Highway 59 – at twenty miles an hour. But he was glad to be off of the Interstate. Maybe they weren't moving as fast as he would have liked, but at least the traffic here wasn't stop and go. He looked at the time. Joe couldn't believe it, but the wreck had cost them almost an hour. He had expected to be at his in-law's house by now and they were just barely out of the city. He turned the radio back on.

" …were low yield backpack nuclear devices. For years, experts have warned that such an attack was not only possible, but inevitable. With many of the weapons of the former Soviet Union missing and unaccounted for, the material to build such a device is available on the black market. The other five bombs were only nuclear laced dirty bombs and pose little immediate danger to those not in the direct blast radius. Officials hope that any further devices are of the dirty bomb variety. They believe that the terrorist used all of the backpack nukes on Washington DC, New York, and Los Angeles. The authorities are asking that everyone stay calm. All of the bombs were detonated in the downtown areas of the attacked cities. Citizens only need to immediately evacuate if they are in the downtown area of a large city. Please listen to your local officials and obey their directions. If everyone

---

[35] Rope, ratchet tie-down straps, flashlight, spotlight, duct tape, jumper cables, crowbar, lug wrench, vehicle jack, vehicle tow strap, road flares, and a few basic tools and other related supplies, should be kept readily accessible behind or under the vehicle seat. You don't want to be digging through your load to find basic items. For more on vehicle oriented bug-out supplies, in Book 2, see *Lists of Gear for GO-Bag and Emergency Kits.*

tries to evacuate at one time, all arteries out of the cities will quickly become clogged."

"No shit," Joe said.

His daughter was now not only cranky, but scared. They were all scared.

As he listened to the radio for the next several minutes, he was slowly able to piece together what had happened. At around noon Eastern Time, seven cities were attacked. New York was hit the hardest; a backpack device on Wall Street, a dirty bomb on Madison Avenue, and conventional explosives at each of Manhattan's tunnels and bridges. Several of the conventional explosives had failed to detonate, but the devastation was nevertheless widespread and the public had panicked. New Yorkers were tough, but this was far beyond anything they had previously had to endure.

The most powerful backpack nuke was detonated in Los Angeles, apparently at the Lakeside Golf Club in Hollywood, but the blast zone included Warner Bros. and Universal Studios, and the intersection of Highway 101 and the Ventura freeway. That was the only target in Los Angeles, as if that wasn't enough.

In Washington DC, the backpack nuke was detonated on the Mall, taking out the White House, Congress, the FBI's J. Edgar Hoover Building, and the main buildings for most of the big government agencies. Deaths from these two blasts were not nearly as high as in New York and Los Angeles. Surviving federal officials had been evacuated to various Continuity of Government sites.[36] The president has been playing golf in Hawaii and was unharmed.

Chicago, Philadelphia, the Mall of America near Minneapolis, San Francisco, Seattle, and Las Vegas were hit with dirty bombs. Widespread panic was proliferating through those cities and others like wildfire.

Reading between the lines, it sounded like the authorities feared that the attacks weren't over. They seemed to be anticipating more terrorist strikes, so the president had not yet mobilized FEMA.

---

[36] More about the federal government's 'Continuity of Government' plan can be found later in this book. See *"Chapter 2, Unprecedented Government Preparations are Underway."*

Each strike was in a densely populated area. Thankfully they were now well outside their metropolitan area and the wind was blowing the opposite direction from their travel. Joe felt they were probably safe, even if the attacks weren't over. They would be okay, he told himself. However, the news still twisted his somewhat large stomach into a golf ball.

Looking down at the speedometer, Joe saw that they were now moving at close to forty miles an hour. He didn't know if it was because they were getting further away from town or if everyone now had more incentive to move quickly. He didn't care what the reason was. He was just happy to be moving.

Thirty minutes later, the radio went silent. Joe punched all of the preset buttons, and then the 'scan' button, but was not able to find even a local station. He turned the dial by hand and found a distant station a state away. They reported that in the last five minutes, two other cities had been attacked, including their hometown. Joe looked south and saw a mushroom cloud forming over what he guessed was downtown. He didn't know why the terrorists would hit his town; it wasn't strategic. Maybe it was just to make sure that the entire nation felt the effect.

The radio said that the bomb that hit Joe's town had been a dirty bomb, but he wasn't sure if that was right. Would a dirty bomb make a mushroom cloud and knock out all of the local radio stations? He wasn't sure. He didn't think so. Everyone in the truck was grimly quiet as thoughts of their friends, and what could have happened if they had not bugged out ran through their minds. They felt almost guilty that they had survived.

An hour later they were at the junction with SH 983. Joe made the right turn along with several other cars. Even though this was just a two-lane highway, it was moving much better than either of the multilane roads he had been on. As he sped toward his destination, relieved that he was making good time, something nagged at the back of his mind. If it wasn't just a dirty bomb that hit his city, where would the fallout go? The wind was erratic this time of year. Would they be safe at his in-laws? How much fallout would a backpack nuke produce? These were questions that he didn't have the answer to. He hoped that someone would.[37]

Panic and chaos were engulfing even those cities which had not been hit. A few minutes later a report came over the air that a dirty bomb had been found and defused in Portland, Oregon. Evidently, panic had also beset the entire West Coast and East Coast. The Freeways in the cities along the both coastlines were grid locked with people who had nowhere to go.[38]

Joe slammed on his brakes as the traffic in front of him came to an abrupt stop. He wondered what could be wrong. They had been moving along so well. Traffic started creeping forward and Joe noticed that an increasing number of cars were coming the opposite direction. He finally crested the top of a hill and could see the problem.

---

[37] Whether we are facing the effects of a natural disaster, or some other form of an emergency situation such as a terrorist attack, there are many things that are simply beyond our ability to control. Forcing yourself to remain calm, while maintaining a flexible, problem-solving attitude, can help keep your mind focused and your spirit resilient.

Occasionally, we will need to remind ourselves of this fact. Nevertheless, we can be problem solvers. We can (and must) make contingency plans, get equipped, and foster an attitude of optimism. Importantly, when others have lost hope we need to embody problem-solving skills and hopefulness. We may lose, but we need to focus on winning.

In the midst of an emergency situation, we need to avoid dwelling on circumstances we can't change. We simply do our best. We acknowledge that mistakes are inevitable, and we quickly forgive ourselves and others. Moreover, we avoid wasting time and mental energy on past mistakes. If we can't do anything to correct a mistake, it is counterproductive to dwell on it. Put them aside. We need to learn from each mistake, and then move on. We need to remain *hopeful* even when our situation looks *hopeless*.

In various research projects which studied *civilians* who had faced disasters and emergency situations, the conclusions are essentially the same. Success and survival does *not* depend on intellectual brilliance, education, fancy equipment, or even physical prowess.

Those who overcome insurmountable odds generally have three things in common: Unwavering **hope**, burnished **diligence** applied to the important tasks at hand, and **perseverance** amidst hardship. For me personally, I've found that it was my **faith in God** which made it possible for me to win an impossible victory.

Therefore, we need to keep these attributes in mind. Preparation is important, but readiness involves much more than just planning and stockpiling supplies.

[38] For more on this topic, in Book 2, read chapter, *Escape 'From' vs. Escape 'To'*.

In the bottom of the draw, between this hill and the next, was a small creek. Over that creek was a bridge, barely wide enough for two cars. A tractor-trailer had been heading south over the bridge at the same time a big motorhome was crossing it to the north. Somehow, they had collided. Both vehicles were wedged so tightly that Joe thought that the guardrails on the bridge would probably need to be removed in order to untangle the mess. Even if they could be removed without disassembling the bridge, it would take a couple of those monster wreckers to do it. It looked like the occupants of both vehicles had abandoned their now worthless rigs. Joe figured that they caught a ride with someone.

There was a wide spot in the road just in front of the bridge and everyone was turning around as they reached it. Joe did not want to turn around and backtrack. He was already much later than he had expected. He also imagined that the interstate would resemble a parking lot by now. As he slowly crept toward the turn around, he pulled out the map. Melissa had been right in that there was no other way to the farm unless he wanted to drive quite a distance. He had the fuel to do it, but then there would be little left for the generator when they got to his in-laws.

There had to be another way. He looked both ways. There were fields on both sides of the road with only barbed wire fences to keep him from crossing them. He wondered if he could find a place to cross the creek and come back to the road on the other side. If he could, traffic would not be a problem. He could really make some time. He pulled the truck over onto the narrow shoulder.

"You all stay with the truck. I'm going to go look for a place where we can four-wheel over to the other side." [39]

---

[39] In recent years four-wheel drive (4WD) vehicles have become very popular, but few of these are suitable for true off-road use. For any terrain other than logging roads, pasture land, and snow or mud covered streets, these vehicles need to be equipped with a lifted suspension and deep-tread tires. If you use a 4WD vehicle off-road in an emergency situation, keep in mind that even lifted 4WD vehicles struggle to fjord a stream or river which is deeper than the distance between the bottom of the tire and the bottom of the vehicle's body. Having a winch, and knowing how to use it, can be the difference between being mobile or stuck.

Off-road vehicles with equal weight on the front and rear tires usually work best. Even beefy-looking pickup trucks need to have weight in the bed.

Joe walked across the ditch to the fence. It was old and rusty. He found a place where the wires were loose and he pushed them down and carefully stepped over. The ground gently sloped down to the creek and he was only mildly winded when he reached the water. He walked along the edge noticing that the water was several feet deep in some places and only a few inches in others.

About two hundred yards from the bridge, he found a spot that looked promising. There were no large rocks and the water was only six inches or so deep. It was flowing over a sandy spot that was only seven or eight feet wide. He hated to get his feet wet, but he had to make sure that the bottom was solid enough. He quickly waded across and was thankful that his boots seemed to be mostly waterproof. The bottom was pretty solid and the truck should have no problem crossing here. The bank on the other side was a little steeper, but his mighty four by four would have no trouble making it back up to rejoin the road. He walked it, just to be sure, and found a route to the fence that would be within the truck's capabilities.

Joe walked back to the truck and pulled his toolbox from behind the back seat. He extracted a large pair of linesman's pliers and walked back to the loose spot on the fence. The four rusty strands of wire popped easily with the bite of the pliers. Joe walked back to the truck, threw the pliers into the seat next to him, and climbed into the driver's seat. He fully twisted the knob on the dash that activated the transfer case, putting the truck into the 4WD 'Low' range.

Dropping the truck into gear, he easily drove across the ditch and slipped through the hole in the fence. He was almost gleeful at his genius. He would now have an uncrowded road to his in-laws' where he could drive at a normal pace. With any luck, they would be there in a little over an hour.

As he approached the creek, Joe wondered if there was anyone back on the road watching. If so, the dolts in the two wheel drive vehicles would be envious of his brilliant plan. But if they had 4WD he knew with certainty what they were thinking. They would be watching to see if he made it. If so, they would follow him.

As Joe approached the river he put these other thoughts out of his mind. Concentrating solely on his driving, he carefully lined up on his spot.[40]

"Everyone, hold on!" he commanded as he hit the throttle.

The truck lunged forward and the front tires plowed through the water, sending a blinding spray up and across Joe's windshield. When they hit the ledge of the bank on the other side, the front of

---

[40] When crossing flowing water, point your vehicle slightly upstream. Then, if the flowing water moves your vehicle, the front-end will likely swing around to your intended direction of travel, giving you the opportunity to increase your speed before the force of the water swings your vehicle around and points you downstream.

A vehicle pointed slightly upstream or downstream can plow through the water more like a boat, with the water flowing along the sides of the vehicle rather than blunt force pushing against it. The power of even a shallow but rapidly moving stream can quickly slide a vehicle sideways. Even a stream flowing at only 4 MPH against a vehicle's body can exert enough force to move it sideways.

The ideal speed is determined by practice. As you might expect, aggressive people tend to use excessive speed which can result in loss of traction or a water-flooded engine, and a stalled or damaged vehicle. Timid people tend to go too slow, resulting is getting stuck if the stream bottom is soft, or if the vehicle encounters a small obstruction. Maintaining momentum is critically important; speed is not. Walking the route first is a must, but if the water is deep or moving quickly, be sure to move across with the protection of a rope tied to the vehicle, to make sure your aren't surprised by the conditions and swept away.

If you need to maximize traction, reduce your tire pressure to 10-12 pounds. This simple technique can double the amount of rubber that is in contact with the ground, thereby giving you twice the traction in snow, sand, lose dirt and for hill climbing. However, this is inadvisable unless you have a way to re-inflate the tires, so buy a small 12-volt tire inflator. One of these portable air compressors costs about the same as a DVD movie, and are handy to have anyway, in case you have a low tire. Warning: Keep in mind that an underinflated tire can come off the rim during cornering. And, understand that this technique will reduce the clearance between the bottom of your vehicle and the ground, and will cause your vehicle to burn more fuel. Bottom line: Only use this technique when you need additional traction, and don't air-down unless you can re-inflate your tires.

In most cases, going off-road even with a 4WD vehicle is not advisable unless you have practiced these maneuvers in advance. The best solution is not to avoid using a 4WD equipped vehicle, but rather to practice prior to needing this skill. For 4WD operation, you need to know your vehicle and its capabilities. Also, an after-market heavy-duty front bumper may come in handy to push stalled cars out of your path whether you are in a water obstacle, off road, or on a regular roadway.

the truck bounced up as if it were doing a wheelie. This surprised Joe, and coupled with the fact that he could not see, he lifted his ten and a half doublewide foot off of the gas pedal. He felt the front of the truck began to fall back toward the earth and he breathed a sigh of relief. It quickly turned into a moan of agony as he felt the back of the truck sink. He stabbed at the throttle, but it was too late. His forward momentum had stalled and the tires only spun, digging him deeper into the creek. He let off the gas and opened his door. Looking at the rear tire, he saw a gray goop covering the half that was not sunk. He stepped out, and his foot sunk into the goo.

It seemed solid when I walked over it, he thought. Joe looked back into the cab of the truck at Linda. She said nothing, but her eyes could have bored a hole through the walls of Ft. Knox. He shrugged his shoulders. He looked under the truck and his heart sank deeper than the rear axle. The truck would not come out easily. He looked back toward the road and heard the other vehicles making an orderly turnaround. No one was watching.

Well, he thought, I can stand here feeling sorry for myself and wondering what went wrong, or I can do something.

"Everyone, out!" he commanded. "Linda, you and Melissa go see if you can find some big branches to put under the tires." He held his hands up in an eight inch circle to show them what he wanted. "Andy, help me get the jack and let's see if we can get these tires up so that we can put the limbs under them." [41]

---

[41] An electric winch mounted on the front of the vehicle combined with a long recovery strap (or stout steel cable of sufficient strength to tow your vehicle) would be the best solution, but if your vehicle isn't equipped with one of these, Joe's solution is not ideal but may still work.

A "Hi-Lift" jack is a basic piece of equipment used by the off-road crowd, and it has many uses. A Hi-Lift jack is far more useful than a regular vehicle jack and has many uses in addition to lifting a vehicle. Yet, even a Hi-Lift jack will need to be supported by a board (or something) to keep it from sinking into the mud.

Military vehicles often carry steel ramps to help a vehicle regain traction, but a quantity of tree branches can accomplish the same thing. However, avoid using branches with leaves or other materials which become slick when wet. Once stuck in mud to the axle, stop spinning the tires, you'll only dig your vehicle deeper. Shift from forward to reverse again and again, with your passengers doing the same by pushing from the sides, forward and backward, repeating until the vehicle can get up onto the branches, and regains traction.

Linda and her daughter walked away from the road toward a clump of trees. When Linda was out of earshot of her husband, she began to complain about the situation they were in. "If we had just stayed home, we probably would have been alright," she said to Melissa. "Now, we're stuck, literally, in the middle of nowhere!" They looked around and finally found a couple of branches that looked like they might work. The two exasperated females drug them back toward the truck.

Linda was surprised when she got back. Both Andy and Joe were covered almost head to toe in the mud. Joe looked at her sheepishly. "It seems solid on top, but once you break through the top layer, it's just soup underneath. We can't find a solid spot to put the jack. I don't see any way to get it out."

"So what do we do?"

"We walk," he said flatly.

"What do you mean, we walk?" Linda asked incredulously.

"We have backpacks. We load as much stuff as we can into them and take off for your folk's. It might take a few days, but we can get there.[42]

"Joe, you must have lost your mind. The kids could probably do it, but my feet are bad and neither one of us is in any kind of shape to hike that far, with or without a heavy pack."

Yet another lower-cost option is to include with your vehicle's bug-out kit a heavy duty come-along, preferably a 4-ton or greater capacity. This hand operated winch is also useful if you need to pull a vehicle's damaged bumper or fender away from a tire, or to force open a gate. It is a very slow process to use a Hi-Lift or 'come-along' to get a vehicle out of the mud, but absent a bumper-mounted winch, a tow truck or another 4WD vehicle to pull you out, you may not have much choice.

Any of these 'winch' or 'tow' options will also require a steel cable or 'recovery strap' attached to a tree or other solid object to act as an anchor for the winch. Most ropes will not be strong enough. If Joe had a steel cable or preferably a recovery strap with him, his best option may have been to go back up to the road and wait for a suitable 4WD vehicle, and ask them to tow him out of the water. When trying to extract a stuck vehicle, be sure to attach the cable or tow strap to the vehicle's axle or frame, not the bumper.

[42] Even when you are using a vehicle to evacuate, each adult and teen still needs to have a GO-Bag readily accessible, not under of all your other gear. Whether you get stuck like Joe, or disabled by a traffic accident like Linda, or you get enveloped by irresolvable grid lock or run out of gas, the GO-Bag is your basic bug-out survival kit. For more on this topic, in Book 2, read the GO-Bag related chapters.

Joe knew she was right. Linda's feet would barely let her go to the mall for half a day, and he was carrying an extra twenty pounds around his waist. They would just have to try to get the truck out. He looked up toward the road and noticed that the line of the cars was gone. Only an occasional vehicle was turning around in front of the bridge. Maybe he could find someone who could pull them out.

Joe stuck his .45 into the back of his jeans and walked up to the road. Every once in a while, a car or pick-up would come up to the bridge and turn around. Joe knew they needed a really big four by four to have a chance at pulling his truck out. Finally, just before sunset, an older Jeep came up the road. It was lifted and had huge tires on it.

As it slowed in front of the barricaded bridge, Joe could see that it held four younger men. He didn't really like the looks of them, but he was desperate for help. He checked to make sure his pistol was in place and hidden, then he stood up and waved at the Jeep.[43]

"Hey man, watcha doin' out here?" the young man in the front passenger's seat asked.

---

[43] It is far better to wait for a respectable-looking Good Samaritan, even if this means camping out at that location until the next day. Unless the situation is so dangerous that you can't wait, don't try to recruit help at night. Wait until morning. If there are no cars on the road, look for a nearby resident who might be willing to help, but don't do this at night. If waiting isn't a viable option, then get going on foot. Unless, of course, you decide you'd like to make your current location your new home away from home.

If not, get going; walk to your retreat location. So your feet are sore and you're out of shape, buck-up and hit the road. Before you begin to hike, use tape or Band Aids around each toe to protect them, and tape those areas on your feet that are prone to blisters. If you can wear two pair of socks and still have your feet fit comfortably into your shoes, this can help protect your feet from blisters. If it can be avoided, don't walk in wet socks. If your feet are weak, wrap your ankle to provide more support. Then, get going. Once you get to your destination, you can turnaround and come back with help and more gear, and hopefully another vehicle suitable for towing your vehicle out (if it's not been looted). An extra pair of dry socks will help to prevent blisters, as will properly fitted and broken-in boots.

In any case, when you seek help it's not about being judgmental; it's about using good judgment. Be respectful, not politically correct.

"My family and I got stuck trying to cross the creek in our truck down there," Joe said as he pointed. "I was hoping that you would try to pull me out."

The four young urbanites drove behind Joe as he walked through the gap in the fence, so they could look at the floundered truck. Upon seeing Joe's plight, the driver turned to his passengers and smiled, then turned back to Joe and flashed a big set of white teeth. "Sure, Mister, we'll help you."

"Oh, thank you so much. I can't tell you how much I appreciate this." Joe relaxed a little. He knew that you couldn't judge a book by its cover, and that is what he had done with these young guys.

Joe began to walk toward his family. He heard the gears grind in the old CJ's transmission and a few mumbled curses from the driver. He turned to look and saw that the Jeep was now lurching backward. Joe wondered what was wrong with it. Probably something wrong with the reverse gear, he figured. The Jeep stopped and then pulled forward much more smoothly, and followed Joe to the edge of the water.

Linda saw Joe and the Jeep behind him. Thank goodness, she thought. As they got closer, she got a little tense about how the men looked.

"Andy, do you see those guys?"

"Yes, Mom."

"What do you think?"

"They look like gang members to me," he replied.

"Grab your sister and take her over there away from the truck. I'm going to go stand next to your dad."

Andy grabbed his rifle and his sister and did as he was told. Linda walked over to where Joe was standing.

"You couldn't find anyone to help but a bunch of gang bangers?" she asked in a whisper. Joe glared at her in his best 'shut-up' look and shrugged his shoulders quickly.

The Jeep pulled into the water and came to a stop behind the truck. The front passenger jumped out of the Jeep and got on his knees in the water, and looked under the truck to inspecting the severity of the problem.

"Damn, Mister, you sure did get stuck. You sure are lucky that we came along."

By that time all four of the men were out of the Jeep and surveying the situation.

"Yeah, you sure are lucky," one of the men from the back seat said. "You sure got a lot of stuff in there. Where was you goin'?"

"We were just on the way to visit some family," Joe replied, not liking the look in the man's eyes.

The other back seater was looking in Andy and Melissa direction. "You coulda been here a long time if we hadn't come along," he said.

"Enough talking!" the driver barked. "You three get the stuff we need to do this out of the back of the Jeep."

The three men walked to the back of the off-road vehicle as Joe and Linda watched them with increasing suspicion.

The driver turned back to Joe. "I think all we need to do is hook a chain onto your trailer hitch. I'll turn the Jeep around and we'll see if we can pull her out this way. I don't want to take the chance of crossing the creek and both of us getting stuck."

Joe relaxed a little. The guys were really going to help them. He began to thank the man again when he noticed that the guy was backing away from him. Joe thought it strange and looked at the man's three accomplices just in time to see an AK-47 with an under folding stock come out of the small space behind the back seat of the Jeep.

Joe tried to scream at Linda, but the words stuck in his throat. He reached under his shirt for his pistol and noticed that the driver was doing the same. Joe wondered how he could have a weapon suspended in the pants that hung below his hips. Joe's right hand came up with his own pistol, and he swung it toward the driver since he was the nearest threat.

Joe grabbed Linda and started to pull her back with his free hand just as he heard the first bullet from the AK zing by his head. He fired his weapon, but didn't think that he had hit his target.

The sound of thundering gunfire became one long deafening boom. Bullets were screaming past Joe as he desperately tried to squeeze not jerk the trigger on his expensive pistol. Aligning his gun's sights on the driver's chest, he pulled the trigger again and again, and then jerked his wife's arm again, trying to get her out of her stupor. They needed to break and run. There was no cover where they were standing. He wanted to rejoin his kids on dry land, and make a stand together.[44]

As they reached the shore, Linda tripped and fell back onto Joe as he heard a sickening smack. The two of them ended up in a pile on the ground. Joe pulled his legs out from under his wife, got to his knees and reached out to help her up as he scanned back to the driver, who was unbelievably still unharmed. Joe had missed.

With his pistol back on target and his sights settled, with new found calmness Joe paused his breathing and forced himself to remain stationary. As he squeezed the trigger, Joe felt the release of the gun's hammer and his pistol fired. The slide immediately locked back indicating that his gun was now empty, but thankfully the driver doubled over and crashed face forward into the water.

Joe pulled on Linda again, but she was not trying to get up. He looked down and saw that part of her head was gone.

If the adrenaline had not been pumping through his veins, he probably would have wretched. He struggled to his feet and turned his attention toward the other three scumbags.

Joe noticed that the rifles they were holding all looked the same. They looked like Kalashnikov AK-47s, the type so popular with street gangs who often got them from the same smugglers who brought their drugs into the country. All three held their rifles in front of them, waist high; with the rifle stocks still collapsed, they wildly sprayed bullets in his direction.

He had to keep moving. He had to get to his kids.

Andy saw his father stand, and continue on without his mother. How could he? If he wouldn't save her, Andy would. Andy stood and continued to fire his rifle as he moved forward.

The slide on Joe's .45 locked back again after he had emptied yet another magazine of ammunition. Joe realized that he didn't

---

[44] Owning a gun isn't enough, nor is target practice. It is important to get tactical training from someone who has actually used a gun in combat or as a police officer.

have another spare magazine.[45] He would have mentally kicked himself, but he didn't have time. He turned to run back to the kids. As he did, he saw Andy advancing on the three shooters.

"No, Andy!" he screamed. "She's gone!"

Andy paused and turned, and looked directly at his father. His son's eyes burned with a look that Joe had never seen in anyone before. He briefly wondered if his children would ever be able to get over the sight of their mother being killed. Suddenly, the look in Andy's eyes turned blank. He crumpled. Joe looked with disbelief at his son and saw his mouth barely moving.

As Joe reached his son and dropped to his knees at his son's side. Two widening circles of red stain were quickly expanding in the center of Andy's chest.

"Go!" Andy barely croaked out, using his last ounce of strength to push his rifle into his father's hands.

Joe saw the wound and knew that there wasn't anything he could do for his son. So he gripped Andy's rifle and fired and few quick shots back at the hell-spawn. He ran to Melissa and pushed her down behind a fallen tree. She didn't have a gun and Joe didn't know how many rounds were left in Andy's black rifle.

"Run!" Joe yelled, pointing up the hill into the wooded countryside. His daughter was frozen, except for her head which pivoted back and forth from her mother to her brother and back.

"Run," Joe yelled again, as he grabbed his daughter's arm and pushed her toward the hillside.

"But, but, but…"

---

[45] In a gun battle, it's not unusual to expend a lot of ammunition. Joe should have taken the time to aim more carefully. That's true. Yet, that is extremely difficult to remember in the heat of the moment when people are shooting at you, especially if you are taken by surprise. When adrenalin hits your bloodstream, taking accurate aim is always difficult. Therefore, extra ammunition is essential.

If Joe had been carrying a high-capacity pistol and at least two extra magazines, which is the standard for most police officers, he would have been far better equipped. The classic 1911 pistol he was carrying is a very fine handgun, but it only holds 7-8 cartridges; whereas a more modern high-capacity pistol can hold 14 rounds or more. This extra ammunition provides a great benefit. A fully loaded high-capacity pistol, plus two spare magazines (clips), will together hold nearly a box of ammunition.

Joe grabbed her again, and twisted her to face the direction he wanted her to go, and pushed. She stumbled slightly, but finally began to run. Thankfully, once she decided to run, she had taken off like a scared deer. He did his best to keep up with her, turning and firing a shot behind him every few steps.

They crossed a tributary of the creek and continued to run. His mind raced. They had nothing. How would they survive? He realized that the firing behind him was slowing. At least we are alive, he thought. It wasn't that far. They could probably make it to Linda's parents. It would be hard with no food, water, or shelter, but they could do it. How far had they run? It seemed like miles to Joe. He looked back and was amazed that they were only about a hundred yards from the truck. Two of the reprobates had quit firing and were bending over their leader.

At least one of them paid, Joe thought. He turned back toward his daughter and saw that she was fifteen or twenty yards in front of him. He didn't know how much further he could run. His breath was short and his side hurt. He tried to call Melissa, but he didn't have enough wind to call her name.

Suddenly the pain in his side traveled to his chest and intensified exponentially. He dropped the rifle and grabbed at his chest, his shoulder hit the ground and Joe rolled onto his back. He couldn't catch his breath. It felt like an elephant was sitting on his chest.

He was in a clearing, and all he could see was the clear blue sky. Not a cloud could be seen. Suddenly, Melissa appeared over him. Her eyes were bloodshot and her face looked as if she were old. She kneeled over him, sobbing. Joe tried to tell her to leave him and keep running, but either she couldn't hear him or he couldn't get the words out. He wasn't sure. She continued to hug him and he could feel the convulsions of her sobs against his body.

Finally, she either heard him or sensed what she needed to do. 'Good girl,' he thought, as he felt her pull the dropped rifle from under his body. He was happy that he had been able to get through to her, as he knew that there wasn't anything else he could do for her, ever. He knew that his time left was measured in seconds.

Following Melissa's gaze, terror ripped through him. It was one of the gang bangers who had pulled Andy's rifle from under him. After slinging the rifle over his shoulder, he saw two dirty hands reach down and tear Melissa away from him. He had to save her, but he couldn't move. The demon with the rifle looked down at him and smiled. As his vision clouded with a mist of gray light, the last thing he heard was his daughter screaming.

Debriefing

Footnotes were appended to the story to encourage reflection on the positive and negative actions of the main character, as well as to provide instruction.

Now that you have finished reading David Crawford's story, we encourage you to turn back to the beginning. This time, just read SIG's footnotes. It's not necessary to re-read the entire story, but since each footnote is adjacent to the narrative, you do have the option of re-reading the portion that provoked the comment.

The bottom line is this: Even though Joe (the main character) thought he was reasonably prepared, he wasn't. Joe had accurately recognized the signs of the times. And, he had thought about the potential need to evacuate. He had undertaken some preparations. Unfortunately, he wasn't adequately ready. He thought of himself as ready, but in reality, he wasn't prepared. He wasn't ready to roll.

Joe paid a hefty price for that mistake.

Are you ready to face an emergency situation? Really ready?

We can all learn from Joe's mistakes. Now is the time to learn these lessons, and to act. Now, in advance of the need, we have the opportunity to make sure we are "ready to roll." We have the opportunity to plan, get equipped, and practice so that our bug-out can be successful.

While it's true that a serious disaster can't always be avoided, by preplanning and preparing we can very often avoid victimization and tragic outcomes. At the very least, we can usually mitigate the effect of a disaster on us, our family and friends.

Isn't this worth the effort?

Chapter 1

Real World vs. Normalcy Bias

For most people the pace of life is fast; maybe even bordering on too fast. At the very least, most of us are busier than we want to be, but what's the alternative? Yes, we are aware that the world is changing rapidly, and yet we feel like we can't handle yet another distraction. Frankly, we don't need additional concerns to add to the load we are already carrying.

This is modern life. Even so, we need to ask ourselves a question: "Are we sidestepping something important? Seriously important? Are we failing to recognize persistent warnings that we need to face?"

Being too busy, as well as carrying a full backpack of problems or responsibilities, is the formula for creating 'normalcy bias.' It may be normal, but more importantly, it may also be dangerous. If we fail to embrace the real world, this has the potential to create serious, negative consequences.

Last Friday, a rancher friend was on his way to visit me and came upon a longhorn steer in the roadway. Since he was driving on a two lane country road, there wasn't much option but to stop, and hope the bull would soon leave the road on its own accord.

However, behind him was a city driver who was less patient. He elected to disregard the big beast standing in the middle of the road and the fact that it was acting belligerent, kicking up its rear legs every few seconds. He ignored the warning signs, and scooted onto the shoulder of the road, expecting to be able to drive around the problem. Big mistake.

As the driver came toward the animal, it stood still and faced the approaching vehicle. As soon as the black SUV was astride the bull, it flicked its sharp horn across the side of the previously pristine Cadillac, gave it a rump butt, a kick with its rear hoofs that activated the side-curtain airbags, and then calmly walked back through the hole in the barbwire fence.

As my friend slowly accelerated past the damaged vehicle, the dazed driver got out and began to massage his neck. He was clearly unhurt, but his car was a different matter.

The outcome was unexpected, but that didn't change the fact that his vehicle was seriously damaged. He had seen the telltale behavior of the bull, the warning signs which indicated a potential problem, but he was busy and in a hurry. He had refused to heed the warning signs and now he would have to pay the price.

Similarly, we are cruising down the road of life amid various dangers; some seen, others unexpected. Unfortunately, in our world today, inattention or an unwillingness to assess circumstances, has the potential for much more serious consequences. Our lack of discernment and poor judgment can cause problems far greater than inconvenience, dented sheet metal, and broken auto glass.

Like the driver of the Cadillac, we have a choice. We can recognize the warning signs of this era or go blindly on and suffer unnecessary, life-altering consequences.

At this point we have a choice. If we wait until the figurative bull drops its head, it will be too late.

Situation Analysis: In the United States, our generation has enjoyed a period of protracted affluence. Combined with years of relative peace inside our homeland, our outlook toward life is predisposed to false assumptions about the future. Most Americans assume that our tomorrows will be similar to our past. We extol the virtue of positive attitude while ignoring negative changes.

This bias has created a mental state which conditions us to filter out the warning signs of serious change. As a result, we continue to think that our life, and circumstances, will remain essentially the same in the future.

It is a preferable viewpoint; we appreciate optimism. However, this orientation hobbles us with an aversion to face unpleasant truths.

Most of us expect ups and downs, but only within the scope of our life experiences. As a result, this limited perception encourages the development of a condition which psychologists call *'normalcy bias.'* Regrettably, this very common response produces a worldview which rules out the possibility of radical change.

This *normalcy bias* inhibits sound judgment, and often brings debilitating surprise when major change does happen. As a result, people infected with normalcy bias fail to take reasonable precautions; they fail to prepare, so they are emotionally *and* physically ill-equipped. They are unable to weather times of serious problems.

Yet, this is still a matter of choice. We can choose to be aware and rational humans as our creator intended or we can be like the ostrich that buries its head in the sand.

Those who have lived their life without experiencing sudden, significant change are particularly susceptible to normalcy bias. For them, when life does change and they are forcibly awakened by circumstance, they tend to react poorly. Not only are they unprepared for the change, they are susceptible to becoming either despondent victims or inappropriately aggressive. With both responses, there is a strong tendency to react emotionally and without strategic forethought.

For most of us, if we do briefly consider the possibility of a life-changing event it is short-lived. When a news story features a talking head warning of an economic meltdown, or a reporter broadcasting from the scene of a natural disaster, we tend to assume that if it ever happens to us, it will be a temporary condition.

We consider our past occasions of modest hardship and project ourselves into the crowd of interviewees who are complaining about the government's slow or inadequate response to the disaster. We acknowledge that it is very different for a few unlucky people. We can imagine that it *could* be a very difficult experience, but we see the situation as manageable. Our media doesn't show us the gruesome scenes.

What if it's more than an inconvenience? What if the scope is larger or the magnitude greater? Are we equipped to adapt to what might become the new normal? Most of us refuse to even think about the possibility, but thinking people do need to consider this growing possibility.

--- The High-Risk Top-13 ---
People Who are Most Susceptible
To a Normalcy Bias

It is part of our culture. Americans and Western Europeans are prone to suffer the effects of normalcy bias. However, there are certain populations within these cultures that are particularly susceptible. Those who fall into one of the below categories need to be especially careful about avoiding this form of self delusion.

1. Affluent people (Generally conditioned to solving problems with financial resources or influence derived from wealth. These assets become irrelevant during a protracted disaster.)

2. Those who have had stable employment and income for a number of years.

3. Individuals who depend on a spouse or someone else for their sustenance.

4. Persons who are politically Liberal or Progressive, as well as single-issue voters.

5. Those under the age of 40.

6. Adults without children.

7. U.S. citizens who have not spent time in an undeveloped country.

8. Those who have little knowledge of world history and U.S. history, or a limited understanding of economics.

9. Excessively busy people.

10. Individuals who watch a lot of television, sports, or live with a primary focus on some other distraction (includes benevolent activities).

11. Healthy people who have been blessed with good health for many years.

12. Christians and Muslims who believe that God will take care of them, thereby absolving them of personal responsibility for their own welfare (a distinctly unscriptural orientation).

13. Those individuals who live in the 'white/gray' mental state (relaxed and unaware) rather than the prudent 'yellow' mental state (relaxed and alert/aware).

Even when confronted with facts which conflict with their perception of the status quo, these individuals resist the need for change. People who fit into two of these categories will often be in intellectual agreement that there is a need to act, but will procrastinate and fail to take comprehensive and decisive action to correct their normalcy bias. Those who fall into three or more of the above categories tend to remain in denial until it is too late to take corrective action.

What are the odds of something "big" happening in our lifetime? Is it possible that momentous change is coming?

Even if you believe that nothing major is going to happen, are you sure? Even if there is only a 5% chance, isn't it prudent to still [46]prepare?

If you were planning an outdoor wedding and the weather forecast indicated a small chance of rain, would you establish a rain plan? Or, would you just 'hope' for the best?

If you are the type of person who doesn't develop contingency plans and just goes with the flow, *you will be swept away if something serious happens.*

It's not an "I have faith that God will protect me" issue. The God of the Bible doesn't promise to protect foolish people.

In today's world, things can change rapidly, so we can't let ourselves be lulled into complacency. We need to intentionally remove the blinders of our normalcy bias and ask ourselves what might happen; what we can do to prepare.

---

[46] Proverbs 22:3

Today we are facing several very negative, and very credible, potential disasters.

For example, many experts are warning that the U.S. economy will likely take an abrupt downward dip and then suddenly get much worse. They tell us that there is a very real possibility that we will experience extreme inflation, deflation or the collapse of the dollar.

If this happens, how will you fare? What will happen to you and your family? Unlike past bailouts, what will happen if the United States itself needs to be bailed out? Who will come to the rescue? Could this really happen? Look what's happened to Greece and other European Union nations.

When the city of Detroit declared bankruptcy in 2013, it was a development which was thought to be impossible in our parent's era. So why do we, in our generation, think that state and national bankruptcy can't happen in the United States? Why can't it?

As bad as it was, thankfully Detroit's bankruptcy was a localized event; 143 square miles of the United States. The fiscal irresponsibility of that city did create an unpleasant situation for its citizens, but the federal government stepped in and provided various forms of assistance. They received outside help

Unfortunately, the fiscal policies of the U.S. Government are equally unsound and very similar to the city of Detroit. The big difference is that the federal government has more money to shuffle—and it can print money to pay its bills, at least for a while.

Unfortunately, it has been printing and shuffling money for several years and this Ponzi scheme can't continue much longer. What if the economy of the United States craters? For many people this sounds farfetched and too horrible to even consider. Yet, as uncomfortable as this thought might be, it is irresponsible to ignore the possibility. A growing number of expert economists assert that it's not only possible, but becoming increasingly likely. Some claim it is inevitable.

But is it, really? Is this just sensationalism, and a way for economists to sell books, or is it truly a looming disaster?

Disaster Aversion

For various reasons, most people never consider the possibility of an extended period of disaster. If we do think about it, most of us quickly conclude that such an event is out of our control anyway, so we put it out of our mind. We conclude that we can't change, so we avoid thinking about it.

Yet, almost daily we are made aware of major changes in the lives of others. We have friends or family members diagnosed with cancer, or a loved one dies in a traffic accident. When these things happen we tend to think, or hope, that bad things won't happen to us. We don't think that disaster will strike us and yet at the same time, we reluctantly acknowledge that personal and wide-spread tragedies do sometimes happen.

If we do experience personal tragedy, despite our inner turmoil, we remain confident that the fabric of society will remain solid and supportive. Family, friends, our church or some government agency, will be there to help. In our society we've always had a safety net, so even sweeping change isn't seen as a serious threat.

Here in the United States, most people expect things to get progressively better, but never much worse. If we suffer one step backward, we anticipate a swift turnaround and two steps forward. If we need help, we are confident that someone will be there to help us recover. It's always been that way, at least in our lifetime.

After all, our standard of living is significantly higher than it was in our parents' era, so we expect this trend to continue. Most expect it to continue forever—or at least throughout our life and the life of our children. Is this a reasonable expectation?

The byproduct of national affluence is a sense of comfortable assurance. Like the sun rising after a night of darkness, we expect stability and safety to automatically appear in our future.

This *normalcy bias* is dangerous, additionally so if we close our eyes to the indicators of change. When our view of reality is clouded by these misconceptions, it obscures the 'red flags' which warn us of trouble.

Yet, this doesn't need to be the case.

Responsible people needn't be caught unawares.

Thankfully, warning signs, often referred to as *signs of the times*, are usually present before major disasters and emergencies strike. Because of this, responsible people actively look for them. We don't need to be an "expert" to see these warning signs.

Still, being aware of the *'signs'* isn't enough. Equally important is the need to properly evaluate what we observe, and then take appropriate action.

For those of us who want to do what we can to prepare for the future, this involves more than planning for health care and retirement. We need to also prepare for disasters and emergency situations. Therefore, it is imperative for us to recognize the key indicators *and respond with fitting action.*

This isn't something magical. It's simply vigilance and wisdom in action.

Those who successfully invest in real estate or the stock market look for indicators of change, particularly those which translate into economic risks or opportunity. Similarly, city leaders look for growth trends to help them plan new streets, expand water and sewage systems, improve electric grid capacity and other predictable needs.

This isn't rocket science. These things are accomplished simply by paying attention to what is happening.

Many of us apply basic planning techniques unconsciously. For example, we avoid driving certain routes during rush hour, or on a holiday weekend we might go to the gas station early to avoid a long wait. In the grocery store, we look for a short checkout line or a cashier we know to be quick. In these situations we have learned to identify indicators, or signs, and we adjust our lives accordingly.

For some of us, from an early age we were taught that we need to plan for unforeseen and unexpected developments. For others, this understanding comes when we embrace responsible adulthood.

For example, responsible people who are able, purchase life and health insurance to protect their family, and fire / theft insurance for their home. They hope they will never need these insurance policies, yet they still make these preparations. Similarly, even if you don't think that economic or social chaos is ahead, preparation is still appropriate. It's simply something that responsible people do.

Prudent people are diligent about personal responsibility. And when they have the opportunity, they are intentional about preparing for all aspects of their future.

Today we have just such an opportunity. We are observing potent indicators of significant economic and social change. These have the potential to be game-changers in our life. Therefore, it is critically important for us to give serious attention to preparing for a time of upheaval. That's what rational, thinking people do.

To accomplish this, we need to do four things:

First, we need to intentionally shed our *normalcy bia*s, and keep shedding it as it has a tendency to return. **Second,** we must be intentional about looking for the *signs of the times* that will help us plan for the future. **Third,** we need to learn how to evaluate those signs. And, **Fourth,** learn how to use them as guidelines to help us actually prepare.

"A prudent person foresees danger and takes precautions. The simpleton goes blindly on and suffers the consequences."

Holy Bible
Proverbs 22:3

"Take a lesson from the ants, you slacker. Learn from their ways and become wise! Though they have no prince or governor or ruler to make them work, they labor hard all summer, gathering food for the winter."

"But you lazy slacker, how long will you sleep?

When will you wake up?"

"A little extra sleep, a little more slumber [ignoring that which is important], a little folding of the hands to rest [relax and contemplate]— then poverty will pounce on you like a bandit; scarcity will attack you like an armed robber."

Holy Bible
Proverbs 6:6-11

Chapter 2

Unprecedented Government Preparations

Risk of Major Threat:
Is it Credible or a Conspiracy Theory?

Is there a credible threat of widespread national disaster? Is it plausible that a large affluent nation such as the United States, can quickly transition from peace to a chaotic national emergency in a short period of time? For most people this is a fantastical suggestion.

Is this reaction due to a 'normalcy bias,' or is it because it's truly fanciful? Where is the truth in this debate?

What do the serious experts have to say about this topic? Conspiracy theories abound, but what is real-world and what is imagined?

Also, what is the U.S. Government's expectation? What are the experts saying, and more importantly, what is the government actually doing?

If actions speak louder than words, then with confidence we can conclude that the U.S. Government thinks the threat is credible. In fact, more than credible; government actions suggest that we are facing serious threats in the not-too-distant future.

This is a jarring but solid starting point on which to build our own analysis of the situation. Let's take a look at what the U.S. Government is doing in regard to disaster preparations. Then, let's see what we can do to identify and mitigate our own risks.

The Federal Government's
Preparations are Revealing

One of the clearest indicators of anticipated major change is the United States Government's massive and comprehensive preparations. Even without delving into any 'classified' projects, we can learn a great deal just by observing.

Currently in progress is a collection of extraordinary activities, undertaken by many different government departments and agencies. Quietly and sidestepping fanfare, these government activities have been underway for more than a decade.

Methodical and with monotonous plodding, these efforts have usually garnered little news media attention. It's no wonder. Viewed individually these activities are mostly unremarkable. Yet, with a little research and viewed together as a package, startling revelations can be uncovered from government sources. These revelations can help guide our own preparations.

Why is this important? Why has this been done quietly? Why isn't the news media connecting the dots?

Judging by the massive scope of the preparations, government officials see a future which will require drastic measures. They clearly want to forestall economic impact of the coming crisis, and mitigate the potential for public panic and backlash. Yet the scope of the preparations is too big to keep secret, so the undertaking has been divided into thousands of pieces. Apparently they are buying time. They want to maximize preparations while they can, without causing alarm.

Yet, you and I have the opportunity to be more discerning. When news stories and government-supplied information is collected and considered together, an obvious pattern emerges. We can learn from it.

Two foundational aspects of
government planning are obvious...

1. The U.S. Government is expecting major problems. Moreover, they anticipate widespread effects and public panic. Therefore, it is only prudent for us to personally prepare for both the anticipated public panic as well as for the emergency situation itself.

2. The government has recently implemented draconian administrative measures to manage what they believe is a looming emergency situation, a state of affairs that will bring about a protracted crisis. These disaster-related presidential Executive Orders are extremely unpopular with both political parties. Therefore, this willingness to suffer universal political push-back, suggests that the administration believes the actions will be necessary. And, they think the emergency situation will emerge in the not-too-distant future. Otherwise they would not implement these universally unpopular measures. Therefore, we too, need to get serious about our own readiness.

If the experts are wrong, and this serious emergency situation doesn't happen, our personal preparations are not wasted. We are simply prepared for a more typical natural disaster. The odds are high that most of us will benefit from disaster preparations at some point in our future.

So there isn't a downside. Why not gear-up and get ready now with extra urgency?

Either way, it would be imprudent to discount that that the U.S. Government is preparing for massive civil unrest and substantial physical and economic devastation. There is considerable evidence that this is the situation they anticipate.

The U.S. Government is currently spending billions of dollars on these efforts, and these disaster preparations are an order of magnitude beyond anything that has previously been undertaken—even in wartime.

As a matter of public record, we note that the Department of Homeland Security (DHS), the Federal Emergency Management Agency (FEMA), the Centers for Disease Control and Prevention (CDC) and other federal and State agencies, are all getting ready for multiple problems. These include: national pandemic, terrorism / warfare, nuclear strike/incidents, major food supply problems, power grid collapse, disruption of internet and communication systems, and widespread violence and anarchy.

How do we know this?

As these preparations are individually reported, it looks like another boring example of government contingency planning. However, when the stories and details are consolidated, what emerges is a powerful indication that a massive, *coordinated,* national preparation campaign is underway.

Presidential Executive Orders issued by both President G. W. Bush and President Barack Obama, provide a framework for these activities. If you doubt the wide-sweeping magnitude of this undertaking, read President Obama's *Executive Order* of March 16, 2012 (EO 13603) which is available in the *Federal Register*, an official website of the National Archives of the U.S. Government (www.Archives.gov). It can also be found in the appendix of this book.

There are a number of Executive Orders which relate to disaster preparedness, but this one illustrates the breadth of the anticipated disaster, and the draconian measures they think will be necessary. These measures are staggering in scope and blatantly unconstitutional. Yet, these Executive Orders have nevertheless been implemented. In these we see a major expansion of federal power and presidential power, all geared toward disaster or emergency-situation management.

Of course, 'Emergency-Powers Orders' are not something new. They have been enacted by past presidents of both political parties. It is not unusual for them to stretch the constitutional authority of the president. However with these recent Orders, the U.S. Constitution, which forms the foundation for governance and law in the United States, is literally set aside. It is effectively suspended.

A Powerful Indicator: A completely new framework for governance has been created in these new national emergency-preparedness plans.

According to the government's Congressional Research Service, "If issued under a valid claim of authority and published in the *Federal Register*, executive orders may have the force and effect of law." Our president is counting on that.

In the last couple of years, a whole slew of Executive Orders on emergency preparedness have been enacted. Plus, the U.S. Congress has passed a number of related laws, as well, such as the National Defense Authorization Act of FY 2012.[47] So we have a wealth of information which telegraphs the government's new framework, and the sweeping scope of the government's new preparation efforts.

Executive Order (E.O. 13603), titled *National Defense Resources Preparedness*, does not give us specifics on "Why?" the government is undertaking these extensive in-depth preparations, but it does contain clues.[48]

Conspiracy theorists see various nefarious agendas behind the "Why?" of these EOs. Some of these theories may be correct, but an elaborate conspiracy can't be proven from the content of the Orders[49] themselves. An intentional disregard for the Constitution and the laws of the land is certainly demonstrated, but we don't find in the Orders themselves a 'smoking gun' that specifically explains what threat, or what circumstance, the government is preparing to face.

In any case, motivation is beyond the scope of this book. We are focusing here on understanding what the government is

---

[47] H.R. 1540 (112th Congress), signed by President Obama on Dec. 22, 2011, when most people were busy with the holiday season.

[48] Forbes Magazine, "Obama's Plan To Seize Control Of Our Economy And Our Lives," by Jim Powell, April 29, 2012.

http://www.forbes.com/sites/jimpowell/2012/04/29/obamas-plan-to-seize-control-of-our-economy-and-our-lives/

planning, so that we can use this information to help us determine if a major catastrophe is likely. And if it is, what we can do to personally prepare for our own well-being and safety.

If we take the time to assess the government's preparations which are already underway, and inspect the legal preparations which run parallel to the government's physical preparations, we can figuratively open a window to see what is anticipated.

When the physical and legal preparations are evaluated together, we gain a clear picture of the results of the disastrous circumstance the government is planning to encounter. Consequently, even if we don't yet have a clear understanding of what will instigate the emergency situation, we can still be forewarned. We can still identify many of the specific problems we can expect to encounter, and solve them. Therefore, we can adroitly engage in our own planning efforts.

Importantly, we can undertake the general preparations which are universal to all major emergencies, and we can also engage in specific preparations, and prioritize our efforts, based on the government's priorities. Savvy planning requires an understanding of the problems to be faced; not an understanding of what initiated the disaster.

For us the axiom, "extreme circumstances require extreme measures," is particularly pertinent. The government's preparations are, without a doubt, extreme measures. So, extreme circumstances are obviously anticipated. For that reason, our preparations need to reflect this same gravity and urgency.

If the government does suspend the Constitution during an emergency situation, that would be illegal. But according to the courts, apparently contingency plans which include this possibility are not. Regardless of your viewpoint on the legality, the bottom line is that these plans paint a picture of extreme measures. Furthermore, these Constitution-suspending actions are not just one of many possible responses outlined; these specific Constitution-suspending actions form the backbone for the extensive preparations that are now underway. This demonstrates the high level of threat the government anticipates.

Since this aspect is distractingly controversial, I need to digress and briefly address the issue. Without a doubt, this is a critically important issue even though it is beyond the scope of this book. Nevertheless, we need to get beyond it if we are going to focus on our own emergency-situation preparations. Our focus here is preparing for an emergency situation, not political commentary. At this point, if we get distracted by the politics we may fail to physically prepare for the looming disaster.

Though I'm now embarrassed to admit it, during my years as a police officer there were a number of times when I violated the Constitution. Never intentionally, and never in a way that generated a complaint, but in hindsight I now see that those actions were inappropriate. My focus was on making the community safe. I was well intentioned—but I was still in the wrong.

Even though the Constitution is the supreme law of the land, in the hot zone of certain dangerous situations, I didn't even think about it. My actions were simply expedient. At the time I thought my actions were justified.

For example, when a police officer is searching a neighborhood for a fugitive, getting permission or a warrant to search a building may not happen. This isn't because the rights of the property owner are not respected, it's because the situation is dire and the officer feels that the risk is high and it's not the time for 'niceties.' Of course, such a search would be totally legal if the officer was in hot pursuit chasing a fleeing felon. However, the legal situation changes when it is simply a search, and the responding police officers don't have a clue as to the whereabouts of the violent criminal.

In a grave and potentially violent situation, most law-abiding citizens are okay with this behavior. That is probably why no one ever complained about my actions.

For the uninitiated this may seem like a minor point. If it was your neighborhood that was at risk you might wholeheartedly endorse such an illegal search. You may think my actions were justified. Nevertheless, this is one of the many important distinctions which separate a free society from a police state. Unconstitutional searches are an anathema to liberty.

Our nation's Founding Fathers had experienced tyranny. When they built our Ship of State, the Articles of the Constitution were the cannon to defend us from government overreach. They knew this was the precursor to the abuse of power which invariably comes in its wake, so they prepared us for it. They also knew that these defenses would be needed most when the Ship was embattled.

Today, as members of the law enforcement community, military, government officials and others prepare for a serious and potentially violent disaster, most are motivated by a sincere desire to bring safety and security to our nation. Unfortunately, mission creep and "facing the challenge" has moved them into dangerous territory. Yet for most of these people, that is not intentional.

For those government officials who do think about the Constitution, many consider it to be a malleable set of guidelines, not the law. Or, they have the attitude that the ends justify the means. Either way, they don't recognize that what they are planning will ultimately do more harm than good.

The survival of our Republic does not rest on expediency. It rests on the firm foundation given to us in our Constitution and Bill of Rights.

Nonetheless, by analyzing the federal government's actions, we can gain important insight into the nature of what the government's experts think is coming. And, what the government plans to do about it.

Naysayers continue to assert that these Executive Orders are innocuous, but they fail to explain "why?" these EO orders were written. If there wasn't some event or eventuality which would lead to their implementation, why were they written?

It would be helpful to know the specifics of what it is the government thinks is going to cause the coming disaster, but at this point we don't have enough evidence to form a verifiable conclusion. We can't be certain if the tipping-point event is an economic disaster, nuclear or biological war, revolution, solar storm or EMP which collapses our power grid, nationwide drought leading to food supply problems, pandemic, or what. This is frustrating, but since we can discern the government's response, we can prepare for what is coming. We don't need to fibrillate in ineffective activity.

NOTE: In addition to Presidential Executive Orders (EO), there are other presidential administrative directives which, according to the courts, have the full power and enforceability of a law passed by Congress. Among others, this includes 'Homeland Security Presidential Directives' (HSPD) and 'Emergency Support Functions' (ESF). These may be unconstitutional and illegal when utilized, they may grant the president powers that the Constitution specifically forbids, and they may be buried and obfuscated in a EO that purports to have a different purpose (such as what President Truman did during World War II, when he used an EO on military base security to arrest and incarcerate without trial Americans of Japanese descent), but the text of these EOs is nevertheless still publically accessible and recorded in the Federal Register. This is not the case with other forms of presidential orders.

In modern times, several Republican and Democrat presidents have used something beyond EOs, when their desired action was far beyond illegal and unconstitutional. These presidential decrees are referred to as Presidential Policy Directives' (PPD). [They are sometimes also referred to as 'National Security Presidential Directives' (NPSD), 'Presidential Decision Directives' (PDD), and 'Security Decision Memoranda' (SDM).] Whichever name the president chooses to utilize, these 'laws' are apparently used to authorize activities and agendas that Congress and the American people would not tolerate.

If you are like me, you may be tempted to relegate this topic to the world of the conspiracy theory crowd. But it's not. Recently, due to a clerical error, a *USA Today* investigative reporter was able to confirm that President Obama has enacted at least 19 secret PPD laws. Though perhaps not as frequent as Obama, presidents Truman, Nixon, Clinton and G.W. Bush have also used this mechanism. [50]

It isn't much of a leap to conclude that the purpose of a PPD is to authorize government entities to engage in illegal activities. However, since EOs are already used to bypass Congress to expedite emergency actions, to grant imperial power to the President, and to create unconstitutional laws, what new 'authorized' activities would be so far beyond these that they would necessitate using a 'secret' law?

---

[50]   These 'Presidential Policy Directives' (PPD) have the full power and effect of a law even though they were not passed by Congress, even though they remain secret. For a brief synopsis of this issue, read the USA Today newspaper article, *"Obama has issued 19 secret directives,"* June 24, 2015.
http://www.usatoday.com/story/news/politics/2015/06/24/presidential-policy-directives-form-secret-law/29235675/

Far Beyond Routine

When we look at the details, the only rational conclusion is that this is far beyond routine contingency planning. These government strategies are too in-depth and too specific, and the physical preparations too massive to simply be general contingency plans.[51]

A close look at the details does give us a number of important insights. It's this framework that we need to focus on first, so that we can prudently design our own response.

---

[51]   For example, National Security Presidential Directive 51 (NSPD-51), the "National Continuity Policy" act, creates a comprehensive plan and implements continuity of government infrastructure for all federal agencies and departments. The stated purpose is to overcome any 'Catastrophic Emergency' and to insure 'Continuity of Government' in any circumstance where the federal government (not the people) might be at risk. NSPD-51 gives the U.S. president the right to unilaterally take any action he deems necessary for the welfare of the national government. It also establishes a 'Counsel of Governors.' Appointed by the president, these Governors will oversee state and local governments on behalf of the President.

An Example: Presidential Executive Order (EO) 13603

As we study each provision of the following presidential EO (and related EOs, see footnote[52]), we need to ask, "Why is this aspect of the Order necessary?" "What does this provision indicate?" "What positive and negative activities and actions might be facilitated by this EO?"

Not only is this informative, the answers to questions such as these can help us build a solid foundation on which to build our own emergency preparations plan. Moreover, since the answers to these questions reveal that these government plans are very specific, not just general disaster preparations, they can help us more narrowly focus our own efforts.

I have included a dozen "indicators" and "clues" in the following section, but I encourage you to analyze this presidential Executive Order and related EOs yourself.

To help get you started, I have included EO 13603 in the appendix of this book. As you read this EO and the others which

---

[52] Other eye-opening presidential Executive Orders which give the president and federal government powers that are not granted by the Constitution include: EO 10995, which provides for seizing control of communications systems and the news media; EO 10997, provides for federal control of all supplies of gasoline, diesel, fuel oil, heating fuel, natural gas, and the mining of all minerals; EO 10999, includes a plan for federalizing all supplies of food and food producing companies, and all food production equipment and materials (seeds, etc.); EO 11000, allows the government to draft civilians into work brigades under federal supervision; EO 11001, allows the federal government to take over all health, education and welfare functions; EO 11002, designates the Postmaster General to operate a 'national registration' of all persons; EO 11003, provides for the seizure of commercial as well as privately owned aircraft; EO 11004, allows the federal Housing and Finance Authority to relocate communities; EO 11005, railroads and rail transportation, any lake river or waterway which could be used for transportation, and any warehouse or storage facility or building; EO 11049, assigns the emergency preparedness function to federal departments and agencies, overriding the States; EO 11051, authorizes the President to implement EOs not just during war, but also during a period of "international tension," or when he determines that an economic or financial crisis exists; EO 11310, transfers control of all penal and correctional institutions to the U.S. Department of Justice; EO 11921, establishes control over all mechanisms of production, energy, wages, and prohibits Congress from reviewing or interfering with presidential actions for six months after their implementation. For specific details, visit the U.S. government's Federal Register website, www.FederalRegister.gov, and download and read the full text of these presidential Executive Orders as officially recorded.

relate to the federal government's preparations for an emergency situation, consider these provisions in light of the government's actual, physical preparations. I have identified several of these in the following chapters.

I encourage you to form your own conclusions. You'll note that I've intentionally avoided telling you mine, as I think the EOs combined with government activities, chart a path to what we can expect. In any case, since this is all so unusual, it is important for you to 'own' your own conclusions.

Publically, the mainstream news media and many elected officials say they are unconcerned, and that they have faith in the government to do the right thing. But privately, the government officials I know, all express grave concern.

Some watchdog groups, such as 'Snopes.com' which exposes urban legends, trivializes these concerns. However, since these are the same people who trivialize Planned Parenthood's harvesting of human body parts and selling them to the highest bidder, their viewpoint seems to be tainted by their political proclivities.

In any case, this is too important and the implications too momentous, to be summarily discounted. I encourage you to do your own research and form your own conclusions, now. I urge you to deal with this right away, while you still have time to be proactive with your own emergency preparations. Our focus here is the need to be prepared, not political commentary.

Regardless of legality and the political implications, these government plans reflect a willingness to ignore the Constitution, and engage in emergency activities and a timeline that suggests grave seriousness and urgency. These EOs and activities express an urgent need for desperate measures.

What do you conclude? Do you find all of this to be highly unusual? Do you think it might be prudent to respond with similar fervor, and get serious about developing your own emergency plan?

The 'National Defense Resources Preparedness' Act (NDRPA)
Presidential Executive Order 13603

You may want to read the full text of this EO yourself, so I included it in the appendix of this book, but here are a few of the highlights. Plus, a brief commentary as to what we can deduct from these provisions.

The administration has rightly claimed that the wording of this particular EO is not very different from those enacted by prior presidents. However, though these disaster preparations began in earnest during the era of President Clinton and have been ongoing since that time, the recent changes and collective contents of these Orders is nevertheless sobering. The changing of a few words is hardly inconsequential. In fact, most Americans find these provisions shocking.

Of course, the underlying issue is trust. If the federal government can be trusted to always do the right thing, then this Executive Order and the other related EOs may not represent a problem. However, in recent years the federal government has repeatedly ignored the constitutional rights of its citizens and failed to uphold the laws of the land, so this level of trust seems imprudent.

In any case, the issue here is what actions are made possible by the series of Executive Orders now in place, and how they will affect us in the future. Since our focus here is disaster preparations and national emergencies, we need to give particular attention to those EOs which relate to these subjects.

There is another aspect of this that can't be ignored. U.S. history includes many examples of EO abuse. During World War II, President Roosevelt issued a seemingly innocuous but open-ended Executive Order [53] on military base security. A few months later, this same EO was used to affect the arrest, and incarceration without trial, of patriotic Americans of Japanese descent. These people lost their freedom, their jobs and businesses, and their property and possessions. This blemish on U.S. history needs to

---

[53] EO 9066 – "Authorizing the Secretary of War To Prescribe Military Areas," February 19, 1942

be remembered, and applied to our current situation which is suspiciously similar.

Throughout U.S. history, Executive Orders have occasionally been misused, but since WWII it has become a pattern. The past three presidents have used EOs to quickly enact fiat 'laws' which bypass Congress and ignore the Constitution. Therefore, we need to remember: Broad open-ended EOs are often used as a mechanism to assert unconstitutional authority for actions, as well as to lay the groundwork for furtive measures like those of Roosevelt.

The 12 Key Provisions of the 'National Defense Resources Preparedness' Act (NDRPA)

With each of these key provisions, I have included a "conclusion" which is my commentary. Other conclusions are certainly possible; mine are simply the obvious, and a place to start as you formulate your own conclusions.

1) This Order makes it possible to easily and quickly invoke martial law in peacetime, without meeting any conditions.

Conclusion: This provision suggests that the anticipated event is not just a response to a terrorist incident. A terrorist attack can be construed to be an act of war, so the provision for 'peacetime' martial law would not be necessary.

2) Authorizes the conscription of any civilian into the military during peacetime, *PLUS*, it gives the federal government the mechanism to force into service anyone who is needed to augment the workforce of any federal agency, without limitations. (This also subjects these draftees to the controls of the drafting government agency, including suspension of various constitutionally protected Rights.)

Conclusion: The government's experts apparently anticipate the need for a massive workforce to combat the aftereffects of the incident. This seems to indicate not just widespread devastation, but also a protracted and labor-intensive recovery.

3) Creates the 'National Defense Executive Reserve.' This new entity, under the unelected secretary of Homeland Security, has the authority to draft into service, and relocate, any private individual or non-federal government employee (such as medical doctors and city police officers).

Conclusion: The scope of the event will be very widespread or national. Or, it will become advantageous to separate these people from family and friends.

4) Makes it possible for the federal government to nationalize any resource or business, control privately owned manufacturing facilities and production, assume control over any business or organization including nonprofits, seize food, water, and private supplies of anything they need, and demand priority procurement from privately owned businesses; all without legislative action or a declared emergency.

Conclusion: Massive quantities of supplies will be needed, far beyond the resources that the government has already stockpiled. Further, since the government has been stockpiling food, ammunition, and other emergency supplies in unprecedented quantities for more than a decade, the magnitude of the anticipated need must be truly staggering.

5) Without any congressional action or declaration of a national emergency, this Act (which functionally has the power of law), gives the federal government the authority to control farming, animals, and any public or private grower of food, as well as any food-related animal, farm and ranch equipment and supplies, food storage, and the distribution of food.

Conclusion: The anticipated situation will include mass starvation, or the threat of starvation, to a vast number of people.

6) Reassigns control of any water supply and water distribution to the federal government, regardless of private or public ownership.

Conclusion: A shortage of drinking water, or water for hygiene or irrigation, widespread drought, or water contamination, is anticipated.

7) It makes it possible for the federal government to seize any privately owned vehicle or transportation equipment, and redirect or seize any supply of fuel or energy.

Conclusion: There will either be a need to quickly transport massive quantities of supplies, or the need for a massive migration of hundreds of thousands of people. Or, the government will find it necessary to stop or limit the public's mobility.

8) Allows the government to control banking transactions, fund transfers, credit and credit card transactions and lending. This provision allows the government to back private loans without the usual checks and balances.

Conclusion: Financial collapse, rapid inflation or deflation, or the devaluing of the U.S. dollar has created financial instability.

9) Creates a 'National Defense Stockpile' of any product or equipment that any of 17 government agencies deem to be in the public interest.

Conclusion: Extreme scarcity of essential supplies, resources, or equipment is anticipated.

10) Provides for the control of any 'technology' deemed to be of critical importance.

Conclusion: Either there will be a need to apply a unified scientific/technological response to the emergency situation; or, control over the use of communication technologies such as the Internet, phones, radio, television and print technologies.

11) Expands the government's subpoena power, and therein provides the ability to force citizens to answer questions, and to force incarceration for those who fail to cooperate.

Conclusion: The government anticipates anti-government sentiment, subversion, new levels of organized crime or gang activity, or large-scale public opposition to the government's efforts.

12) It delegates presidential authority to a number of unelected cabinet members who are not subject to oversight or congressional controls.

Conclusion: The government response will not simply be a mop-up type response such as what happens after a natural disaster like a hurricane. Rather, it will be an event which hits and then expands in severity. The government either expects their response to be controversial, or there will be such great potential for further devastation that normal administrative chains-of-command will be inadequate. Moreover, the pace of developments and the need for rapid decision making and implementation will require a decentralized executive branch with eighteen president-like leaders.

What do *you* think these provisions indicate? Do you think this is simply contingency planning on steroids? Or, are these preparations based on expert analysis and actual expectation?

Clues to Help Identify Operational Plans and Patterns

If we follow the clues and look for a pattern, we can gain a good idea as to what the U.S. government thinks is coming. Though we may not be able to identify the specific type of incident which will launch implementation, we can reverse-engineer the federal government's preparations so that we, too, can more effectively prepare.

In addition to NDRPA, there is a collection of other Executive Orders and administrative directives which we can use to understand the federal government's response plan.[54] However, in the interest of brevity, I will focus here on NDRPA since it is representative of the government's planning efforts.

For those who are concerned, it needs to also be understood that a presidential Executive Order remains in effect until withdrawn. A change in the presidency does not nullify an EO. Moreover, even if the public forces the cancelation of one presidential EO such as NDRPA, there are many other Orders and administrative policies which include the same or similar provisions. These would all need to be reversed, as well as the laws which have similar provisions buried in them.

In the NDRPA Executive Order and related federal regulations, the president of the United States is granted powers the Constitution specifically prohibits. Supremely troubling on one hand, yet we do want the government to be able to respond promptly and effectively to save lives and maintain peace.

For some, this looks like a Catch-22 situation. For others, the negative aspects far outweigh the positive. Moreover, they fear that once implemented, these measures will be impossible to reverse.

Regardless of your viewpoint and your level of trust in the government's intentions, the illegality of Executive Orders (EO) such as NDRPA, does not come into play until the President uses these powers. Therefore, there is little that can be done in advance of the implementation of the Order.

---

[54] This includes these presidential Executive Orders: EO 12148 (FEMA), EO 12656 (emergency powers), EO 10990 (transportation), EO 10995 (media and communication), EO 10997 (energy and raw materials), EO 10998 (food and food production), EO 11000 (civilian work brigades), EO 11001 (health, education and public welfare), EO 11002 (mandatory registration and draft), EO 11003 (airports, aircraft and air travel), EO 11004 (forced relocation), EO 11005 (railroads and waterways), EO 11049 (federal department assignment, consolidation), EO 11051 (emergency authorizations), EO 11310 (enforcement, incarceration, tribunals, internment), EO 11921 social and financial control), EO 13603 (grants sweeping new powers to President and his representatives).

One additional provision which is beyond sobering, is that if the president does invoke this Order and puts these powers to use, various provisions of the Order use the full weight of government to stop opposition. Therefore, we cannot expect corrective measures using the courts or Congress.

The separation of power being necessary to maintain freedom, was instituted by the Founding Fathers of the United States, who established three distinct branches of government: Executive (President), Legislative (Senate and House of Representatives) and Judicial (Supreme Court and lower courts), for the purpose of maintaining a system of checks and balances. These are built into the U.S. Constitution, with the express purpose of providing balance and the mechanism to stop the abuse of power. This has been eliminated in this Executive Order. Further, the legal maneuvering built into this Executive Order makes it functionally impossible to stop implementation of these provisions, as well as the provisions of other presidential EOs.

Additionally, the Executive Order we are focusing on here (EO 13603), stipulates that anyone who gets in the way of this emergency plan can be arrested, and they can be held without trial for the duration of the emergency. This would even include State governors, elected officials such as members of State legislatures and the United States Congress, Supreme Court justices and judges, and military personnel who refuse an unlawful order.

So, though we can appreciate the need to streamline the government's response, and we resonate with the desire to react with effective and timely action, this may create a bigger problem: It is the formula for creating a disaster with far more serious and long term repercussions.

Apparently, the government's disaster plan also has the capacity to become a self fulfilling prophecy. As bizarre as this might be to contemplate, this is yet another disaster we may actually need to face. Therefore, we need to prepare for this eventuality, too.

The plan that has been implemented is not only prone to serious abuse; it can also bring a lengthy time delay in abatement. Once implemented, it will be very difficult to reverse and return things to our current 'normal.'

For those who understand why our Founding Fathers created our checks and balances system of government, which guarantees constitutional protections and the separation of power, they are horrified when they read this Order. This is no surprise, yet the Order remains in force despite complaints from all quarters.

The practical ramifications include the denial of justice, loss of liberty and private ownership, and other momentous changes. Importantly, this isn't just a proposed change that is being considered, this has already been enacted. It is poised for immediate implementation.

Notwithstanding, it is not an onerous political maneuver we are focusing on here. Rather, it is the preparations we need to undertake for what may transpire. When the United States eventually recognized that it had abused Americans of Japanese decent during World War II, the damage had already been done. A presidential apology was eventually issued, but restitution wasn't possible.

The U.S. Government is ready to roll. We need to be, too.

What I am trying to do here is open a window to help us catch a glimpse of what the government is anticipating. We need to know the provisions of their emergency response plan, so that we can understand the magnitude, scope, and nature of the disaster they think is coming. Armed with these details we can do a better job of drafting our own preparation plan.

For example, if the government started buying millions of gasmasks we would not automatically know why they are making these purchases. They might be anticipating the outbreak of an airborne disease, street riots in which they intend to use teargas, terrorists who are planning a biological warfare attack, or some other airborne threat. Still, even when we don't know the specifics of "why?" they are doing something, we can conclude that our personal emergency plan should include protection for the air we breathe.

The "why?" is important, of course. But knowing "what?" the government is doing, gives us important clues that we can use to guide our own preparations. These clues can help us get ready to face specific types of problems.

12 Clues We Can Use to Jump-Start
Our Own Preparations

As we consider the topics from the prior section (12 Key Provisions of the National Defense Resources Preparedness Act), we can form conclusions and identify the actions the government is likely to take. This can be very helpful for us as we formulate our own personal plans.

The below 'clue' numbers correspond to the topics and numbering used in the prior section:

Clue #1: Suggests that the anticipated emergency situation will require the quick implementation of martial law. Since martial law can already be enacted in a time of war (including a terrorist event), or when civil authority has broken down as a result of something such as a natural disaster, we can assume that the government is anticipating some other type of situation in which martial law would be helpful for attaining their objective.

Clue #2: Suggests that the anticipated threat will: a) require a massive amount of manpower; or, b) precipitate desertion or decimate the existing military or government employees; or, c) the public will be opposed to the action of the government and not want to help; or, d) this can be used to suspend various civil and constitutional Rights when an individual becomes a federal employee.

Clue #3: Suggests: a) A situation of such magnitude that specialists from one part of the nation will be needed in another part of the country, and that normal recruitment and humanitarian appeals will provide insufficient motivation for recruitment; b) The 'hot zone' will be so dangerous that absent force, these experts will refuse to go to where the government needs them; c) the federal government anticipates that they will need to quickly establish preeminent authority over state, county and municipal workers, as well as forced service and relocation of civilian experts such as medical workers and engineers.

Clue #4: Suggests that the demand for food, water, and essential resources will be so great that: a) the federal government will want to choose where these resources are sent, and to whom they are allocated; and b) force unwilling manufacturers to produce the goods which the government feels it needs, including the voiding of patents, and the subordination of contracts previously made with civilian buyers. We need to note that a portion of this, or all of this, can be implemented even without a declared 'state of emergency.'

Clue #5: Similar to #4, but specifically controls the production of food, the food distribution and storage systems, and to take over any private food production on both public and private land. Coupled with #3, this can be used to force companies, and individuals, to produce food and deliver it to whomever the government stipulates. Failure to obey a federal directive can result in arrest and imprisonment, or detention without trial for the duration of the emergency.

Clue #6: Similar to #4 and 5, but specifically controls all state and municipal water supplies, including reservoirs, lakes, rivers and supply lines. This gives the federal government the right to control the allocation of water for human consumption, sanitation, irrigation and for farm animals. It gives the federal government the right to seize municipal water supplies and their water sources, the output of wells on private property and water wells used for private residences. The federal government can not only seize water and water-sources, it can also stop people from using their own wells, their own stored water, and even stop rainwater collection for personal use.

Clue #7: Gives the federal government the ability to nationalize any car, truck, trailer, railroad engine or railroad car, airplane, and any other mechanized equipment that moves. Though this section specifies any fuel that is used by any vehicle or transportation equipment, the wording is such that it can also be applied to all forms of energy, such as electrical power. It also includes the production of energy in any form. This also provides for the control of roadways, both public and private, and for the seizure of any vehicle or mode of transport. This includes vehicles such as trucks which are in the process of hauling goods for the private business which owns the vehicle. Even a private car that is currently in use by a parent to drive their children home can be seized on the spot. Once again, there is no appeal process or legal recourse.

Clue #8: Gives the government the right to freeze bank accounts, and to use the private funds of individuals and corporations, and to exert total control over the monetary system.

Clue #9: Identifies 17 federal agencies and gives them the right to procure and stockpile any supplies or resources they deem necessary, all without review, oversight or spending (budget/debt) limits. Gives these agencies the right to give, sell, or deny resources to any local government entity, as well as nongovernment organizations, companies or individuals.

Clue #10: Grants the federal government the right to expand their governance of certain technologies without any underlying legislation. This also makes it possible for the federal government or its agents to secure or deny the use of these technologies. This includes force multipliers, the use of radio and satellite bandwidth, it makes it simple to block access to the internet and communication tools by opposition, controls vaccine and medical developments, and provides for government control over any research and development effort, irrespective of the negative ramifications on that private company, its stockholders, or any individual or group of individuals. Again, no appeals.

Clue #11: By the suspension of habeas corpus and other legal rights, the government can seize people without arrest and incarcerate them without trial. This paves the way for all sorts of abuses, but it would also be useful if the government finds it necessary to force the quarantine of a large part of the population.

We already have legal mechanisms for quarantining individuals and groups who pose a health risk to others, but there are legal steps in this process, including the right to counsel and access to the court system. So, since we already have laws which provide for public health needs, this seems to be in anticipation of some dangerous development; probably other than medical, which involves such large numbers of people that the existing mechanisms are too cumbersome to accomplish the government's objective.

Moreover, the expansion of subpoena power gives the government the right to interrogate people without any evidence of wrongdoing, and to hold them in jail for contempt if they fail to answer questions.

Clue #12: Suggests that the President expects to be overwhelmed by a multitude of urgent tasks and the enormity of the emergency situation, and that quick, decisive response will be absolutely necessary to maintain control.

These provisions essentially make it possible for our Commander and Chief to not only command the military, but to also command the nation like a general delegating operations to field commanders, and imbuing them with his full authority to act on his behalf. In this case, not military generals who have come up through the ranks, but rather his own appointees who answer to no one other than the president.

The provisions within this one Executive Order essentially suspend freedom and our Bill of Rights, eliminates private ownership when it's expedient, and abolishes our legal system as we know it. Under these conditions no longer would a person be presumed innocent until proven guilty, but rather assumed to be guilty until they prove themselves innocent. The separation of power between the Executive, Legislative and Judicial branches of government would be suspended. By decree, primacy is granted to the Chief Executive (U.S. president).

It seems totally farfetched to think that this could happen. Yet, this is what is provided for in this one Executive Order. This is why Republicans and Democrats alike have been outspoken critics of these sweeping Executive Orders. Nevertheless, they remain in force.

Why were they enacted? What is the looming crisis that motivated these 'legal' preparations? What are we facing? Is all this routine contingency planning, or something which is truly unusual and unprecedented?

"When people are saying, 'Everything is peaceful and secure,' then disaster will fall on them as suddenly as a pregnant woman's labor pains begin. And there will be no escape."

Holy Bible
1 Thessalonians 5:3

Chapter 3

Routine Planning or Highly Unusual?

The legal preparations discussed in the prior chapter provide the structure for the government's plan, but to properly understand the legal maneuvering, we need to also look at the physical preparations. We are not talking here about planning, but rather plans that have been implemented. These represent billions of dollars worth of spending on physical preparations, which when combined with what we know about the legal side, seems to paint a clear picture of what is anticipated.

However, first we need to ask two questions: "Do these government preparations simply represent routine contingency planning and preparation for traditional disasters?" And, "Are these physical preparations, which have been undertaken over the last two decades, something unusual?"

It seems odd that the government's preparations would be so extensive and far reaching, not to mention specific, if these efforts are routine. Also, since these physical preparations are devouring billions of dollars during a time of serious budget crisis, when there is no demand for it by other elected officials or the public; it makes this situation highly unusual.

Further, there is no evidence that the related expenditures are pork barrel allocations, nor is it crony politics. These disaster preparations do not provide a political advantage either, at least not prior to the activation of the plan.

Moreover, the physical preparations are highly orchestrated, unified strategies which reach across federal departments and leap over the fences between federal agencies. Without question, this is a vast, comprehensive, strategic undertaking.

Beyond this, and perhaps even more telling, it is extremely odd for a politician to put to paper and implement, odious and unconstitutional Executive Orders which are not supported by any political party or constituency group. In the case of NDRPA[55] this Executive Order, and related government activities, offend liberals and conservatives alike.

When was the last time you remember organizations which were politically polar opposites, to be on the same side of an issue? With NDRPA and related Executive Orders, conservative organizations such as the American Center for Law and Justice (ACLJ.org) and liberal organizations like the American Civil Liberties Union (ACLU.org) are on the same side. Similarly, the informed members of the general public are unhappy with these developments as well, yet they continue unabated.

Even notoriously liberal media outlets, such as the *Huffington Post* which has a history of always being supportive of President Obama's policies, expressed shock at these actions. After the president signed his *National Defense Resources Preparedness* Act (NDRPA), the Huffington Post was aghast. Their news report said that the President has "quietly placed the United States on a war preparedness footing."[56]

The *Huffington Post* is right. This does put the United States on a war footing, and this should be a wake-up call for the general public. But what kind of war is the President anticipating?

NDRPA was instituted at the time when President Obama was widely proclaiming that the threat of terrorism had greatly diminished. So what is the threat that he was addressing? What was his motivation for implementing this presidential Executive Order?

---

[55]   EO 13603, "National Defense Resources Preparedness Act," is included in the appendix of this book.

[56]   Huffington Post, "Barack Obama Prepares for War Footing," by Edwin Black. March 19, 2012. http://www.huffingtonpost.com/edwin-black/obama-national-defense-resources-preparedness_b_1359715.html

Additionally, it's important to understand that President Obama was not acting alone. This era of extensive preparation did not start with his administration. Nor is this a Democrat vs. Republican issue.

Though not nearly as controversial, Presidents Clinton and G.W. Bush both initiated major new initiatives aimed at preparing the nation for a catastrophic event.

It is true that President Obama ratcheted-up these preparations in a major way, but his efforts did not begin the massive new emergency preparedness effort. He just accelerated the existing momentum, and used it to build a much bigger 'preparedness' machine with much more elaborate Presidential controls.

One example of the ramped-up preparation efforts undertaken by President Obama's predecessors is the development of new 'Continuity of Government' (COG) bunker facilities.

Prior to George W. Bush's presidency, these preparations focused on Presidential succession; to maintain continuity of government if the nation's top leaders were killed or incapacitated. During the Bush era, we saw a major departure from this historic purpose.

Originally conceived by President Harry S. Truman in the 1950s as part of his Cold War civil defense plan, *Continuity of Government* (COG) preparations were undertaken to protect the President and his successors in the event of a nuclear war.

However, in 1991, after the fall of the Soviet Union and the perceived end of the Cold War, most of these facilities were closed. A decade later President George W. Bush inaugurated a new era of major expansion of COG preparations, yet his efforts were fundamentally different.

The Bush-era continuity plans included protecting government leaders, and also the national resources which would be needed by the government after a catastrophic event. It wasn't about the continuity of Presidential leadership; it was the survival of government.[57]

During the presidencies of Bill Clinton and G.W. Bush, COG was expanded to include certain scientists, and hundreds of civilians who are considered 'essential' for national leadership and recovery after a calamitous event. Whereas President Obama, has not only expanded these earlier efforts, but has added to them by implementing new, ramped-up preparations aimed at controlling the population.

The nation's original COG facility, built under the Blue Ridge Mountains of Virginia, was a massive bunker with state-of-the-art communication capabilities. That secret facility, known as Mount Weather, was designed to house a score of elected officials, some department heads, and hundreds of support staff. However, in this new era of contingency planning it was not big enough, nor sophisticated enough for the new expanded mission, so it has been replaced.

As a result, dozens of new and much larger not-so-secret 'secret' installations have been built. There are now dozens of these bunker facilities, primarily in Virginia and Maryland, but also in other parts of the country, apparently conjoined with the ten FEMA regional districts.

Though extensive, and built at a cost of billions of dollars, these Continuity of Government installations are only one element of the new, ratcheted-up National Preparation Plan.

Since 2004, there have been annual exercises in which thousands of government workers and 'essential' civilians are whisked to COG bunkers around the country. These training exercises are undertaken to test the readiness of the people, transportation, and the facilities themselves.

---

[57]   The primary documents which provide a feel for this new COG era, include NSPD 51 (aka / PDD-51 and HSPD-20), National Security and Homeland Security Presidential Directive, implemented by President G.W. Bush. The key parts of this directive remain Classified despite efforts by Congress to gain access, but a public summation document is available. President Obama has significantly expanded these COG operations through various executive orders, such as PDD-21 and a host of other Orders which focus on Critical Infrastructure Security and Resilience and COG operations.

Now, *every* department of the federal government is required to have a COG plan, as well as suitable facilities and equipment—and to train for COG annually.

However, testing the government's ability to engage in strategic retreat isn't the only training which is underway. We are now observing joint military and police actions in every major city in the U.S.; "war games," with scenarios which purport to use terrorism as the reason for the exercise, but don't generally have a credible relationship to acts of terrorism.

Another startling development: The government has established SWAT teams in federal departments that are not law enforcement agencies; organizations that do not have a military or law enforcement purpose. Plus, they have been providing military training and large quantities of military equipment to local law enforcement agencies.

New Military Technologies for Domestic Use

Jade Helm[58] is an annual military training exercise for joint forces and special operations warriors. From the onset of these domestic operations in summer of 2015, it was controversial, but the most interesting aspects were reported but not by the mainstream news media.

Military insiders publically admitted that an underlying purpose of this exercise was asymmetric warfare training—and also to condition our troops and the public. These two purposes were debated publically, and many felt the exercise was inappropriate and illegal, but that was only the tip of a very chilling iceberg.

Jade Helm attempted to normalize the concept that American citizens can be the enemy. It was also designed to desensitize the American public to an armed military presence within the United States. This is important for the National Preparedness Plan that is being implemented, since troops would need to operate in a martial law environment. Of course, that's not all there was to Jade Helm, there was much more built into this training exercise.

It is the 'Classified' aspects of the Jade Helm operation that are the most interesting. This is particularly relevant as we focus on the topic of "highly unusual" government preparedness efforts.

Since this training operation involved 7+ states, the scale of the operation made it impossible to keep the lid on all the 'Classified' aspects of the exercise. The technologies themselves remain Top Secret, but the Jade Helm operational structure has been leaked, so these details are now available in the public domain. It is this operational framework that is noteworthy, as it is a custom fit with the controversial 'civil unrest' portions of the National Preparedness Plan.

---

[58] UNCLASSIFIED//FOUO, US Army Special Operations Command, "Request to Conduct Realistic Military Training (RMT) JADE HELM 15," June 15 – September 15, 2015.

Tellingly, even though this was billed by the military as a training exercise for foreign conflicts, the news media was refused access. We now see why. Reporters were not allowed to observe these operations for a very good reason; the special operations portions of this exercise used a bevy of new, top secret, high-tech tools.

It is no accident that the official motto for the Jade Helm 15 operation was *"Master the Human Domain."* This term is widely known within the intelligence community to describe the technologies used to amass intelligence, data mine using all forms of electronic data collection from public and private sources, all to accomplish a military objective. Since terrorists use few of these conduits, this process is largely irrelevant for antiterrorist operations overseas, as well as those conducted within the United States.

For the first time on a large scale, with Jade Helm 15, the military put to use new asymmetric warfare technologies for field operations. Particularly relevant was the use of new artificial intelligence (AI) aids for battlefield strategy and decision making, and new technologies for gathering domestic intelligence. This is why the news media was not allowed to observe the training.

These new technologies were used to identify and track 'hostile' targets in real time—*from the field.* It is the A.I. and "from the field" aspects which are unusual, as these surveillance missions have historically required large teams of people based at a distant computer center. What was also unusual was that these 'simulated' exercises focused on American citizens and domestic groups with no ties to terrorism.

One of the tasks for these elite troops was to use these technologies to identify 'previously unknown' individuals who are *potentially* hostile. Once identified, these were either surreptitiously watched using A.I. surveillance tools, or deemed to be an immediate threat. Those in this second category were covertly abducted in the middle of the night or when no one is watching. These 'threats' and 'potential threats' would simply disappear.

Much like the movie *Minority Report*, spec-ops teams, in this case Navy SEALS and other special operations teams, were transformed into "Precrime" operators. The idea was to track down dissidents before they were able to act. The concept was simple, but operationally it was hugely complex. The scheme was to find links between 'known' suspected hostiles and not-yet-identified 'unknown' hostiles from the field in real time.

Using a new bag of tricks, these operators applied advanced high-tech tools to the task. New software technologies were used to merge hundreds of sources of information and different types of hardware and software, to help field operatives find and evaluate targets, and then pinpoint the location of these potential dissidents. They would then track movements, intercept communication, and intervene as they autonomously thought appropriate.

The strategy is to look for evidence of pre-crime, and grab pre-criminals before they are able to act. It is a brilliant concept if used appropriately, but as Tom Cruise discovered in the movie *Minority Report*, this power is prone to abuse; thus the controversy and the government's secrecy.

In the Jade Helm 15 exercise, these diverse tools were combined for the first time in a major field operation. These special operations troops were able to vacuum-up public and private surveillance camera feeds, automatically process these through advanced facial recognition software, as well as software which identifies people through their gait and mannerisms, couple these with voice recognition software, and activate surveillance systems in the proximity of a targeted individual. Or, the *Precrime* warriors could suddenly descend on the site and grab the person or people of interest.

This bag of tricks also includes technologies for intercepting email and text messages, monitoring purchases, watching Facebook, tweets and other social media, tracking websites visited, identifying locations and proximity via mobile phones, and RFID chips (Radio Frequency IDentification as used in newer forms of ID, credit cards, etc. which can be read from a distance), etc. Through the use of artificial intelligence, these sources of intelligence were not just monitored, but also analyzed, all without the need for any human effort. At least this was the goal.

The A.I. computers constantly monitor targeted individuals, and look for 'transactions' by these *suspects* including interactions with other people, as well as key words and the names of other individuals that would surface throughout this hodgepodge of information sources. At the same time, the A.I. system would constantly update relationship charts and behavioral indexes to maintain a 'profile' on each individual.

In addition, the plan was to also use these intelligence gathering tools to facilitate sending out false messages which look like they came from the 'target' individual's computer or phone. This classic disinformation technique was made famous by FBI Director J. Edgar Hoover in his rout of American communists, but the new version includes far more sophisticated abilities designed to discredit or confuse an enemy, instigate false flag operations by a group, or to manipulate the general public.

These new technologies also make it possible to turn "on" the microphone and/or camera on a phone or computer and automatically listen to and watch everything within range. Filtered through software that is designed to look for names, specific voices, or video images (photo recognition software), this computer program can, all on its own, locate people of interest, and notify a spec-op team if the target is within their field of operation.

Other related tools are able to look backward in time by using NSA's data collection, to track the prior locations of mobile phones, and look for points of intersection; pauses, which indicate a meeting between the dissident they are tracking and a new person. In other words, produce a new "Precrime" suspect to tag, track, and watch. Since these troops are connected by satellite to massive government computer complexes, the capacity is almost limitless.

In case any of these capabilities sound like science fiction, I assure you they are not. I am no one special, but I do have personal knowledge of these systems. The existence of these tools is not secret. What is 'Classified' is how they work, their capabilities, the integration of these tools, and the use of Artificial Intelligence to increase speed and improve results.

What made Jade Helm 15 noteworthy was not the simulated midnight abductions of dissidents and people of interest, nor was it the objective of desensitizing troops and the public, it was this Precrime function.   This undertaking required merging and integrating hundreds of types of data sources, overlaying them with automated controls to coordinate different computer systems that have different functions and operating systems, all to find suspected dissidents, identify new potential threats, and disrupt the activities of these 'enemies.'

Jade Helm 15 did demonstrate that diverse technologies can be combined with automated A.I. analysis, and used to advance military objectives on battlefield USA.   Importantly, most of this is not transferable to other parts of the world, except to a limited extent Western Europe, so the primacy is evidently domestic operations.   This fits with the National Preparedness Plan, specifically the blueprint for utilizing the U.S. military during a national crisis.

Overall, the success of Jade Helm 15 was marginal, I understand, except to prove the validity of the concept (and the prepositioning of military materiel).   For us however, the undertaking exposed abilities and a perceived need which is so significant, that it justified this monolithic allocation of resources. In the eyes of the National Preparedness Plan strategists, with Jade Helm 15, the U.S. Government got a major payoff from DARPA[59] and its many years of investing in breakthrough technologies for national security.

If not to counter terrorists in the U.S., what would be the military's objective if they were called upon to operate inside our borders? Let's not forget that major police departments, the FBI, and other state and federal law enforcement organizations already have well-trained antiterrorist SWAT teams.

In regard to the U.S. military, its seasoned special operations troops who are veterans of the Iraq and Afghanistan wars, hardly need more practice—unless the practice is to train them to operate targeting U.S. citizens and using these new battlefield technologies at home.

---

[59]   Defense Advanced Research Projects Agency: www.darpa.mil

According to the military, Jade Helm 15 was a *"US Special Operations Command (USSOCOM) sponsored exercise to improve the Special Operations Forces' Unconventional Warfare capability as part of the National Security Strategy."* [60]   So, since the main focus of this training mission was Special Operations Command, we need to look no further than the role these warriors play to understand their responsibilities in the National Preparedness Plan.

What the government's public relations people say about Jade Helm is not supported by what these troops actually do when deployed.   As Ronald Reagan was fond of saying, "trust, but verify."   We need to take this to heart if we are going to identify and analyze government preparations.

Just as with the new powers the President has given to himself through the Executive Orders he implemented, joint military and local police operations currently sponsored by USNORTHCOM[61] have historically been prohibited by law.   In the past, the United States military has been forbidden from conducting domestic military operations against American civilians.   (Apparently practice for such an event is acceptable.)   In any case, in the last decade each major U.S. city has been the center for some type of major military-federal-state-local war game exercise.

These exercises have now become so commonplace that the media has nearly stopped reporting on them.   At the time of the Boston Marathon bombing, an active joint exercise was underway in Boston and was immediately re-tasked to help with the incident.   Yet, none of the major news organizations drew attention to this unusual coincidence.

---

[60]   PowerPoint presentation created by US Special Operations Command, *"Request to Conduct Realistic Military Training (RMT), JADE HELM 15,"* May *2015,* UNCLASSIFIED//FOUO

[61]   The U.S. military's "United States Northern Command" provides command and control of Department of Defense (DOD) homeland defense efforts.

What is additionally troubling about these training operations is that civilians are often unapologetically swept-up and forced to unwillingly be a part of these exercises. In the process, they routinely have their privacy rights, constitutional protections from warrantless search and seizure, unlawful detention, and other protected rights trampled. If you happen to be in the area of the training exercise, everyone, willing or not, is considered to be a participant in the exercise. This is also illegal.

Beyond the constitutional and legal issues, these encounters are frightening for the surprised civilians who get caught-up in them. So, for the authorities to ignore these legitimate concerns and complaints, the situation must be sufficiently important that they are willing to suffer public ire.

Since the American people have not asked for anything such as this, and neither the U.S. Congress nor State governments have requested these maneuvers, we need to recognize that these developments are highly unusual. It is still unclear why these exercises are being conducted, but the fact that they are being conducted is itself informative.

Moreover, neither Homeland Security (DHS) nor the Federal Emergency Management Agency (FEMA) has the charter authority to conduct these operations. So, presidential Executive Orders are used to authorize these exercises, and the reason is cited as national security needs.

What aspect of national security? It's certainly not terrorism. For example, the core operations of operations such as Jade Helm 15 are not oriented to stopping Muslim terrorists, which is our only significant terrorism threat.[62]

Furthermore, most of these exercises are totally unnecessary. Soldiers and police officers can learn how to fast-rope out of a helicopter at a training base. They don't need to do it in downtown Los Angeles or Miami. So why conduct these shock-and-awe operations in areas populated by civilians, unless one of the objectives is, well, shock-and-awe intimidation.

These unannounced show-of-force exercises intimidate and desensitize the citizens who live and work in the area. Exercises such as this occurred in Miami, where military helicopters also fired blanks in their machineguns in the middle of downtown, which was unnecessary – unless the objective is unprofessional showmanship or intimidation.

Since these activities don't provide a commensurate training or political benefit, experts who are high-ranking former military, conclude that these exercises are in anticipation of an escalation of hostilities in U.S. cities. At the very least, the federal government is preparing the public for some future crisis, an unthinkable occasion for which they deem it necessary to communicate a clear message; resistance is futile. The kid gloves have been left at home.

---

[62] Note: The federal guideline for the identification of homeland terrorists no longer includes any Muslim groups. Currently there are nearly 100 domestic groups /categories of potential domestic terrorists. To give you the flavor of the new Watch List categories, here are a few of the listed threat-groups: Religious extremists generally, but the only groups specifically mentioned are: Evangelical and Bible-believing Christians, anyone who believes in end-times Bible prophesy, and anyone who believes in obedience to God over obedience to the State. Also, donors to the Family Research Council, American Family Association, or the Christian Action Network, and anyone who identifies as a political conservative, Libertarian, or with the Tea Party movement. The list also includes those who opposes abortion or special rights for homosexuals, those who seek to preserve the U.S. Constitution, those who support the 2nd Amendment or gun ownership, people who display patriotic bumper stickers on their cars, those who display the Gadsden Flag (Don't Tread on Me), and all military veterans who served in Iraq or Afghanistan.

The Department of Homeland Security (DHS) is stockpiling vast quantities of food, military gear and disaster-oriented supplies.

DHS has been quietly purchasing enormous quantities of freeze dried and dehydrated food, along with millions of dollars in other disaster supplies. The purchase of these items is not unusual, but the quantity of goods being purchased is odd.

I have a personal friend who tried to start a business which included the packaging and retail sales of freeze dried food, such as the food packets used by backpackers. After contacting the top 12 U.S. producers of this type of food, she was unable to find a supplier for these products. In each case she was told that they couldn't accept a new wholesale customer. They explained that the federal government was buying their entire production capacity for the foreseeable future. She finally had to give up, since she was unable to secure a source for this type of food.

Yet another indicator is the acquisition of military equipment, not just by DHS, but also by other federal agencies.

Not only have innocuous, previously benign government agencies such as the U.S. Post Office, the Department of Education, and the National Oceanic and Atmospheric Administration (NOAA) which has no security or law enforcement responsibilities, established SWAT teams, they are also stockpiling quantities of military gear, arms and ammunition. Why? These agencies now have SWAT teams that are equipped with advanced technology military weapons. This is a perturbing development, additionally so since there has not been anything to justify these actions.

In April 2014, there was an incident in southeastern Nevada in which a Bureau of Land Management (BLM) SWAT team nearly ambushed a group of protestors. The BLM SWAT team and other armed BLM employees held nonviolent protestors at gun point, and BLM snipers aimed their high-powered sniper rifles at family members, as these government agents seized and killed animals belonging to a local rancher.

This altercation was initiated as a result of a civil dispute between the BLM and a lone, family rancher. Regardless of your opinion as to which side was right, the more serious issue is that the BLM was ready to use deadly force rather than the courts to enforce their agenda. Why?

Experts conclude that this is what their military-sponsored training prepared them to do. Fortunately, widespread exposure of the incident 'live' using cell phone-transmitted video, along with the circumspect actions of the local sheriff, stopped the bloodshed.

Various media outlets reported on the story, but no one asked why the federal Bureau of Land Management had hundreds of heavily armed SWAT officers, or why they immediately resorted to the threat of deadly force rather than utilize the court system? These are important questions. I suspect the answer has more to do with training these BLM people for a nationwide emergency situation or disaster, than it does training them for land disputes with harmless ranchers.

Government agencies are stockpiling massive amounts of ammunition and military gear.

Contingency planning is the duty of every responsible government. Yet, the sheer magnitude of our government's spending during a time of fiscal crisis, exposes an orientation of urgency.

We may not know the specifics of what is expected, but the timing and pattern of government spending does telegraph a perceived need for haste. These preparations also give us a clear picture of the violent working environment they expect for federal agencies and law enforcement officers, and the possibility that these SWAT skills and military gear may be needed in the not-too-distant future.

Since there have been widespread rumors regarding the Department of Homeland Security (DHS) purchasing incomprehensible amounts of ammunition, I decided to see if I could uncover the truth. Since most government purchases are a matter of public record, spending patterns can shed light on perceived need. In this case I thought it might also spotlight the extent and duration of civil unrest they anticipate. As I learned when I was a police detective, *"Follow the money."*

In regard to ammunition, what is often missed is that due to liability concerns, law enforcement officers need to train with the same ammunition that they carry in their guns. I expected this extra quantity of ammunition for training purposes, to be how these rumors started. From past experience, I've learned that the general public doesn't understand that this expensive ammunition is needed for training, so I wasn't expecting what I uncovered.

Most Department of Homeland Security (DHS) procurement details are available on the government website, www.FedBizOps.gov. With the help of some research assistance, I discovered that the rumors I expected to disprove are in fact, true.

I was able to verify that federal law enforcement agencies have purchased unprecedented amounts of ammunition. Just in the past three years, DHS and other federal agencies have purchased

2,118,002,000 rounds of ammunition. This is primarily hollow-point ammunition, a type which cannot be used in other countries as it is prohibited by international law (which the U.S. endorses). Therefore, there can be no misunderstanding. This ammunition was purchased for domestic use.

Moreover, these statistics do not include ammunition purchased by non-law enforcement federal agencies, nor state, county and municipal law enforcement agencies. Many of these agencies are also purchasing large quantities of ammunition. For example, in July 2015, the obscure Bureau of Reclamation requisitioned 52,000 rounds of ammunition[63] ostensibly to protect Hoover Dam, even though there is no indication that the dam has ever been seriously threatened.

Nevertheless, despite no evidence of need, thousands of state and local law enforcement agencies have received grants from Homeland Security to increase their local stockpiles of ammunition, military arms, and military equipment. These purchases are not included in these statistics.

---

[63] Las Vegas Sun newspaper, July 9, 2015, "Agency's request for 52,000 rounds of ammo for Hoover Dam prompts inquiry," by By *Kyle Roerink*.
http://lasvegassun.com/news/2015/jul/09/fed-agency-wants-52000-rounds-ammo-hoover-dam-prom/

To put these ammunition purchases in perspective:

During the years of war in Iraq, the U.S. military expended an average of 66 million rounds of ammunition per year. Therefore, the amount of ammunition purchased by federal law enforcement agencies, *for domestic use,* is equivalent to 32 years of war in Iraq. Keep in mind, too, that these are law enforcement agency purchases, not Department of Defense military purchases.

As another point of reference, it is worth mentioning the number of federal law enforcement officers in the United States. According to the U.S. Department of Justice, there are only 45,000 federal law enforcement officers in the U.S. who perform criminal investigation and law enforcement duties.[64]

Contingency planning is important, but why do we need 2.12 billion rounds of ammunition for domestic law enforcement use? This number is so staggeringly large that it's hard for us to get our head around. Look at it this way: This is enough ammunition to shoot every adult in America 9 times. It is enough to kill every man, woman and child in the United States, and still have nearly 2-billion rounds (1,799,142,944) of ammunition left over.

Thankfully, the general public seems to be waking up to these odd developments. When we started our blog site on preparedness (www.36ReadyBlog.com) three years ago, it was in response to requests from former students in our firearm self-defense classes. In those early days, our preparedness blog had an average of a dozen visitors per month, primarily former students. Now, just three years later and without any promotion, we have 70,000 users.

Americans may not know what's coming, but they are experiencing a sense of disquiet about the future. Apparently, there is good reason for their anxiety.

---

[64] U.S. Department of Justice, Bureau of Justice Statistics, Bulletin, June 2012, "Federal Law Enforcement officers 2008" by Brian A. Reaves, Ph.D., BJS Statistician http://www.bjs.gov/content/pub/pdf/fleo08.pdf

More SWAT Teams?

Why does the federal Bureau of Land Management (BLM), Department of Agriculture, the federal Railroad Retirement Board, Tennessee Valley Authority, the federal Office of Personnel Management, Consumer Product Safety Commission, Department of Education, U.S. Postal Service (USPS), National Oceanic and Atmospheric Administration (NOAA), and similar agencies, which are not law enforcement entities, need SWAT teams?

These and other federal agencies that are not law enforcement agencies, now have SWAT teams which have been trained by the military and armed with military weaponry.[65]

Military Tanks for Domestic Use?

Why do federal, state and local law enforcement agencies in the U.S. need thousands of military tanks designed for urban combat?

---

[65] Gertz, Bill (May 28, 2014). Memo outlines Obama's plan to use the military against citizens. *The Washington Times*.

Portraying Ordinary Citizens as the Enemy?

Why has the Department of Homeland Security (DHS) developed new "no hesitation" shooting-training targets?

In addition to the billions of rounds of ammunition that the Department of Homeland Security (DHS) has purchased, they have also developed new shooting targets for training. Rather than use the standard "silhouette" practice targets used by law enforcement agencies around the country, DHS has had special targets made. DHS refers to these as "no hesitation" targets.[66]

Take a look at the photo which illustrates three of these new "no hesitation" targets, positioned above three standard law enforcement "silhouette" targets. What does this change in training suggest to you? Why do you think DHS feels that these new ordinary citizen, "no hesitation" targets are needed?

With the entire collection of photo realistic "no hesitation" shooting targets, none of them look like Islamic terrorists. None of them depict street gang members. All the images are of ordinary looking Americans. Why?

---

[66] Public outcry against DHS for commissioning these targets was substantial, but it was the public pressure applied to the manufacturer which succeeded in stopping the production of these anti-citizen targets. This responsiveness was in stark contrast to the reaction of DHS, which was to look for a new manufacturer.

Top Row: New DHS "No Hesitation" shooting targets. Bottom Row: Standard targets used by most state and local law enforcement agencies.

What is going on?
What is the federal government preparing to face?

This is far more elaborate and extensive than just routine training and disaster-prep stockpiling. Nor does it have any relationship to what is needed to secure discounts by placing large orders. That could be accomplished easily without any increase.

Again, considered individually perhaps just an oddity, but when considered together a demonstrable pattern emerges. It paints a discordant picture of the future they anticipate.

These purchases of weapons, massive amounts of ammunition, urban tanks, and the labeling of ordinary citizens as domestic terrorists, suggests that the U.S. Government is expecting a new type of domestic emergency situation. The evidence indicates that they are preparing for domestic upheaval beyond what the American people experienced during the four year American civil war (1861-1865).

On the local level: In every state and urban area, we see federal funding of military training for law enforcement officers. We also see the delivery of advanced weaponry and military hardware to state, county and local police departments throughout the nation.

This includes funding to expand the number of local police, county sheriff, state, and federal SWAT teams. Even small no-crime rural communities are receiving funds to arm, equip, and train SWAT teams, and to purchase armored vehicles (in addition to the MRAP urban-combat tanks they have been donated by the military).

Not only is DHS providing funding for military-style body armor and tactical gear, they are also distributing and funding the acquisition of high-tech weapon-equipped robots and surveillance drones equipped with FLIR systems.

These unmanned nearly-silent aerial drones can not only track movement with cameras capable of identifying people on the ground, they also use body heat and other high-tech sensors to find people who are hiding. These FLIR systems can also identify camouflaged structures, supplies buried deep in the ground, and they can look through the walls of buildings to watch the activities of the people inside. This isn't new technology, but the broad distribution of these tools is new and highly unusual.

DHS is distributing a new generation of technologically advanced surveillance gear.

In addition to distributing military hardware, DHS is also funding the research and development of all sorts of ultra high-tech surveillance gear and other, people-control technologies. These items are being widely distributed to local law enforcement agencies—*even though these cannot be legally be used.*

These "donations" to local law enforcement include: devices to facilitate remote surveillance, facial recognition software, license plate reading and vehicle-tracking tools, equipment which makes it possible to track the movement of *all* vehicles in a region, surreptitious DNA collection from children and those who are not criminal suspects, cellular phone signal disruptors, the spoofing and manipulation of email, telephones, and radio signals, social media manipulation tools, equipment to monitor and remotely search computers and phones, wide-area communication disruption gear (TV, radio, Wi-Fi, etc.), selective Internet blocking and automated denial-of-use tools, remote vehicle-engine disruption transmitters, high frequency sound generators for crowd control, quick-deployment razor-wire walls, and portable incarceration centers.

Millions of dollars of this high-tech equipment have already been distributed to state and local law enforcement agencies. And, more of this equipment has been ordered and will soon be on its way.

What is especially odd is that if these resources were used to gather evidence to make an arrest, most of the cases would be thrown out of court. Why? It's because most of this equipment is illegal for law enforcement use. They certainly can't use it without a warrant, and they aren't even requesting warrants. So why is this equipment being distributed? Why is the federal government training state and local agencies to use this equipment that cannot be used for crime fighting?

If these technologies were used for law enforcement purposes, including traditional antiterrorism investigations, specifics on the capabilities of these technologies would become known as details must be revealed in the court mandated 'disclosure' process. To counter this, DHS is requiring recipient agencies to sign nondisclosure documents. In violation of the law, DHS has repeatedly refused to honor court orders of disclosure, citing national security[67] concerns. However, since crime and the apprehension of criminals are not within the scope of their national security mission, there must be another reason.

The questions which persist:

1) Are these tools supplied to law enforcement agencies intended for illegal use? Or,

2) Is this equipment being supplied to meet a future, not-crime-related need?

Why is the federal government distributing this advanced technology equipment to law enforcement agencies if they can't legally use it? If these expensive resources are not being used to apprehend and prosecute criminals, why are they being bought, and why is DHS providing training to law enforcement agencies in how to use this equipment?

The Department of Homeland Security, an agency which was created solely for domestic security within the United States, is engaged in highly unusual preparations. Why are they doing this? What is it they are expecting? What are they preparing for?

---

[67] According to President Obama's Executive Order 13526, to invoke "national security" as justification for secrecy, the situation must directly relate to, and have a compellingly negatively impact on, the nation's security. It must also fall into one of these categories: a) military plans, weapons systems, or operations; b) foreign government information, c) intelligence activities (including covert action), intelligence sources or methods, or cryptology; d) foreign relations or foreign activities of the United States, including confidential sources; e) scientific, technological, or economic matters relating to the nation's security; f) United States Government programs for safeguarding nuclear materials or facilities, vulnerabilities or capabilities of systems, installations, infrastructures, projects, plans, or; g) protection services relating to the nation's security; or h) the development, production, or use of weapons of mass destruction. / When in doubt, the stated policy is that all information should remain available to the public. The criteria for invoking national security to maintain secrecy, is that there must be a compelling need present which relates directly to protecting the nation.

It has become apparent that disaster preparations which include hunkering down at home with the FEMA-recommended 3-day supply[68] of food and water isn't going to be enough. We need to start planning for serious upheaval, the potential of widespread violence, and a protracted emergency situation.

---

[68] www.ready.gov/food

"Let no one deceive you with empty words"

Holy Bible
Ephesians 5:6a

"When people are saying, 'Everything is peaceful
and secure,' then disaster will fall on them as suddenly
as a pregnant woman's labor pains begin. And there
will be no escape. "

Holy Bible
1 Thessalonians 5:3

Chapter 4

Looking for the
Story Behind the Story

When it comes to an urgent topic such as preparing for an emergency situation, understanding the cause is always desirable, but it is knowledge of the disastrous results which are actually far more useful to us. It is the anticipated outcomes of the incident which we can use to help us navigate and find safe passage through the calamitous event.

The keys for unlocking the chain of problems are found in the outcomes, not in the cause. Therefore, we need to gain a firm grasp on the anticipated results of a future disaster. Only then can we move beyond *general* preparations to *specific* preparations. It is in these details where we will find what is needed to become wholly ready for what is coming.

In this era we are facing many potential causes of disaster, so we look to the various signs of the times, and the conclusions of informed experts to help us. Sadly, one source of expert opinion that we often neglect is the federal government. We tend to ignore this source of information because government officials are known for being economical with the truth. Yet, the government does pour millions of our tax dollars into analysis, and billions more into solving the problems it has identified. So how can we get the information we have paid for?

Unfortunately, the conclusions of government research are often either 'Classified' or 'sanitized,' so we never get the real results. Yet, there is a way around these obstructions. We can look at what the government is actually doing. If the anticipated problem is big, we should be able to see the planning which is taking place. Even though we are not able to gain access to the research itself, we can see the conclusions if we take the time to look closely. They are evident in the government's actions.

Since we don't have access to the top tier of government planning, it is the story-behind-the-story which will often give us the important but elusive details. This back-story is often our best opportunity to deduce information about the government's expectations. As the saying goes, "actions speak louder than words." With this in mind, we can expect the government's actions to be more candid than what the officials talk about publically.

For thinking people, the story-behind-the-story gives us the opportunity to identify what the government is really thinking vs. what they say. Insider trading is illegal when it comes to the stock market, but that's because others don't have access to the same information. In this case, everyone has the opportunity to gain "insider" knowledge by watching government actions. However, we need to look for it.

The mainstream media isn't going to do this for us. In their quest for ratings and advancing their own agenda, television news shows and newspapers are increasingly irrelevant. Even FOX News, which independent research has identified as having the most balanced viewpoints, only presents a small fraction of the important news stories. Because of this, it is critically important to find reliable alternative sources of news, and to constantly look for the story-behind-the-story. Only then can we accomplish our own, reliable analysis. If you haven't already come to this conclusion, the following pages will make it clear why this task is too important to neglect. Your future well-being will likely depend on it.

Except when the government is trying to influence public opinion, mainstream news reports on a subject such as disaster preparedness, typically feature spokespeople who espouse soothing rhetoric. The underlying goal of these representatives is twofold: First, to nurture being prepared for minor disasters, a task accomplished by stockpiling basic necessities and being ready to evacuate to a community shelter. Second, and even more importantly from their viewpoint, they want to calm fears, instill confidence in government, and maintain the status quo—*normalcy*.

Both objectives are understandable. Likewise, even when they don't tell the whole story, the motive of the spokesperson is often benign.

For example, when I was a police crime scene investigator, I remember working a high-profile serial murder case which generated a great deal of public fear. With no apparent pattern the suspect was killing women in their homes. These were gruesome crimes and women who lived alone in the Los Angeles area began to panic. Vigilance was important, but panic and living in constant fear was not productive. Terror would not help us catch the murderer. In fact, it would serve to feed his demented ego. So we engaged in a media disinformation campaign to calm fears.

In hindsight I think this was inappropriate and paternalistic, but our motive was honorable. More to the point, in our minds we didn't lie. However, we did intentionally obscure the truth. The facts were provided, but we eclipsed the uncomfortable story with other details. We essentially hid the truth behind other information. By focusing on a different storyline, we diverted the interests of the news media.

In the process I learned an important lesson: Truth is not the absence of a lie. Truth is when the story told, and the important details and ramifications, are all aligned and communicated with clarity.

Unfortunately, Madison Avenue, Wall Street, the mainstream news media, and the U.S. Government do not embrace this definition. Therefore, if we are looking for the truth we need to ferret it out ourselves.

What is the story-behind-the-story?

Today we see this same *disinformation* approach applied to various domestic dangers. This means that responsible people are not getting the facts they need for decision making. As a result, we don't have what is necessary for insightful preparation to meet the challenges we will face in the future.

At best, when our nation's leaders don't think the public can handle what is coming, or they want to avoid the inconvenience of public scrutiny, they sidestep the truth and with it, the oversight of those they are employed to serve. As a result, they hobble responsible people. This is true even when they technically tell the truth but bury it by distraction or deep inside another story.

In this vein, the leadership of the Department of Homeland Security (DHS) and the Federal Emergency Management Agency (FEMA), routinely give their spokespeople watered-down details to present to the public. Even the middle managers, who are implementing plans, only get a slice of the truth. In government and military circles, everything has become compartmentalized. Originally this technique was to improve security, now it is also used as a matter of convenience to avoid scrutiny. As a result, employees only get what they need to do their job; rarely much more. The unvarnished truth is reserved for the top leaders who have increasingly become elitist.

As a result, the news stories accomplish their intended purpose. They assuage fear and sidestep details which would provoke undesirable public reaction. These agencies consistently avoid anything which might cause public panic. Anyone familiar with how government agencies operate will recognize this as standard operating procedure.

From their viewpoint and given the current circumstances, they know that public awareness will make their erudite plans more difficult to implement. They are already working feverously to prepare. Moreover, they understand that negative public reaction and public pressure will not help them with what they are trying to accomplish. So, though their approach isn't forthright, it is commonplace.

At the most basic level, we need to understand that their motivations and agenda may be different from our own. In the case of big government, we need to understand that their agenda is often different from ours. Sometimes it is very different.

Notwithstanding differing agendas, if these government leaders were to speak clearly to the general public, and plainly explain the emergency situation they are anticipating, what would happen? Would people accept their responsibility to personally prepare, or would they sit back arrogantly, whine, and demand that the government do more?

Based on past experience, we would expect the public to insist that the government do something different. Many would take to the streets and demand a change in direction; not to better help the nation, but to benefit them, personally.

Since you are reading this, you are probably part of the 1% of the population who would welcome the opportunity to astutely prepare. Conversely, if the other 99% knew what was coming, they would become apoplectic. Their demands and wailing would impede the agenda which is quietly being implemented.

The general public would be confused, scared, enraged, and ultimately unhelpful. Since the government recognizes that this response would become a counterproductive distraction to their agenda, they actively promote preparedness, but remain silent in regard to the severity of what is coming.

For us, our situation can be different. We can discern the truth, and then we can use it to formulate our own action plans.

Though government representatives aren't talking about what is coming, their actions do speak clearly. Therefore, we have the opportunity to listen by observing.

The federal government's disaster preparations are undertaken quietly to avoid opposition and public panic, but these machinations are not secret. It can't be; the operation is too big. Therefore, the truth is hidden in plain sight. We just need to look for the various story-behind-the-story truths, and identify the patterns which emerge.

If we want to differentiate between the government's encouraging words and the actual planning that is taking place, we need to be both observant and discerning. We need to understand that it is government actions which communicate the details of the plan, not their verbiage. Looking for the story-behind-the-story is the place to start.

Looking for 'patterns' to clarify and validate the story-behind-the-story

In the prior chapters I focused on presidential Executive Orders, new laws, and the federal government's activities which connect to disaster preparedness. I also included a number of odd news stories which, combined with these other details, suggest that the disaster the U.S. Government is expecting includes massive civil unrest and anarchy on a national scale. If my conclusion is accurate, we should be able to find other facts which provide additional support to this viewpoint.

Sound judgment requires preponderance of evidence. When we find links which connect related and unrelated facts, we can assemble an orderly explanation which will help us with our own decision making.

Since we appear to be standing with our family and friends on the edge of a precipice, this is an important task if we want to escape from our dangerous predicament. Like when I was a police detective proving a case using circumstantial evidence, we need to gather the facts and see what fits together.

As we pull together the jigsaw puzzle pieces of story-behind-the-story truth, we will have our evidence. We don't need all of the pieces of the puzzle, we only need to fit together a sufficient number to produce a clear picture of what is coming.

When we only have a few minor facts the best we can do is arrive at an educated opinion. If it is important for us to understand the true story, the whole story, as it is in this situation, we need more than just a best guess. We need to know what the government is actually planning. Since we don't have relationships with the government decision makers, the next best thing is to observe the implementation of their plans. These actions telegraph the details of the scenario.

Dependable conclusions require facts not conjecture. For example, if the story-behind-the-story on militarization of the police is caused by something else, such as a social shift caused by large numbers of military veterans becoming police officers, that will become obvious when we study the details.

If we are unable to find corroborating evidence, that lack of evidence is also noteworthy. Not being able to find any other facts to support a different premise, is also noteworthy and another form of evidence.

In the situations I have related, one of my conclusions is that violent civil unrest is coming. Importantly, it is not just validated by the militarization of the police, but by a preponderance of other evidence. There are many factors and story-behind-the-story details which direct us to this same conclusion.

In addition, as various story-behind-the-story conclusions are considered together, a distinct pattern emerges. As a number of puzzle pieces fit together, unrelated stories and news developments fit together as something more than a collection of oddities. When viewed together, we see a pattern made by compelling pieces of evidence which fit together, documenting that a worst-case National Emergency Plan is being implemented.

If I am right, since my conclusion requires large government-sponsored initiatives, we should be able to find other story-behind-the story news reports and/or facts to validate this conclusion.

Sound Conclusions Are Affirmed
by Additional Evidence

It is foolish and harmful to retain a viewpoint that is disproven by new facts. We need to be careful that our desire to be 'right' does not overshadow our need to be correct. We need honest analysis, not tally points in an academic debate.

Here are a few of the stories addressed in the prior chapters, which I used to support my conclusion that the U.S. Government is preparing for widespread, extremely violent civil unrest and anarchy or civil war. Let's see if we can find other stories, or evidence, which either provides a reasonable, alternative explanation to refute my conclusion, or, builds on the pattern I previously presented:

Story #1: Presidential Executive Orders and laws which pave the way for the easy implementation of martial law and other extreme measures which are in violation of constitutional law and the separation of powers which forms the basis for American government.

Story #2: Large scale, multi-state joint training exercises with the U.S. military and civilian law enforcement agencies, are occurring nationwide in rural areas and in all major cities.

Story #3: The Department of Homeland Security (DHS) and other federal agencies, including those which do not have a law enforcement mission, have established SWAT teams and purchased billions of rounds of extremely deadly antipersonnel ammunition; a type of ammunition that cannot be legally used outside of the United States.

Story #4: DHS has designed a series of new gun training targets, which by their own admission, are designed to desensitize the shooter; teaching them to shoot ordinary-looking citizens without hesitation.

Story #5: DHS is supplying civilian law enforcement agencies with high-tech surveillance gear, communications control technologies, and other equipment which cannot be legally used by police officers in their crime fighting and criminal investigations. Moreover, citing 'national security' as justification, these civilian law enforcement agencies are prohibited from sharing any details with their local government officials who employ and pay them, as well as the court system which holds them accountable and insures that they are obeying the law.

Additional Evidence: Other on-topic news stories which fit this same pattern

Story #6: Distribution of Thousands of Military Tanks to Police Departments.

Thousands of MRAP military tanks have been donated by the federal government to civilian law enforcement agencies nationwide. These expensive, modern tools of urban combat have quietly been given to state, county, and local law enforcement agencies over the past few years. These 'gifts' have been reported, but generally only as local news stories. Largely unreported is the fact that there is a multitude of similar stories. When considered together, there is a story-behind-the-story which remains largely unreported, a staggering national program which remains unexplained.

MRAP, an acronym for Mine-Resistant Ambush Protected, are towering military tanks designed for urban warfare. Our troops in Iraq and Afghanistan used them for asymmetric warfare missions. These tanks are not designed for fighting a foreign army, but rather for fighting civilian insurgents who are armed with IEDs (Improvised Explosive Devices) and rockets.

In the last few years, the Department of Defense has donated more than 13,000 MRAPs to 780 local and state law enforcement agencies around the United States. The combined cost of these MRAPs exceeds $8 billion. Each major city and region of the United States now has a fleet of these mammoth military tanks, with many rural areas having at least one.

At the same time, several thousand new MRAPs have been purchased by Homeland Security and other federal agencies. At an average cost of $700,000 each, this represents a major expenditure.

Why is the Department of Defense giving away thousands of these fully operational tanks to local law enforcement agencies, when at the same time, the Department of Homeland Security is purchasing thousands of new ones? Is the federal government simply inefficient and generous? Or, do they think thousands of these urban tanks will be needed here in the United States?

Size Comparison
Top: Military Jeep (Old Style). Middle: MRAP Urban
Tank (Protection from rockets and IED bombs).
Bottom: Humvee (Armored versions are bulletproof).

Unlike the military's versatile Jeep-like 'Humvee' which weights 2-1/2 tons, the MRAP weighs 17-40 tons (depending on model) and is ungainly to operate. Its weight and burgeoning size, 8' tall (not including gun turret), 8' feet wide, and 21+ feet in length, makes it a great tool for urban warfare but overkill for crime fighting.

Though an MRAP may be ideal for soldiers who are engaged in urban combat, or traveling highways which might be peppered with improvised explosive devices, this type of equipment is counterproductive for use by American law enforcement. These are not needed even for encounters with the most ruthless criminals. *These aren't simply armored cars; they are a type of military tank.*

Further, since MRAPs are extremely top-heavy and can easily tip over in off-road conditions, they aren't suitable for any use other than as an urban tank. Since their operation is generally confined to established roadways, they are useless for the off-road needs of search and rescue missions and most disaster relief efforts. *These are not dual-use vehicles.*

If the only use of an MRAP is as a military urban-combat tank, why do local police and sheriff department's need them?

This story is more than unusual. The substance of the story is of such a size and scope as to be extremely provocative. It is a disturbing development, and obviously there is much more to this story than that which is being reported. This is yet another powerful example of an important story-behind-the-story.

Is there a different, reasonable explanation that trumps my conclusion? Maybe, but in all my inquiries I've been unable to find another explanation.

This isn't an example of government waste. It fits neatly into a pattern of government spending on military gear for law enforcement agencies and federal departments. Moreover, it's too big and too public.

This is not an example of overkill problem-solving. The MRAP is very different from the military's Jeep-like vehicle, the Humvee, which is peerless for off-road operation. The Humvee is ideal for rural use, as well as for search and rescue operations. It can fjord flooded rivers, climb mountainous areas, and go where no other vehicle can operate. It is therefore perfect for law enforcement, wilderness medical aid, wildland firefighting, and the natural disasters that our preparedness efforts have concentrated on in the past.

Similarly, armored Humvees (technically referred to as 'up-armored'), have done a great job of protecting our troops against rifle and handgun bullets, and even grenades. These would amply meet the needs of police SWAT teams which deal with drug cartels and other well-armed criminals.

Despite these factors which make the Humvee the clear choice for domestic use, and despite the fact that the military has 100x more Humvees than MRAPs, it is the MRAPs that are being donated to local law enforcement agencies.

Another option for distribution would have been the Stryker. It is the military's high-tech armored personnel carrier which is capable of operating off-road. These have fallen into disfavor as insurgents in Iraq were able to successfully attack these using rockets and high-explosive IEDs, so they were replaced with the larger and more heavily armored MRAP-type vehicles. These Stryker vehicles would still be overkill for use by domestic law enforcement agencies, but it does demonstrate that there is an intermediate step between an up-armored Humvee and a MRAP tank.

What can we reasonably deduce from this odd development? It's worth noting that the Department of Defense (DoD) rarely sells its surplus Humvees. In fact, it usually cuts them up and sells the pieces as scrap metal. Yet, it donates its tank-like MRAP vehicles to local law enforcement agencies. This includes donating MRAPs to rural sheriff's departments and no-crime small towns. The DoD often even picks-up the $14,000+ shipping cost of the MRAP.

Why does the DoD have radically different policies for these two military vehicles? Why make it nearly impossible to acquire Humvees which are so agile off-road and in high water, while at the same time facilitating the acquisition of urban tanks which are nearly useless in a natural disaster?

The answer is important.

Why are thousands of these MRAP tanks being donated to cities and counties for law enforcement use? Why is the Department of Homeland Security, which only works within our nation's borders, buying thousands of *new* MRAPs when at the same time, thousands of used MRAPs are being discarded by the military?

Why does the Department of Defense cut-up its surplus Humvees, selling them as scrap metal, while MRAPs, which are made of expensive high-grade ballistic steel, are donated? Is this just the action of a clueless government bureaucracy or do they think the MRAPs will be needed domestically? Might they be needed for use in the event of mass terrorism or a domestic war against civilian insurgents? Certainly. For crime fighting purposes? Certainly not.

The Problem of Militarizing Civilian Police: History teaches us an important lesson. The militarization of law enforcement is not compatible with a free society. When I was a young police officer in the Los Angeles area and a member of the police SWAT team, I saw militarization as a good thing. We were fighting well-armed criminals, drug cartels, and various terrorist threats. In my mind we needed this gear and military training. To a certain extent this remains reasonable. What isn't reasonable for a free society is how these teams and advanced technologies are being used.

Our current situation of rampant militarization creates a serious, insidious problem. Absent strong leadership within these agencies, we see that military gear and military training of law enforcement often produces heavy-handed war-like responses to solve peacetime problems. It has now become routine to use heavily armed SWAT teams to serve simple search warrants and make arrests in situations where there is literally no threat of violence.[69]

In every state within the U.S. it is a crime, a serious felony (assault with a deadly weapon), to point a gun at a person if there is no threat of grievous bodily injury. Yet police officers daily commit this crime, particularly through the antics of militarized

---

[69]   John W. Whitehead, JD; President of the Rutherford Institute; "Government of Wolves: The Emerging American Police State," Select Books, New York, NY, 2013

local, state, and federal SWAT teams. This reasonable military tactic for a theater of war is a totally unacceptable tactic for domestic law enforcement.

Somehow we have come to accept this criminal behavior when the perpetrator is a police officer. Conversely, if a civilian was engaged in the same behavior in the presence of a police officer, they would likely be shot and killed.

Another problem which relates to the militarization of law enforcement is that these 'gifts' of military equipment come with strings and these tie into federal control. With this comes unwarranted, and unhealthy, influence over local law enforcement operations and tactics. Police and sheriffs' departments should be beholding solely to the community they serve, not an amorphous federal government. This is yet another insidious problem that is getting worse.

No longer is officer safety the reason a SWAT team is deployed. Originally, Special Weapons And Tactics (SWAT) teams were organized to increase officer safety in high-risk encounters with dangerous criminals. Their use was reserved for apprehending armed violent criminals, as well as for potentially deadly situations such as a criminal gang being armed with tactical firearms.

Today, SWAT operations have changed radically. They have become military operations, even when there is no threat of violence. It's important to understand that SWAT teams are no longer just a mechanism to increase officer safety.

It's also important to understand that this isn't the fault of the Teams. It is a problem created by inept leadership, politically motivated governmental agencies, and financially-strapped police departments which see 'free' federal money as a way to solve their fiscal woes.

The story-behind-the-story is that local, state, and federal law enforcement agencies are being equipped with military hardware and given military training which has no relationship to crime fighting or terrorism. These preparations can only relate to violent and protracted civil unrest or war. There is no other reasonable explanation.

Story #7: A New U.S. Military Unit - *USNORTHCOM*

The Pose Comitatus Act of 1878[70] is a law which has served us well. It was instituted to insure that the U.S. military was not used against its own citizens. Notwithstanding, USNORTHCOM was formed in October 2002, and the legal prohibition for USNORTHCOM military operations on U.S. soil was made 'legal' a few years later when HR 6166, the Military Commissions Act of 2006, was signed into law.

It is USNORTHCOM that is providing military training for civilian law enforcement agencies, as well as leadership for joint military and civilian law enforcement operations. It is also USNORTHCOM that is responsible for military-unit training operations such as Jade Helm, which readies U.S. military units for operational missions inside the borders of the United States.

To be clear, having military units train within the homeland is nothing new. What is a radical change is to have military troops engage in operations which target American citizens. These military maneuvers are directed toward individual Americans and groups of U.S. citizens. They are fighting 'bad guys' who are Americans.

These types of operations currently fit into four primary categories: 1) Military and SWAT operations that are "shock and awe" demonstrations, designed to intimidate the public; 2) Operations to create a spirit of federal unity, trust and esprit de corps between military and police units; 3) To develop uniformity in tactics and communication; and, 4) Spec-operations military missions which involve the neutralization or abduction of high-value Americans who are considered dissidents.

The stated purpose of U.S. Special Operations Command is: direct, small unit action; special reconnaissance; counter terrorism; internal defense; civil affairs; psychological warfare; and, unconventional warfare. It is not traditional warfare.

When all of these news stories and government actions are considered together, a clear pattern is evident: The U.S.

---

[70] The Posse Comitatus Act is a federal law (**18 U.S.C. § 1385**) which has been in place for nearly 150 years. The stated purpose of the act, in concert with the Insurrection Act of 1807, is to prevent the federal government from using **military** personnel and military equipment in domestic law enforcement-type operations.

Government anticipates massive social unrest or insurrection. This will be of such magnitude that our existing 929,000 gun-carrying law enforcement officers,[71] and 462,000 National Guard troops, will be insufficient to handle the problem. Together, these law enforcement officers and National/State Guard members total 1.4 million armed defenders. These are already operating in the United States, but apparently this won't be enough. That's why USNORTHCOM was formed.

The situation will be truly dire if 1.4 million armed defenders aren't enough to protect us. Yet the institution of USNORTHCOM is itself a forecast for a bleak future, one that is rife with government expectations of violence and suffering in many forms. Such a move suggests the anticipation of hostilities which exceed those of America's deadliest conflict, the Civil War (1861-1865).[72]

Alternately, if the anticipated situation isn't widespread civil warfare, the other alternative is that our law enforcement officers will oppose the federal government's actions. Either way, the situation will be extreme. This suggests new dangers that must be anticipated and planned for in our disaster preparations.

USNORTHCOM was formed for a self-evident specific purpose: The U.S. Government anticipates that the combined forces of the U.S. military will be needed inside the United States. The only viable conclusion is that they anticipate a catastrophic situation. The purpose of USNORTHCOM, which is evidenced by their training operations, is not to defend our borders or fight

---

[71] U.S. Department of Justice, FBI Criminal Justice Information Services, Unified Crime Report for 2011, indicates that there are 809,000 sworn officers employed in local, county, and state law enforcement agencies in the U.S., plus 120,000 civilian federal law enforcement officers who are authorized to carry a firearm. Total: 929,000 civilian law enforcement officers who are authorized to carry a firearm. Link:. https://www.fbi.gov/about-us/cjis/ucr/crime-in-the-u.s/2011/crime-in-the-u.s.-2011/police-employee-data

[72] In that war, 2,000,000 Americans from the North fought against 750,000 Americans from the South, resulting in the death or serious injury of more than a million combatants and perhaps as many civilians. Revised estimates of Civil War deaths and injuries: Guy Gugliotta, "New Estimate Raises Civil War Death Toll," April 2, 2012.

http://www.nytimes.com/2012/04/03/science/civil-war-toll-up-by-20-percent-in-new-estimate.html?_r=0

Muslim terrorists. It is to conduct operations inside the U.S. which target American citizens.

The list of stories which fit this pattern of violence and disaster goes on and on. You don't need to be an expert to see that there is a story behind these stories. When considered together and in context, a pattern has emerged. This pattern exposes a key component of what the government is expecting. It doesn't tell us what will initiate the emergency situation, but it does make it clear that they expect an outcome that is catastrophic. The U.S. Government is getting ready for nationwide civil unrest and urban warfare.

What can we reasonably deduce, that will help us personally prepare?

In spite of official denial, the facts shout loudly. The truth is unpleasant, but we need to let it overcome our natural tendency of normalcy bias and embrace the facts, letting them overwhelm the false scorn and calming rhetoric of the government's representatives and news media. Like pieces of a puzzle put into place, when we pull together the disparate facts a clear picture has been revealed to us:

The U.S. Government is expecting a specific emergency situation or sequential disastrous events. The ramifications will include widespread social and economic disaster, as well as anarchy or domestic insurgency.

Moreover, these stories are tied to a comprehensive National Emergency Plan that has not been made public, and there is a reason for this silence. This federal disaster plan is not just a hazy "what-if" scenario. It is highly detailed, massive in scope, and goes far beyond routine contingency planning. It is a plan that is now being implemented.

Therefore, not only do we need to prepare for traditional natural disasters, we need to get ready for a big incident, as well as the possibility that we will face a multi-phase, progressively worsening sequence of disasters.

Thankfully, we don't need to do this in a vacuum. Our preparations can be informed by what we see happening around us. And, by observing what the government is doing, so that our personal preparations provide a counterpoint to what the federal government is doing.

We need to prepare for historic dangers and for a future danger that has a high likelihood of striking us in the months or years ahead. If the government's experts are right, this will be an occurrence that is different and far more troubling than anything the United States has previously endured – including the Civil War and two world wars.

What do you think?

Does this sound farfetched? Is all this simply out-of-control government contingency planning for routine natural disasters? Or, is it something else? Do these preparations point to an emergency situation that might be huge and life changing?

It is time for you to decide. If you agree that this might be a credible threat, it's time to take decisive action. It's time to get beyond fear and talk, and take steps to respond by implementing a personal action plan.

From my perspective, what the U.S. Government has been doing for nearly two decades is a major, comprehensive undertaking, designed to deal with a society-shattering emergency situation. As I consider the cost, mindshare, manpower, and resources that have been dedicated to these efforts, I recognize that this is unprecedented.

Government leaders must think their preparations are necessary. We are in the midst of a major fiscal crisis, yet they have found it necessary to quietly implement a supremely expensive plan, a plan that no constituency group is requesting.

In the process, the federal government has borrowed billions of dollars and is continuing to borrow billions more to finance these ongoing preparedness efforts. They aren't just spending money that the government has collected from taxes; they are borrowing $ .46 of every $1.00 they spend on these preparations.[73]

Are these the actions of an out-of-control government? Or, do you think it's reasonable to conclude that these preparations are in response to serious analysis and credible threats? None of this information is secret. These 'indicators' are all readily available to anyone who is willing to take the time to look. This type of information is under-reported by the mainstream media,

---

[73] www.usdebtclock.org

but it is nevertheless easy to find by anyone willing to take the time to investigate.

Do your own checking. You will find that what is presented here is just the tip of the iceberg. You don't need a security clearance to accomplish this research. There is plenty of information in the public domain if you're willing to dig for it.

Considered individually, not remarkable.
Considered together, shocking.
When a pattern emerges, we need to pay close attention.
A Pattern Has Emerged.

This chapter has focused on U.S. Government actions which are hidden in plain sight; a series of unreported story-behind-the-story developments which the mainstream media has ignored. When these stories are considered together, undisputed facts compound to expose a federal plan designed to make it possible for the government to overcome a disastrous emergency situation.

Beyond this, there are many other ominous indicators of a coming major disaster which come from nongovernmental sources. These "signs" relate to various potential causes, whereas the federal plan only exposes the response.

There are many non-governmental indicators which point to the same conclusion. Various signs-of-the-times support the deduction that a major national disaster is around the corner. These all portend life-altering disaster. This is sobering, but these details can be helpful for developing our own preparedness plan.

With a few notable exceptions, the cause of the disaster may be of secondary importance. So for most of us, it should be general preparations which are our initial focus. It is the likely 'general' effects that should drive our initial reparations, and then we progress to the specific threats. Step-by-step, this planning and preparation can help us win over adversity.

It's a Question of "When?" Not "If?"

Whether a single disastrous event suddenly crashes down on us or a confluence of unrelated events snowballs over the span of a few months or years, we are currently facing a major disaster. That's a given. That's the bottom line.

Experts agree that we are facing many threats and each of more than a dozen issues has not only the capacity, but the likelihood to become a tipping-point for disaster. Each of these problems has life-changing potential.

We can't afford to be mollified by our normalcy bias. Nor can we allow ourselves to be castrated by those who heckle and insist that everything is fine. It's time to face the facts and spread the word among those we care about. It's time to get busy preparing for our own safety and the welfare of our family and friends.

We don't know all the details about what is coming, but there is sufficient evidence to conclude that the threat is credible. Inaction is irresponsible.

Are you going to be part of the 99% of the population that depends on the largess of the government during a disaster? Or, are you going to be part of the 1% that accepts personal responsibility to prepare?

The federal government has been working on this for many years. Unless you've been keeping pace with them and making your own preparations, you are seriously behind. Yet, we still have the opportunity to get busy and get serious about preparing. It's not too late.

Don't let yourself be sidetracked by apocalyptic fatigue. We don't know how long this window of opportunity will remain open. Now is the time for decisive action. If you still have doubts, make it a priority to conduct your own investigation.

Investigation Principle #1

There is a principle which is a bar against all information, which is proof against all argument, and which cannot fail to keep man in everlasting ignorance. That principle is contempt [condemnation] before investigation.

-- William Paley (1743-1805)

"He who gives an answer before he hears, it is folly and shame to him."

"The first to plead his case SEEMS right, until another comes and examines him."

Holy Bible
Proverbs 18:13, 17

Chapter 5

Tools of Deception

'False Flag' Operations:
An Increasingly Popular Tool of Deception

There are many tools of deception and this could easily be the topic of an entire book, but 'false flag' operations are among the most insidious, so this technique is worthy of special mention. A 'false flag' deception diverts attention from the real agenda of the instigator, while focusing the blame for a terrible deed on someone other than the true perpetrator. Then, the perpetrator often orchestrates retaliation against the innocent party as if it is a necessary public response. All of this is done to divert attention away from what the perpetrator is doing in the background.

In essence, a false flag operation is an elaborate con. It is a way to beguile and cajole the public into believing something, or doing something, which is in opposition to their best interests.

This mechanism of deceit isn't anything new. The term is thought to have originated in naval warfare, when a warship hoists the flag of another nation before staging an attack, thereby diverting blame to an uninvolved nation.

The fledging United States government sanctioned such acts of piracy during its war of independence from Britain. False flag attacks against America's enemies have been a tactic of U.S. military operations ever since.

Today, modern practitioners have transformed this simple trick of war into a domestic art form, using choreographed events to deceive or distract the public. These 'false flag operations' are one of the best examples of the modern deceiver's skill. Unfortunately, this has not made it any easier to detect.

Alongside this problem we have another: When this advanced tool of deception is combined with a lack of trust in leaders, it becomes easy for various watchdog groups to eagerly suggest that there is a story-behind-the-story. This story may, or may not, actually exist.

Whether the incident is a terrorist attack, a new infectious disease, or something like a decline in the bee population, there is always some individual on hand to promote the explanation that it is a false flag operation. It's akin to grabbing media attention by blaming the devil rather than evil people. These weak arguments without adequate evidence aren't helpful.

Other times, those who use the hot button term 'false flag' have more accurately encountered a problem that is an unintended consequence; an unexpected outcome which is the result of some imprudent, arrogant or even unlawful action. In this situation there may be an important story-behind-the-story, but it's not a false flag operation.

There are Many Tools of Deception

There are many forms of organized deception but these do not rise to the level of being a false flag operation. For example, 'Operation Choke Point.'[74] This deception was conceived by the Obama Administration, and used government agencies such as the U.S. Justice Department (DOJ) and banking regulators, to carry out their scheme.

In this deception, banks were told that for them to do business with certain types of businesses would jeopardize their bank's reputation. Banks which persisted in doing business with these 'high risk' customers would receive added scrutiny, additional audits, and they would be required to pay higher fees to the FDIC, etc.

---

[74] "Congress launching hearings on complaints businesses targeted by 'Operation Choke Point,'" March 24, 2015, by Ruth Ravve, FOX News:

http://www.foxnews.com/politics/2015/03/24/congress-launching-hearings-on-complaints-businesses-targeted-by-operation/

Initially, government controls such as these may sound reasonable, but what if the underlying premise is false? It is faux reasonableness which is central to manipulation, and for orchestrating an effective deception.

With 'Choke Point' this deception was further validated as reasonable, because all the bankers knew that this operation was (initially) legitimate. It was conceived to stymie the efforts of criminal cartels which were using banks to help them launder drug money.

Just as in the infamous DOJ operation 'Fast and Furious,' a legitimate program was hijacked and used as cover for an illegal deception. This is a brilliant mechanism for validating legitimacy, and it secures the willing participation of many good people who are essentially tricked into participating in the scam.

With both 'Operation Choke Point' (OCP) and the 'Fast and Furious' gun-walking scandal, these government-sponsored deceptions involved a quiet switch in emphasis inside an existing program. With 'Operation Choke Point,' this was a transition from targeting drug cartels and illegal gambling operations, to other companies the administration claimed were similarly high risk. The new additions to the OCP list were companies such as gun manufacturers, guns stores, and retailers of precious metals. (Owning precious metals like gold and silver, takes control of the money supply out of the hands of the government, so this is presumed to be the reason these were included.)

Until exposed by the Wall Street Journal in 2014, many of these gun and precious metal companies found it very difficult to operate. Some were actually forced to close their doors or substantially cut-back their operations.

In many cases, banks closed the accounts of long-term customers and called their loans. Companies caught in this trap were often unable to find a different bank which would accept them as a customer. At best, banking became much more expensive for these targeted companies.

In reality, OCP had nothing to do with risk. The government simply used this subterfuge to target companies they didn't like; businesses which they considered to be impeding the implementation of their Progressive political agenda.

In this case, the government's deception was based in a claim that this new government requirement was based in scientific risk analysis, when in reality there was no such analysis. The government used the Department of Justice and federal banking regulators, to target businesses solely on ideological grounds.

Example of Deception:
GMO Food (Genetically Modified Organism)

Another example of a deception which is reprehensible, but not a false flag operation, is the use of Genetically Modified Organisms (GMO). It appears that the genetic manipulation of food crops is responsible for the major decline in the bee population. However, the goal of the business endeavor was not to harm bees. The deception came after the fact, apparently as a way to avoid reputation-damage and costly legal liability.

If it could be proven in court that the seed company was responsible for the decline in the bee population, it is likely that the serious human health risks of GMO foods would be exposed at the same time. So though the problem with the bee population seems to be an accidental byproduct of corporate avarice, it is not itself a deception.

In a situation such as this, the big deception seems to have come in the form of a cover up. Deception was apparently also involved to accelerate bringing GMOs to market, but the big deception began when the unintended consequences became apparent.

These deceptions are different from those used in a 'false flag' operation. In a false flag operation the planners intentionally expose the misdeed, and then use deception to divert blame away from the perpetrator and onto an enemy. So though the damage to bees and our food supply is blameworthy and seriously threatens public health, and despite the fact that this situation seems to involve illegal activities including collusion by government agencies and perhaps payoffs, it does not meet the criteria for a false flag operation.

Sophisticated false flag operations are less frequent than other forms of deception and manipulation. This is because successful operations require tremendous insight in both conception and planning, and they generally require at least tacit support from within the top echelons of power.

When watchdogs overuse the term 'false flag' their veracity comes into question, too. As a result, the public becomes suspicious of them as well. When the public trusts no one, they fail to act.

Moreover, if the watchdog is unable to produce evidence that the public finds compelling, they become discredited as a news source, even when they are right. Therefore, even when we have cause for believing some exploit is a false flag operation, it is to our advantage to not use this term until we have assembled enough evidence to expose the deception.

On the other hand, just because this tool of deception is frequently not in play, does not mean that these 'false flag' assertions are always unfounded. These operations are increasingly common and they are progressively becoming more insidious. This makes them all the more dangerous since these operations can be used for purposes beyond escaping blame, misdirection and deception.

Modern 'False Flag' Operations

False flag operations are increasingly being used to destroy ideological enemies, and manipulate good people to engage in counterproductive or harmful activities. When such a ploy is successful, time, energy and money is wasted—or worse. Increasingly, undiscerning people are being manipulated to engage in unhealthy, inappropriate actions. This creates new dangers.

We are also witnessing the advent of 'false flag' operations designed to neuter the police and encourage lawlessness and violence, all for the purpose of advancing political agendas. This is particularly evident in inner city areas where politicians and self-serving activists foment anti-police crimes and race-based or poverty-based social unrest.

When good people succumb to the promptings built into this type of false flag operation, we play right into the hand of the perpetrator. Discernment and restraint have never been more important.

For example, an anti-gun President without scruples, could issue a presidential Executive Order mandating the confiscation of all black rifles. The U.S. Attorney General, who is a presidential appointee and therefore prone to collusion, could then set-up a confrontation between the police and some pro-gun group. If such a plot works, the president wins. If it fails, no one is the wiser.

Over time this president can count on eventually winning. Good, honest, patriotic, and God-fearing people are not always discerning. This is what unscrupulous leaders are counting on.

At some point, one of these groups will respond to such a situation by killing several police officers who are attempting to enforce the president's illegal Executive Order. At that point, the next phase of the false flag operation is activated.

The news media is used to make the defenders of the 2nd Amendment look like the Christian version of al-Qaeda. As a result, the general public, which has also been duped by this false flag operation, responds with horror and demands that the government do more to disarm the population.

Once the possession of guns has become prohibited, and public opinion supports this unconstitutional action, the plotters are free to implement their hidden, tyrannical agenda. Resistance has become impossible.

In this example, fear is used to manipulate the public in phase-1 of the operation. In phase-2, new governmental power is used to accomplish some other agenda which the public would not otherwise accept, but resistance and backlash is minimal because the people now fear the government.

"When the people fear the government, there is tyranny; when the government fears the people, there is liberty."
—Thomas Jefferson
3rd President of the United States.
Principal author of the U.S.
Declaration of Independence

Intrinsic to the success of a false flag operation such as the one used in this example, is that neither the police officers involved, nor the police department's leadership, nor the citizen defenders of the Constitution and their organizations, know they are part of a false flag operation. After the fact, they may become suspicious because everything flowed so perfectly to the conclusion the government leaders wanted, but no one can prove duplicity.

A false flag operation which is increasingly likely is one that will sow seeds of discord between Conservatives and the police and/or the military. When operating in harmony and in support of each other, as these groups have historically done, they are a social anchor for holding firm to law and order, national defense, and support of the original meaning of the U.S. Constitution. Therefore, it is to the advantage of political 'Progressives' (currently in many top positions of power), to create a rift between citizens and those who provide security and enforce the laws; those who have pledged to support and defend the Constitution.

Gun ownership would be an ideal target for such a divide-and-conquer operation. If an individual false-flag attempt fails, no one is the wiser. But if it succeeds, the perpetrator has created division and infighting, sapped energy and resources, and distracted good people from the hidden agenda.

If good people have killed other good people in the process, the perpetrators of the false flag operation win. When the police and military are confused and revert to obeying orders that are unconstitutional, they are also victims, and again the perpetrator wins.

Unless other actions can't be avoided, good people need to target the police and military with education campaigns, not physical action. Police officers and military personnel need to be taught the Constitution, Bill of Rights, and that they can refuse an illegal order. Unfortunately, by design, the situations are often not black and white, and they are often charged with emotion. This is by design.

The Enemies of Truth Are Shrewd

When I was a police officer, a silent alarm summoned the police to a bank before the robber could exit the building, but the criminal was resilient. He concocted a very clever plan.

The robber seized a poorly dressed bank customer, and made him appear to be the bad guy. After he tied the hands and gagged his innocent victim, he covered his hostage's head with a ski mask. The ruse was to make the police think that the bank-customer hostage was the robber.

As they exited the bank the robber went first. With his hands behind him as if he was a restrained victim, his hands were actually busy with another aspect of his plan. With one hand he held the rope which was tied to the hands of his hostage, and with the other he held a gun pressed into the stomach of the hostage. He had warned his victim, if he tried to run, the robber would shoot him before he could escape. With a gun pressed into his belly, it was prudent for the hostage to comply.

The bank robber knew that the police SWAT team was outside. As he cried out in feigned fear, he expected the SWAT sniper to shoot the hostage. This would give him the opportunity to escape in the pandemonium that would follow. Fortunately, the scheme didn't work. The criminal was arrested and the victim freed, but only because the police were discerning.

We need to be similarly discerning. We need to identify the real criminal, and not falsely target those who were duped into taking part in a false flag operation.

Perpetrators of false flag operations know that a "divide and conquer" scenario weakens opponents. Since Progressives generally distain Conservatives, police, and military personnel, they would like nothing better than to see these groups fight against each other. This represents 'false flag' perfection when the goals of the initiator are advanced, and at the same time their antagonists are distracted and coerced into fighting with each other.

Those involved in orchestrating a false-flag tragedy usually can't be connected to it. Integral to their success is their ability to maintain deniability. In a situation such as the one described, the organizers created the fertile ground for the altercation. They pulled the strings in the 'false flag' puppet show, but will have made sure that there aren't witnesses who can expose their machinations. Everything is compartmentalized. By design, they make sure there is no smoking-gun evidence which ties them to their trickery.

This Isn't Just a Theoretical Threat.

Since we are usually unable to produce incontrovertible proof in modern false flag operations, I will relate a true story; one with which I have personal knowledge. This is a real-world example which illustrates how a sophisticated false flag operation actually works. It also shows that these operations are being used by the U.S. Government, so this is not just a hypothetical or abstract 'potential' threat.

The following situation is one in which I have personal knowledge of the behind-the-story facts. I was involved. I'll try to keep the story brief, but I need to provide sufficient detail to demonstrate how a false flag operation works in real life.

As I relate this story, keep this cycle of 'false flag' development in mind: First, a fictitious narrative is invented by the perpetrator. It is then supported by actions which give it the appearance of validity, even though factual evidence is usually sparse, conflicting or nonexistent. Then new details are added which may even be factual, but aren't actually germane evidence. These 'facts' are nevertheless used to add weight to the veracity of the narrative, so that it seems reasonable. Whenever possible, heart wrenching testimonials and graphic photos are presented by the news media. This flows into making the desired conclusions plausible, and the coveted public response appropriate, even necessary.

Interestingly, a false flag operation can be perpetrated by a relatively small number of people. In this particular case, it was probably only about 20 people who were behind this false flag operation.

Note: A false flag operation can be orchestrated by anyone in a position of power. This tool is used by governments, corporations, political activists, scientists looking for funding, and even nonprofit charitable organizations. However, when used by a multi-national corporation or government, a handful of leaders can literally change the future of an entire nation. The following true story is an example of how this can be accomplished.

A True Story of a U.S. False Flag Operation

When I was a police officer in the Los Angeles area, there was a homicide in Costa Mesa which the investigators believed to be a professional hit. The victim was found in his car which was parked in a nice, middle class neighborhood. As he sat in the driver's seat, he was shot by an assailant that he probably knew. The line of fire supported the premise that the shooter drove up to the victim's vehicle from the opposite direction, driver's door to driver's door, and shot him point-blank before the victim realized what was happening.

What was especially unusual about this crime was the lack of evidence. All the investigators could ascertain was that the murder weapon was a 12-gauge short-barreled shotgun, probably a double-barrel model with the barrel cut-down to about 9-inches. The victim was shot twice. Some of the shotgun pellets passed through the fully open car window to strike the victim, while others first penetrated the door of the car, just below the open driver's window.

With this type of weapon the result was devastatingly destructive. This added further support to the conjecture that the murderer also intended to communicate a clear message to others. It appeared to be a graphic warning to other associates of the victim who would undoubtedly hear about this death.

Since both barrels were discharged simultaneously, the gun produced what would have sounded like a single gunshot, a situation which is far more likely to be ignored. One gunshot is often dismissed by those in the area because they are not positive that it was actually a gunshot, whereas multiple gunshots tend to validate the cause, so they are reported to the police.

Since this type of weapon doesn't automatically eject the spent shell casings after it is fired, and since a shotgun barrel doesn't have rifling to make distinctive marks on the projectiles, even if the gun is eventually recovered it cannot be definitively linked to the crime. In other words, these details fit the profile of a professional killer.

The shooter didn't leave any distinctive evidence at the crime scene, except for the shotgun pellets themselves. Rather than use commercially-made shotgun ammunition, the assailant had replaced the buckshot in the shell with bullet-size steel ball bearings. Unlike the standard soft-lead pellets, these steel ball bearings would reliably penetrate the body of a car. At point blank range, this would guarantee an instant, no nonsense kill, also consistent with a professional hit.

The detectives assigned were unable to come up with much in the way of helpful leads. The steel ball bearings were of a common industrial variety and couldn't be traced. All that they were able to learn was that the victim may have had connections to mercenaries.

To simplify this rather involved story, I'll only explain that my partner and I were involved in a separate investigation, but we were able to connect the dots between our case and this homicide. Leads in our case had led us to several caches of military weapons and explosives and these were buried in the desert east of Los Angeles. While engaged in aerial surveillance, we discovered that these weapons were in the same vicinity as a collection of stolen motorhomes and speedboats. Needless to say the situation was unusual, suggesting that there was more to this story than gun trafficking.

One of the motorhomes was unoccupied at the time of our arrival, but obviously in use. In it we found a briefcase containing a gun, false IDs, and other documents. As we looked it over, we realized that the photo on the IDs depicted a well-known mercenary. The briefcase also contained maps of Central America plus a thick stack of papers which described in detail, the invasion of Belize. Initially we didn't know what we had stumbled upon, but we knew it was something significant.

As we looked over the documents it became clear that the recreational vehicles, pleasure boats, and military hardware we had found in our aerial reconnaissance, were to be used in this operation. We had in our hands, marked-up maps, diagrams depicting military strikes against targets in Belize, details about the mercenaries involved, a timeline, and other specific operational details. We had it all. It was a goldmine of incriminating evidence, much of it with handwritten notations.

Obviously we had fallen into the middle of something big. Something that was far more significant than illegal weapons, stolen vehicles, and the murder of a fringe criminal.

As the investigation progressed, we learned why the man in Costa Mesa had been killed. It was to silence a loose-lipped mercenary. The victim had foolishly talked with someone about his involvement with this mercenary operation.

He was killed to silence him. As a side benefit, the Colonel who was in charge of the operation, apparently decided to use the murder to send a message to the others involved. He wanted them to understand that operational security was to be taken seriously.

After finding the plans for the invasion of Belize, we contacted the U.S. State Department and the Central Intelligence Agency and briefed them on what we had found. They wanted to borrow the evidence to validate its veracity and pledged to help us with our investigation. We also contacted the producers of the national television show, 60-Minutes. Apparently they had recently interviewed the Colonel, so we wanted to see what else we could learn from the interview.

Our first indication of a problem was when 60-Minutes stalled, essentially refusing to release to us the raw footage of the interview with the mercenary leader. Next, we learned that the federal prosecutor was blocking our arrest warrant, as well as warrants for various pieces of evidence. We went over his head, and still the stalling tactics continued. While we fought these delays, the Colonel somehow got wind of our actions and slipped out of the country.

My partner and I were flaming mad, but there was nothing we could do. We didn't know why, but it seemed like the federal government was actively stonewalling us, as well as doing various things to torpedo our investigation.

It didn't seem possible. We had trusted our contacts at the State Department and the CIA. They apologized and explained that these things sometimes happen with a big bureaucracy. None of it made sense. Why would they obstruct our investigation?

After weeks of gridlock we acknowledged that the investigation was dead. Our evidence and all of our suspects were gone. We did foil the invasion, but for us that was a shallow success.

We concluded that the CIA was somehow involved in this imminent invasion of Belize. They were either behind it, or they had decided to let it happen. Beyond this, we couldn't figure out why anyone would want to invade this sleepy underdeveloped nation.

During those years, Cuba and Russia were involved in promoting the spread of communism in the region, but we hadn't found any connection to communism. So that didn't seem to fit the scenario, either. We couldn't find a viable explanation. It remained a mystery.

As interesting as the case was, we were not only baffled by the circumstances but stymied and unable to make further progress. I'd like to tell you that we persevered and eventually broke the case, but that isn't what happened. Our commanding officer was supportive, but without additional leads to work, we were forced to inactivate the case. My partner and I turned our attention to other matters.

Two decades later and again by accident, I stumbled upon the answers which had previously been so elusive. At that time I wasn't familiar with the term 'false flag operation,' but that is what we had stumbled into.

Years later, I was living in Guatemala after taking an early retirement from the police department. Guatemala is the Central American country adjacent to Belize, but my presence there had nothing to do with my old, inactive investigation.

However, as a result of my work in Guatemala, I had the opportunity to develop a personal relationship with the former president of the country, General Rios Montt, and a number of other top military leaders and government officials. Over time, I became privy to additional information about my old investigation. What I learned was fascinating.

In Guatemala, locally printed maps of the country also include Belize. I had noticed this, but assumed it was simply due to geographic proximity. However, these friends explained that the people of Guatemala consider Belize to be part of their country. Through subterfuge, the British had stolen the land from Guatemala, making it possible for British corporations to exploit Belize's forests of exotic-wood trees and other natural resources.

Years later, when the United Kingdom was forced to stop its environmentally unfriendly exploitation of Belize, the British gave the country its independence. This further exacerbated the territorial dispute which still remains unresolved.

What I learned was that my old criminal case, which involved mercenaries and the invasion of Belize, had been part of a CIA 'false flag' operation. Their goal was to use the invasion to not only resolve the territorial dispute in favor of Guatemala, but to also advance U.S. interests in the region.

By restoring Belize to Guatemala, the unified nation would gain more influence in the region. This was something the CIA could exploit. So they struck a deal with Guatemala's leaders. The CIA would facilitate the reunification, and in return Guatemala's leaders would become more active in fighting the expansion of communism in Latin America.

A few years prior, Colonel Mike Hoare and 43 mercenaries, invaded the Republic of Seychelles, a small archipelago in the Indian Ocean that had fallen victim to a socialist coup d'état. Apparently this incident is what gave CIA planners the idea for how they could restore Belize to Guatemala.

Their plan was similar to what had happened in the Seychelles. They would use a group of mercenaries to invade Belize. But in this situation, the Guatemalan military would heroically come to the aid of their weak neighbor. Guatemala's army would engage and defeat the small mercenary force and liberate the people of Belize from the hostile invaders.

With a little help, the news media would naturally draw an obvious parallel to what Colonel Hoare had attempted a few years earlier in the Seychelles Affair. It was a tight package of deception and manipulation.

After defeating the mercenary force, the plan was for Guatemala's military to remain in place "temporarily," ostensibly to protect the people of Belize. However in this secret CIA deal, Guatemala would be allowed to progressively absorb the small independent nation. The plan was for it to eventually become a de facto State within the Republic of Guatemala.

It was a shrewd plan. The U.S. would expand its influence in Latin America, Guatemala would regain its stolen state, and the lackadaisical people of Belize would benefit from economic revitalization that would naturally come from reunification. In the eyes of the CIA, everyone would win, but for them the most important aspect was that the U.S. would secure an important new beachhead in the Cold War against communism.

Interestingly, in the documents we recovered in the California desert, there was nothing to indicate that the mercenaries knew the whole plan. Such is the world of politics and false flag operations, where friends and employees eventually discover that they were witless pawns. All along, the plan was to use the mercenaries hired by the CIA as sacrificial lambs. Very likely, many of the mercenaries, as well as many civilians, would have died in the exploit.

Of course in the eyes of the world, the mercenaries were just Wild Geese, so who would care? As a result of this 'staged' mercenary invasion, the Guatemalan government would have the excuse they needed to justify their own, permanent invasion of Belize. In the process, the world would herald them as the good guys who helped a neighbor in need.

Guided by the CIA and the Guatemalan leaders, the media would tell the story the powerbrokers wanted told. No one would be the wiser. Even if a talented investigative reporter became suspicious, there would be no evidence to prove that the U.S. had sponsored this false flag operation.

Even the leader of the mercenary group apparently had no knowledge of the real objective, nor would the field commanders of the Guatemalan army. As a result of shrewd contingency planning, when the operation fell apart, the CIA instantly switched gears and helped the Colonel and his mercenaries escape from the United States. As a result, these soldiers-for-hire became beholding to the CIA. The mercenaries had been involved in gun smuggling, vehicle theft, possession of explosives, murder, and a host of other felonies, so the mercenaries understood that the CIA had protected them from many years of imprisonment. The CIA plan was not only clever, it was resilient.

It would be impossible to prove government collusion with the mercenaries. Everyone knew that to talk would mean ending up like the victim in Costa Mesa. This sophisticated contingency planning insured perpetual secrecy. There is no statute of limitations on murder, so even the hapless mercenaries would remain silent. It was a slick plan.

As you see with this joint CIA-Guatemalan operation, a well conceived and implemented false flag operation is difficult to expose and impossible to prove. Successful false flag operations have many layers of insulation between the people pulling the strings and the puppets who carry out the operation.

We Need to be Discerning and Circumspect

When I was a police detective, I was once called to a bank as a teller believed that an elderly patron was perhaps in the middle of a con referred to as a 'bank examiner' fraud. Apparently this customer of many years, who lived a very frugal and solitary existence, had just come to the bank and withdrew her entire savings of $25,000. This was extremely unusual, as the teller knew this woman never withdrew more than $100. The bank manager wanted me to make sure this customer wasn't being swindled.

Since this woman lived nearby, I went from the bank directly to her home to talk with her. She graciously welcomed me into her home after I showed her my badge and identification, even though I was dressed in plain clothes and had parked an unmarked police car in her driveway.

She was warm and friendly, and had insisted that I sit down and join her for a cup of coffee. Once I broached the topic of her large, unusual withdrawal from the bank, she became nervous, but eventually told me that she was working with the FBI to nab a thief who was an employee of the bank. She told me that her favorite teller was apparently a crook, and had been stealing money from the bank for years.

At least that is what the FBI agent has explained to her when he had visited her home, to enlist her help in nabbing this criminal. He had asked her to withdraw her life savings. He would come by to get the money, take it to have the cash marked with infrared dye, and then return it to her. The plan was for her to redeposit the funds, and the FBI would be able to determine if she had skimmed any of the money and taken it from the bank. She was promised an official receipt in exchange for the funds, and promised a letter of commendation. The local newspaper would likely send someone to do a story on how she had helped the FBI arrest this embezzler.

Once I explained to this gentile woman that this was a scam, a con routinely perpetrated on trusting seniors, she became argumentative. Even though I wasn't asking her for anything, she concluded that I was the con, and she threw me out of her house. I was barely able to convince her to call the police department and ask for a uniformed police officer to come, to validate my identity as a police officer.

Once the uniformed officer arrived in his black and white police car, emblazoned with the word 'police' and with a light bar on the roof, she finally conceded that I was, in fact, a police officer. But I was still unable to convince her that she was being duped. In this case, the criminal was so convincing that he was able to deceive her even after she had been given incontrovertible evidence to refute the scheme of the conman.

Fortunately I had arrived in time, and was able to arrest the con, and escort the woman back to the bank where she could redeposit her money. Others aren't so fortunate.

Similarly, today the perpetrators of false flag operations are very convincing. With the potential for deception in mind, we need to carefully discern the truth, and be circumspect in how we respond to situations.

For us as individuals, when we observe that some event ignites or adds fuel to social upheaval or crisis, we need to look for evidence before we respond with what might be untoward action. We need to make sure we aren't being manipulated into a prescribed response that is harmful to us or others.

Whether it is the tactics of former FBI Director, J. Edgar Hoover who was a false flag expert, the CIA in collusion with the Guatemalan government, or a lightweight false flag operation conducted by a current politician who is fomenting racial strife just to advance his Progressive agenda, we need to be circumspect. When possible, our response to chaos needs to be thoughtful and reasoned. We may not be able to prove intentional deception, but we can discern when it is appropriate to stand back and avoid personal involvement.

The same mentality which let U.S. Government leaders justify the Guatemala operation is now being used domestically. Unfortunately, many of today's top-echelon leaders are even more morally bereft than those who were in positions of trust during the Guatemala affair.

Keep in mind, those leaders were willing to fund the creation of a vehicle theft ring in California, and the smuggling of weapons and explosives which they knew would be used to kill people (including innocent Belizean citizens). Those same U.S. government leaders obstructed the murder investigation of an American citizen in Costa Mesa, they betrayed their mercenary partners who they had recruited for their operation, and they were willing to capriciously orchestrate a change of national borders of two friendly countries and violate their national sovereignty, all for the 'greater good.'

False flag operations and other forms of deception are a constant threat. Shrewd manipulators such as these have agendas which are not compatible with a free society.

Moreover, this mindset is capable of justifying any action. And, it is the prevailing self-centered intellectual will, which drives modern elitism. We do need to be concerned.

> "The 10 most dangerous words in the English language are, 'Hi, I'm from the government and I'm here to help.'" [75]
>
> - Ronald Reagan
> 40th U.S. President

> "Man is not free unless government is limited. There's a clear cause and effect here that is as neat and predictable as a law of physics: As government expands, liberty contracts." [76]
>
> - Ronald Reagan

---

[75] Remarks to Future Farmers of America, July 28, 1988.

[76] Presidential Farewell Address, Washington, D.C., January 11, 1989

Dangerous Words: "The Greater Good"

When the people in positions of power are guided by the nebulous principle of the "greater good" rather than morality and the rule of law, any machination can easily be justified. Whether we contemplate the implications of my Guatemala story, the various IRS scandals which targeted conservatives and Christians, or any of the thousands of less visible underhanded activities perpetrated by other government agencies, someone's concept of "the greater good' is often used to justify their illegal or immoral activities.

This does affect us, personally. When a government agency is willing to violate the law, and betray their nation's Constitution and their own colleagues, why do we think our situation will be different?

Further, whether it is the proponents of the deception who talk about "the greater good," or weak-thinkers or rabble rousers who indirectly infer a similar justification, we need to be careful.

When either side infers justification for their actions based on "the greater good" we need to see this as a 'red flag' of warning. We need to proceed with extreme caution.

Why the Focus on 'False Flag' Operations?

To drive a vehicle while under the influence of alcohol or drugs is known to be dangerous. Everyone understands that beer, wine, mixed drinks, liquor, legal and illegal drugs can all impair a driver's judgment. Similarly, there are various forms of deception which alter our judgment and accelerate us toward danger. False flag operations are but one example.

Any deception can corrupt sound thinking and actions. This is very true, but I've singled out 'false flag' deceptions here because they are insidiously effective for accomplishing more than just deception. These operations often stimulate fighting between friends, or misdirect thoughts and actions by focusing our attention on superficial issues or benign foes.

By featuring this form of deception here, my hope is that we will remind each other of the need to be evidence oriented, and circumspect in our response. Manipulation is the goal of the deceiver, so we need to proceed thoughtfully when we plan any action. Absent due care and caution we can easily fall into the deceiver's trap.

Please indulge me as I recap the obvious: When we commit ourselves to righteousness and justice, and apply due diligence to ferret out the truth, making important decisions prayerfully and after seeking wise counsel, only then can we foil the Machiavellian plots of those who devise evil.

This process of discernment isn't just the responsibility of leaders. It is the duty of each of us. It is our personal responsibility.

We need to remember, too, that the perpetrators of false flag operations can be very cleaver, but in the end they are simply vainglorious cowards. Nevertheless, these people and their schemes can be extremely dangerous for us personally and for our families, as well as for the United States or any nation.

As we prepare for the future, we shouldn't become survivalists; we should be revivalists. We need to hope and work for the best, while we also prepare for the worst. We need to prepare so that we can continue to work for a revival in our homeland, never forgetting that we need it in our own lives, too.

We can't defeat this enemy by behaving like our opponents. They are our nemesis, not our exemplar. The weapons we need to defeat these adversaries are truth, personal righteousness, shrewd strategies, and a commitment to justice. If we are to win, we need to respond with the better Way. We need to make sure that we are on the right track; the higher road.

With God's help, we can discern he truth and live as purveyors of the truth. We need to be selfless, genuine peace-*makers,* understanding that the peace process now requires us to forge peace. We need to be like the skilled blacksmith with a plan, who wields his hammer accurately, with the force of his whole body behind each blow. With divine wisdom and appropriate force we can overcome the deceiver.

"They conceive mischief and bring forth iniquity, and their mind prepares deception."

Holy Bible
Job 15:35

"See to it that no one takes you captive through philosophy and devoid-of-truth deception, according to the tradition of men, according to the elementary principles of the world rather than according to Christ."

Holy Bible
Colossians 2:8

"... we have made falsehood our refuge, and we have concealed ourselves with deception."

Holy Bible
Isaiah 28:15b

"He [Satan] will use every kind of evil deception to fool those on their way to destruction, because they refuse to love and accept the truth that would save them."

Holy Bible
2 Thessalonians 2:10

"They speak falsehood to one another; with flattering lips and with a double heart they speak."

Holy Bible
Psalm 12:2

"Through knowledge the righteous are rescued."

Holy Bible
Proverbs 11:9b

Chapter 6

Watching for Key Indicators of Looming Disaster

The U.S. Government is obviously preparing for widespread disaster or a life-altering nationwide incident. What is it they are preparing for? What is going to happen? What are the signs-of-the-times? Can we identify the key indicators of major change and discern the actual threats the government is contemplating?

We can't know with certainty what government leaders are thinking, but we can make an educated guess. Regardless of the specific scenarios they are envisioning, we can identify the signs-of-the-times and engage in our own targeted preparations. Since we are preparing for ourselves, our family, and friends, we don't need to know everything. We just need to know enough to develop our own response. This is a much simpler task.

To do this we still need to identify the key signs-of-the-times because these will guide our planning. It's these 'warning signals' which will give us the framework for our own preparations.

Since 'signs' are *signals* of change which effect economic, social, and political developments, we need to give particular attention to identifying them. Particularly those changes which build on each other; those which may not be hugely significant when considered alone, but in combination, can alter community and family life, our livelihood, health and well-being.

We routinely check weather reports in anticipation of a storm. Similarly, we need to watch other indicators which can help us monitor social and economic pressure.

These are discerned through reading news reports, blogs, and timely books, by sharing information with knowledgeable friends and coworkers, locating savvy insiders, and exposing ourselves to sound thinkers and cutting edge sources of news and relevant information.[77] These activities are necessary for responsible living as well as essential components for vigilant contingency planning. No longer can we afford to sit back and only concern ourselves with our own little world.

The U.S. and world economy is in serious trouble, but our life-altering impairments are much broader than just economic. We need to remember that a serious problem can suddenly become a disaster as a result of other deficiencies which have entered into the mix. Past financial mistakes are compounding, but it may not be the trending of these problems which eventually rattles us. It may be intersecting fault lines, such as dishonesty and greed which are suddenly exposed. These overstress the system and can trigger a financial earthquake.

Trends are worth watching, but don't let them tranquilize your vigilance. Very often it is some other factor which causes the loss of equilibrium. A tipping-point is often reached when some other event suddenly adds new weight and leverage to the problem. This sudden imbalance can topple the system.

To identify the signs of our times, we need to also look for changes in culture, such as attacks on family life, religious freedoms, the singling out of specific social groups rather than the acts of individuals, and blaming inanimate 'things' (like guns) rather than the individuals who carry out reprehensible acts. We need to look for threats such as war and terrorism of course, but also internal problems such as attitudes of entitlement, hubris toward God, abuse of power, belittling the U.S. Constitution, and injustice and liberty denied.

---

[77] The mainstream media is useless for this purpose. We need alternative news sources which report on meaningful news stories and developments. These will provide early warnings of trouble. In the appendix of this book you will find examples of news sources known for breaking important news stories and for providing links to original source documents and resources. News commentary may be interesting, but gleaning facts is far more useful for discerning the signs of our times. Our decisions need to be based on fact not commentary. See the appendix for more.

In the process we need to ferret out indicators of malaise. This includes the standard concerns of community decline and social change, health and safety issues, and the deterioration of literacy and education. It also includes disparate issues such as the public's loss of interest in news that is relevant, the decline in civic responsibility, as well as fundamentally different issues such as voter fraud, the increasingly tenuous availability of essential goods and services, and problems with water and food.

We need to search for meaningful developments, not those which capture the interest of the major media outlets. We need to develop our own sources of information so that we aren't dependent on traditional media sources.

Plus, we need to look for harbingers of social storm. This includes the loss of trust in government and leaders, abuse of the law and activist courts which thwart the law, systemic lawlessness, and lack of interest in the First Principles[78] on which the U.S. was founded. This may also include declines in morality and civility, devaluing of human life, advancing the welfare of the collective by trampling the rights of individuals, attitudes of unearned entitlement, manipulation of the government, and misuse of its institutions. Unnecessary intrusion by government into business and private life, corruption in various forms, new taxes as a scheme to redistribute wealth, and increases in tension among racial and other social groups can also be overlooked warning signs.

Approached diligently as part of everyday life, we can learn to discern significant new developments, find trends, and identify where a confluence of different factors might combine to produce a crisis. Confluence,[79] or the 'multiplier effect' where several issues merge and gain power and momentum, is a key.

Empowered with this approach, and fortified with solid information, we have the opportunity to make informed decisions of both substance and timing. We can formulate plans and incisively prepare for the future. At the very least, with this advance warning, we can often avoid the full impact of a crisis.

---

[78] www.firstprinciplesjournal.com

[79] See Chapter 6 for more on confluence events.

As we learn how to recognize the key indicators; the *signs of the times* which can help us make savvy forecasts, we need to look for the precursors which indicate a potential 'tipping point.' The events or developments which threaten the status quo have the capacity to destabilize, and these can slide us into a disastrous situation.

Positive change is also possible, but significant improvements that reverse the trends are unlikely at this point. In any case, it's not an issue of outlook. It's not an issue of being pessimistic vs. optimistic or seeing the glass as half-empty or half-full. It is a matter of watching the key indicators and trends and honestly embracing truths that are exposed.

If we aren't looking for indicators of change, and if we aren't aware of our weakened condition, we will be surprised and caught off guard. We can be easily duped by the Neville Chamberlains[80] of this world who tickle our ears with shallow, baseless optimism, if we aren't discriminating.

Not only do we need to embrace the truth, we need to also understand that harmful change can be progressive or it can occur suddenly. While we enthusiastically work toward positive change and improvements, we also need to methodically prepare for the unpleasant.

If things turn around, it will be a surprise which we relish. However, if things continue to slide downhill, our response will need to be quick, deliberate and decisive. That situation will not take care of itself, so we need to be vigilant. We need to be prepared and ready.

---

[80] Arthur Neville Chamberlain was Prime Minister of the United Kingdom prior to World War II. His policies of appeasement, and his refusal to face the truth about Adolph Hitler, resulted in the UK and Europe failing to stop the Nazis early and perhaps avoiding worldwide war. He was also responsible for a lack of national preparedness, which made the disaster of war far more devastating for the British people. In his pre-war era, Chamberlain was extremely popular with the people. Now, he is used as an example of wishful thinking and clueless leadership.

We need to be ready for two responses.

When disaster strikes, we need to be ready to "batten down the hatches" at our well-equipped home or the home of a nearby family member or friend, so that we can live in a protected environment for several weeks if necessary. With this response we need to also have a GO-Bag[81] ready, just in case we find that it is necessary to evacuate to a community shelter. This response covers the bases for most traditional disasters.

However, if we look at both the signs of the times and the U.S. Government's preparations, and conclude that there is a viable threat of a much larger disaster, we need to do more. In fact, we will need to do far more. We need to have the ability to evacuate to a prearranged rural place of safety; a retreat location that we have prepared in advance to serve as a longer-term "safe haven" refuge.

In other words, we need to be prepared to operate in a protracted disaster environment such as the one the government envisions. In addition, we need to be prepared and ready to shrewdly counter or coexist with the federal government's response.

If past experience is an indicator, the government's actions will help some people, while producing a new set of problems for others. This will be particularly evident for those who want to remain independent and self-reliant, in a world that will have become hyper-controlled by government agencies following a pre-prescribed disaster-response plan.

One incident may very well spark three distinctly different disasters: The natural or manmade disaster which kicked-off the chaos, the public's response and the effect of their lack of preparedness, and lastly the government's response which has historically created yet another disaster. A brief study of the events surrounding Hurricane Katrina provides a good example of this three-fold disaster phenomenon.

---

[81] For more on Go-Bags and evacuation, see Book 2 in this "Prepared: Ready to Roll" series.

In regard to a looming major disaster, if you don't believe that the government's analysis is accurate, at least prepare for a more traditional, major disaster like Hurricane Katrina. This is a minimum, bottom baseline of preparedness for responsible adults.

The first level of defense, the "batten down the hatches" response, is comparatively easy to prepare. It needs to be based in a solidly-built home or business situated in a safe area in your community. It needs to be defensible, and equipped with sufficient stockpiles of water and food, and outfitted with alternative power and other supplies, to live independently and ideally invisibly, for two weeks.

The second level of defense, a "safe haven" retreat location, requires substantially more preparation. It is this second site that will be required if the government's predictions are correct. Without our own safe haven, we will be relegated to whatever help we can get from overwhelmed state and federal bureaucracies.

If a serious emergency situation develops and the event is nationwide in scope and protracted in duration, as federal preparations suggest, the government will only be able to provide comprehensive, meaningful help to a small number of people. Probably no more than 1 in 40 will receive adequate help. These are worse odds than using your paycheck to gamble in a Las Vegas casino.

Furthermore, in this case the game you are playing is Russian roulette. You are literally gambling with your life. If you don't come out the victor in this game, you will be on your own; essentially left to fend for yourself with millions of other abandoned people. This will not be a pretty situation, especially in urban areas. In this government-care vs. no-care environment, even the winners of this lottery will be losers. Ending up in one of the government's I/R Centers[82] will be a miserable win.

If you are a Christian and think God is going to protect you, it's time to start reading the Bible to see what it really says. God does not promise to care for his people if they fail to do their part.[83]

Recovery after a Major Disaster is Slow

With Hurricane Katrina, many displaced people were still in emergency housing three years after the hurricane. Imagine what it will be like if a disaster of similar severity is nationwide rather than just regional. In such a situation, resources would not be sent to your area from another part of the country. Every region would be on its own. You and your neighbors will need to fend for yourselves.

---

[82] I/R Centers, aka Internment/Resettlement Centers or FEMA Camps, are sponsored by FEMA, DHS, CDC and other federal agencies, but are routinely run by the U.S. Army. These facilities are described in the Restricted but Unclassified government document, FM3-39.40 'Internment and Resettlement Operations.' The updated, February 2010 version of this document includes provisions for interning American citizens inside the United States. (This U.S. Government document can be found on the Internet.) As this field manual makes clear, these are prison-like facilities without privacy or basic freedoms. Residents will apparently work for their keep, as described in Army Regulation 210-35, which can also be found on the Internet. It is estimated that the government has now built a sufficient number of these semi-permanent 'Centers' to warehouse 8 million Americans, i.e. 1 out of 40 people. Some sources claim that the government will be able to accommodate far more than 8 million refugees, but the author was unable to locate official documentation to validate a larger number. Regardless of the number of people which can be accommodated, I/R Centers will not provide a pleasant refuge.

[83] For Example: Luke 22:35-36; Proverbs 6:6-11; 13:14; 22:3; Matthew 16:2-4; Ezekiel 38:7.

Of course, life in an I/R Center is better than starvation. Thankfully, today you have another option. Another choice is available to you, but only if you get busy now and prepare your own safe-haven retreat.

So the story-behind-the-story here is not that these Centers exist, but that the government, despite its years of preparation, is still not in a position to provide material aid to the millions of people who live in the United States. This is why the new 'Continuity of Government' (COG) plan includes highly secure housing for selected government employees and 'essential' civilians who will be needed for a national rebuilding effort.

These fortunate few will be housed in felicitous locations on military bases with accouterments and congenial management. This will be in stark contrast to the 'I/R Centers' which are built to warehouse people. Unless you're one the elite who are already pre-assigned to a COG center, an I/R Center is the best you can hope for if you have failed to prepare your own safe-haven retreat.

Government documents such as FM 3-39.40 make it clear that life in these Centers will resemble incarceration. This will include minimal food, little privacy, and assigned manual labor jobs, primarily agricultural.[84]

Despite years of preparation, it is impossible for the U.S. Government to help millions of people. They can't do it. Frankly, we have no right to expect it. The task is simply too big.

There is yet another pattern here. In the Cold War days, the U.S. Government established neighborhood nuclear bomb shelters for short-term protection of the general public. However, we need to recognize that today's government has only given serious attention to meeting the needs of Continuity of Government employees, plus an elite group of civilians which it has identified, and prequalified, as essential for rebuilding. The reasons for this can be debated, but it is without a doubt a major change in approach to disaster preparedness.

If you aren't already part of the COG preparations, you are considered redundant. Conditions will resemble a hospital engaging in triage after a disaster. Therefore, if you aren't prepared to be self-reliant, you will very likely be a victim.

---

[84]   U.S. Army Regulation 210-35, "Civilian Inmate Labor Program," Unclassified, 14-January-2015.

If the federal government's risk assessment is accurate, we have a figurative gun pointed at our head. The threat is imminent and serious. Like the movie character Dirty Harry, I need to ask, "Do you feel lucky?"

You will need to be either supremely lucky or suitably prepared. Without adequate supplies and a "safe haven" retreat location which has been prepared in advance, only a few very fortunate people will survive unscathed.

Maybe you will be one of the lucky ones. If the big event does happen, perhaps you will find that you are living in a part of the country that isn't hit as hard. Maybe the emergency situation will be far less severe. Are you willing to accept this risk?

The U.S. Government and military do prepare for worst case scenarios. True. Yet, worst case scenarios do happen. Based on the U.S. Government's 20+ years of full-steam ahead preparations, they expect the coming event to be major—beyond anything the U.S. has ever experienced.

The nature of the government's preparations reveal that the expectation is for an event which adversely impacts the entire population, a problem that is simply too big to handle using normal but ramped-up preparations. This is why the major effort has been focused on Continuity of Government (COG) preparations. COG preparations are still large scale undertakings, but the scope is manageable.

The government's preparations for the bulk of the population may seem massive, but they are totally inadequate when you consider the need to care for the entire population for an extended period of time. Their plan is akin to packing as many 'important' people as possible into Noah's Ark (COG), then giving a bag of Styrofoam to 2-10% of the rest of the population, while hoping the rest can swim.

Hope for the Best, Prepare for the Worst.

The old adage *"hope for the best, prepare for the worst"* is the U.S. Government's mantra. Their preparations do reflect a worse-case scenario, so a major disaster that is less cataclysmic is quite possible; maybe even likely. Yet the question remains, *"Do you feel lucky?"* If you don't want to depend entirely on dumb luck, some level of safe-haven preparation is necessary.

Those who have not prepared to face a major disaster will probably not survive a protracted, widespread, catastrophic event. Yet, with a little luck (or divine intervention) and some serious preparation, it is totally possible. It is do-able. We can do it.

Furthermore, we don't need to live in fear. And, we don't need the deep-pockets of the federal government to provide for us, either. This is something we can manage on our own. We can do it.

Nevertheless, most people will not succeed if they try to do this alone. This is an undertaking which needs the cooperative efforts of a group of likeminded people who have foresight, the willingness to prepare in advance, and the mindset to work cooperatively with each other in an Intentional Community (see the chapter, "Community is Essential" in Book 3.)

Hope is justified. If you are proactive there are ample reasons to remain hopeful. However, it is only when we combine hope with adequate preparation that we can expect success.

Each of us has a choice. We can mentally check out and escape into a normalcy bias. We can ignore the signs of the times, and discount U.S. Government preparations as being overzealous. Or, we can be responsible, self-reliant, and prudent people who *hope for the best but prepare for the worst.*

Which one are you? It's time to decide.

When we seek out the truth and do what we can to prepare, we can experience the freedom that comes from being independent and self-reliant (as opposed to being government dependent). This is the cost, and a responsibility, that comes with liberty. As our Founding Fathers understood...

"Eternal vigilance is the price of liberty." [85]

Vigilance, self-reliance and preparedness aren't something new. This approach is just a return to the age old, tried and true virtues which our ancestors embraced.

---

[85] Variations of this statement are attributed to a number of the Founding Fathers of the United States, but Thomas Jefferson is often cited as the one who popularized this truism. Source: "The Union," *Pennsylvania Inquirer and Daily Courier*, January 4, 1838, Issue 4, column B.

*"And you will know the truth,
and the truth will make you free."*

Holy Bible

John 8:32

Chapter 7

A Confluence Disaster is Increasingly Likely

Experts debate amongst themselves as to which of our looming problems will eventually cause a major meltdown. However, they all agree that the situation we will face may not be caused by one single, tragic incident. Rather, it will likely be a combination of factors, or a series of events which intersect to build a stair-step of lesser disasters which lead to a blow-out crisis. This is referred to as a "confluence disaster."

The experts agree that it's no longer a question as to "If?" a major disaster is coming, it's now just a question of "When?" Likewise, they agree that a combination of festering problems can quickly morph into a 'confluence disaster' of major proportions.

Since a confluence disaster can develop with little warning, prepared people need to be vigilant and observant of the sparks which are the flashing lights of change. It is these hot-spot problems which can suddenly become a blaze.

Since these developments can escape notice, we also need clear channels of communication with other 'watchers,' so that news about developments can be shared and discussed. We also need to be ready to move quickly to implement our emergency plan at the first indication that circumstances are getting out of control.

Confluence disasters often start with a single, isolated, burning island of a problem. It can be a social issue like racial unrest, or an economic problem such as a crash in the derivatives market. With a confluence disaster, the fire of this burning problem is then fanned by something else, like a news media which is eager to grab the attention of new viewers, or panic selling in the stock market. This adds extra energy to the problem, and effectively fans the flames, which in turn transports sparks from the isolated incident to ignite a different problem.

Once the fire jumps to another problem, it has the potential to spread further and more rapidly, becoming a nationwide wildfire. If unchecked, these fires can be further fed by other, totally unrelated but smoldering problems. These add more fuel to the blaze, and the fire burns brighter and begins to consume everything in its path. If the news media, social networking, Internet or some other mechanism stokes the blaze, this increases the heat and the intensity, creating even more disastrous results.

Overnight or over a few months, this progressive stair-step of incidents builds. In each case, this "confluence" mechanism takes a modest problem, legitimate or baseless, and transforms it into a flashover conflagration.

In each confluence disaster, it is the other related or totally unrelated problems which intensify the heat and progressively add more fuel to the fire. It is this *confluence* of added fuels which can turn a hot problem into one with almost explosive force.

A few years ago, one of my close friends was doing a controlled burn on his ranch. The fire he set was isolated and distant from trees and other flammable materials. At first, everything was fine. It was a hot fire but totally under control. Then the wind suddenly shifted direction and increased in intensity, carrying sparks into tinder dry grass. He was prepared. He had water and other firefighting equipment on hand to extinguish these small fires. Unfortunately, the weather forecast did not include high winds. Gusts ignited more and more grass in the area around his controlled burn; more than he could extinguish. Suddenly, the small grass fires began to ignite the drooping branches of cedar trees, which then lifted the flames into the dry branches of the nearby oak trees.

Within a few minutes, a wildfire spread up the hill, erratically expanding as the changing winds spread the fire. A few hours later the fire was extinguished, but not before acres of land were charred and a number of majestic oak trees had been destroyed.

It has taken the intervening years, but new growth has finally repaired the unsightly damage. However, the beautiful oak trees which previously graced the area are still gone. It will take generations to replace those.

This ranch fire wasn't a confluence disaster, but it does illustrate how a small fire can become a big one unexpectedly, with little warning. In just the same way, a small problem can unexpectedly become a big disaster.

Unlike watching a trend where we can monitor change over time, a confluence disaster can transition from a bonfire to flashover in a few days with little warning. It can shake the very foundation of a society, and burn down even those things which were previously considered fireproof.

An important characteristic of a confluence disaster is that the sources of volatility may be only tangentially related, or even totally unconnected to each other. Yet, it's the combination of these different fuels (problems) which are ignited at the same time, turning separate distinct problems into a single major disaster. It is this combination of fuels which powers a confluence disaster.

Since this framework fits the U.S. Government's unprecedented disaster preparations, we need to watch for these kinds of developments. Those who focus their attention on one threat, or even a false-flag incident, need to be watchful for this type of disaster which can spring up quickly, and which may not be initiated by the topic of their concern. In any case, absent a major incident which initiates widespread disaster, the set of dominos which form the basis of a confluence disaster is a likely scenario. At this point when we have so many major problems tottering, one problem can impact another sequentially, and soon everything starts to topple.

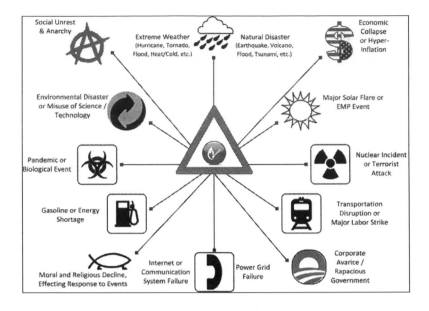

This illustration includes a selection of a dozen current problems. Each of these, over time, has the potential to develop into a major disaster. However, when any of these are combined together, or with some other burning problem, this can become an volatile mixture that has the potential to explode in the immediate future.

As two or more significant problems expand simultaneously, or back-to-back sequentially, they draw energy from each other and a multiplier effect kicks-in. Each intensifies the effect of the other, forming a *confluence disaster*.

Individually, problems may be serious but not disastrous. However, when they feed off each other, they can cascade with a powerful surge effect. Like atoms bouncing into each other in a nuclear reaction, this dramatically increases explosive force.

An emergency situation created by a confluence of events is not only possible, it is increasingly likely. In our society, and in our world, there are many serious problems smoldering.

When an individual twig such as racial strife is ignited, it may be distressing, yet the problem may still be correctable. However, when a pile of twigs (problems) is lit at the same time, it can become a flash fire.

Similarly, if a burning problem is provided with more fuel, such as a multi-city terrorist attack, the devaluing of the dollar, a cyber attack which cripples the Internet or compromises online security, or even the threat of a pandemic, any of these can envelop a previously modest blaze and transform it into a firestorm.

When the right combinations of factors come together at the same time, this is both the kindling and fuel needed to create a life-changing flashover event. In both situations, it only takes a little spark and an unexpected gust of wind to get it started. At that point, a major disaster may not be far away.

Is a confluence disaster farfetched?
Think about it. It's not.

Study the illustration on the prior page. Consider how easy it would be for several of these problems to flare, intersect, merge and suddenly snowball, picking up momentum as they roll along together to emerge as a major disaster.

Are you prepared for a chain-reaction series of events? Few are, in spite of the many warnings that a confluence event is very likely in the months or years ahead.

What are the odds of something big happening? Is it one chance in five? One in twenty? One in a hundred? Even if you think a major disaster is unlikely, and the odds are in your favor, isn't it prudent to take action to protect yourself, your family and friends?

Do you have car insurance? The odds of getting into a major traffic accident are less likely than a confluence disaster. So, isn't it a good idea to insure that you have protected yourself from a major disaster as well.

Examples of how a confluence disaster might play out...

Example #1: War in Israel or the Middle East.

The world's supply of gasoline and fuel is disrupted. Even though the U.S. gets little of its oil from the Middle East, it is a world market so the cost of fuel spikes. People have a hard time getting fuel as well as paying for it, so they have difficulty getting to work. They also limit their shopping to necessities, so the economy begins to falter.

After a few weeks, portions of the electric grid fail as many power plants are unable to get fuel to operate their generators. A few days later, emergency generators at the mobile phone companies and police/fire dispatch centers stop running. As the fuel tanks run dry at water districts, fresh water stops flowing to the faucets and sewage is no longer pumped so toilets don't flush.

Lack of sanitation breeds disease, but the hospitals are only operating at 5% since their generators are also without fuel and the trucks which deliver medical supplies can't make their rounds. (Hospital generators typically have enough fuel to run for 3-5 days.) Local government makes essential services like hospitals and water plants a priority, but fuel delivery is still spasmodic. Since hospitals have few windows which open and are wholly dependent on HVAC for ventilation, most patients must be released and new patients are rarely admitted.

As a result of increased demand and decreased capacity, most people are turned away from hospitals. Minor illnesses begin to fester and disease begins to spread. Slowly at first, but conditions are such that disease spreads faster and faster. An epidemic emerges and, without power and other resources, the snowballing problem of disease can't be stopped.

Many people die of simple diseases and injuries because they went untreated. Entire communities are quarantined and left without sufficient food and water. People aren't working, so society comes to a standstill and then crashes.

Example #2: Sleeper-Cell Terrorism

In cooperation with various Islamic State organizations, groups of Muslim 'sleeper cell' terrorists who are already living in the United States, strike on the same day. This time the weapons are everyday items.

Vehicles are driven into crowds of people, simple improvised explosive devices are detonated in stores, poison is added to food in grocery stores and public water supplies are contaminated, axes and swords are used for beheadings, and other unsophisticated but dramatic weapons are used in ordinary places, all to prove that no one is safe—*anywhere*.

Dozens of soft targets are hit such as busy shopping centers, office buildings, sporting events, public transportation, schools and churches. There is no apparent pattern, and these targets are hit within hours of each other, but located in more than twenty metropolitan and rural areas across the country. The public's fear is palatable.

People respond by hunkering down at home and many people stop going to work. As a result, many businesses are unable to operate. Paychecks stop coming. Transportation is affected and groceries and other essential products aren't delivered to the stores.

Panic buying and hoarding empties the shelves of groceries and other essential supplies. Hyperinflation strikes as people are forced to pay outrageous prices for food and other goods.

As these problems intensify nationwide, the world questions the viability of the dollar and the American stock market. The value of the dollar drops and the stock market nosedives. The economy goes into a freefall. Property values plummet as a large portion of the population is unable to make their mortgage payments. The economy is topsy-turvy; the price of food and essential goods skyrockets, while the value of other things such as businesses, houses, and cars drop abruptly. Fear is infectious. Widespread violence erupts in the inner cities, and rapidly expands into suburban areas.

Example #3: Economic Crisis

Envision an economic crisis caused by our unsustainable national debt, and the disclosure that the Federal Reserve is unable to return foreign depositors gold reserves which have been stockpiled in the United States. (We can't return it because the Federal Reserve sold the gold to prop-up our national debt.) As these stories develop, new scrutiny is applied to other financial institutions. The derivatives market is exposed and collapses, followed by five too-big-to-fail banking institutions. The public will not tolerate yet another round of bailouts, so large companies begin massive layoffs of employees. Worldwide the economy wavers as unemployment skyrockets. New austerity measures by federal and local governments are too little, too late; confidence in government is gone. Frustration reaches explosive levels and civil unrest grips most Western nations. In the U.S., the federal government clamps down with heavy handed measures which backfire. Chaos reigns.

Example #4: Internet Breakdown
An event which initiates a cascading series of crises.

The Internet stops operating and the experts are unable to reboot the system. No one knows what caused the Internet blackout. It may have been anonymous hackers or a foreign government, but China is blamed since their prior 'test' attacks are widely known. The American people feel angry and impotent.

Quickly, the debate on culprits is overshadowed by the widespread effects of the loss of all Internet-dependent services. People who previously lived with an umbilical attachment to social networking are the first to panic as they became relationally isolated. Since Internet-based telephone and email services stopped, contact between friends and family cease, and a national sense of disquiet escalates while business-to-business and business-to-customer communication comes to a screeching work-throttling halt.

Online retailers have stopped selling, so they have laid-off their workers since no one can access their website stores.

Neighborhood stores, large and small, are dependent on Internet-based point-of-purchase credit card processing for their sales, so they are also forced to close their doors. A few small businesses remain open, but cash in the hands of consumers is soon exhausted. Bank branches have difficulty verifying funds on deposit, so they refuse to give their customers the cash they have on deposit. This makes the public anxious and angry, so many bank branches close, too.

Banks are generally unable to continue their operations. Financial records, information on loans, ATMs, credit and debit card operations, are all heavily based on Internet-based data transfer, so banks are forced to limit or even cease consumer-level operations.

Automatic deposits of paychecks, social security checks, SNAP and welfare checks were all lost in the Internet blackout. Since most of the population lives paycheck to paycheck, they do not have cash on hand to make purchases of food, gasoline, and other essentials. Even those people with hefty bank accounts are unable to access their funds. Barter becomes the only mechanism for trade.

Transportation, inventory, and delivery systems for goods, are all Internet dependent, so these have stopped working. Stores are no longer being restocked. Grocery stores remain empty, so FEMA steps in to help with emergency supplies of food and water. Unfortunately, the scope of the need is far beyond their ability.

To stop hording and violence, FEMA emergency centers are opened to house and feed the public. These become centers of violence and abuse despite the presence of National Guard troops. Frustrated and tired police officers and military, begin to overreact. Shootings become commonplace. FEMA centers are locked down like prisons.

In a desperate attempt to restore order and services, the federal government announces that it has created a new, better and more secure Internet. After several more weeks of delay, Internet-2 is operational. The public responds with a sigh of relief but it is a short-lived reprieve. The replacement systems are quickly infected and collapse. The public becomes desperate, and a sense of hopelessness emerges.

Parents can't get adequate food for their families. Children are hungry and becoming sick. Looting is theft on a grand scale and normally honest people find it easy to get lost in a crowd of looters, justifying theft if it is to assuage hunger and care for their family.

Theft to alleviate hunger morphs into the theft of other goods to use for barter. Those who resist these thefts are overrun, injured, or killed. Initially, it's others in the gang of looters who are the ones perpetrating the violence, but need begins to jade the outlook of the normally good person, so violence expands. Then, even the looters become victims as larger and more powerful gangs vie for dominance and the dwindling supply of goods. Government services are in disarray, but somehow the criminal gangs are increasingly organized.

The police are overwhelmed and officers begin to stay home to protect their own families. The entire military is mobilized but soldiers are inadequately trained for this type of scenario. However, once attacked, their war-training kicks in and they begin to shoot their fellow citizens. The people retaliate.

The military has become the face of government and the people are fed up. Military bases are where food supplies are stored, so our troops are increasingly seen as the enemy since they are guarding food but not distributing it. Military bases and convoys are attacked by citizens, and the federal authorities respond with heavy weaponry. The de facto state of martial law is replaced with a formal declaration and the implementation of the federal Continuity of Government Plan (COGP).

Ordinary people are afraid and caught in the crossfire. As in the aftermath of Hurricane Katrina, death is so widespread that bodies are no longer even moved. Public health problems increase exponentially.

Anarchy becomes rampant. In the ensuing chaos, law-abiding citizens are abused and their rights trampled in a panic-filled effort to restore order.

Guns are confiscated from law-abiding citizens, while criminal gangs become increasingly well armed; including advanced military weaponry stolen from the convoys they ambushed. Citizens are no longer able to defend themselves from criminals since their legally-owned guns were confiscated by the government. (Also like during the aftermath of Hurricane Katrina, but on a national scale).

Businesses have closed. No one is going to work. Enclaves of people band together for mutual aid, but are unable to protect themselves from prowling gangs of criminals. The police and military are busy with other priorities.

Money becomes useless. Bartering with criminal gangs becomes the only way to get food, water and essential supplies. Government services have collapsed. Remaining supplies are going exclusively to the institutionalized people living in FEMA Centers.

FEMA Centers have become fiefdoms; some merely exploitive, others appalling. The country becomes a feudal state. The only noticeable recovery is in isolated rural areas where the people are self sufficient and have been left alone by the government.

Does this Sound Unreasonably Bleak?

Actually, these are the scenarios and effects which are forecast in the Federal Emergency Management Agency's (FEMA's) national disaster response plan. This "Continuity of Operations Plan" (COOP) strategy is not talked about publically.[86] But privately, DHS and FEMA insiders explain that these are outcomes they expect to face. This is what keeps them up at night, as they design and implement strategies designed to counter these problems.

Have you ever wondered "Why?" FEMA seems to respond so poorly, even to a major natural disaster? And, why heads don't roll after huge blunders in the handling a major natural disaster?

Apparently it is because the top people at DHS and FEMA are assigned to work on implementing COOP. It is estimated that top-level managers at FEMA spend 40% of their time inside "Classified" projects that are part of 'Continuity of Government' efforts, and the implementation of the 'Continuity of Operations Plan.' They perceive these tasks to be so urgent, that to spend time on a routine disaster is antithetical to the higher priority of getting ready for the larger, looming national catastrophe they think is coming.

Is such an event really on our doorstep? I don't know, but they certainly think it is.

---

[86] The Department of Homeland Security has even refused to show the plan to the Homeland Security Committee of the House of Representatives, which is supposed to provide congressional oversight of their work.

Reaching a Tipping Point

Like the block-stacking game *Jenga*, our society has grown in prominence but has become increasingly unstable. While most people look at what appears to be a growing tower of affluence, the foundation of our society has been progressively weakened. Just as in the game of *Jenga*, we will eventually reach a tipping point and the tower will, to one degree or another, collapse under its own weight. Restoration remains possible, but it will take revival within the citizenry not just a new batch of politicians.

Whether the coming changes occur as the result of an abrupt bump or a cascade of problems which become a confluence disaster, at some point the structure of America will not just wobble, it will topple. We can't be afraid to embrace the facts: This disaster may be soon or in a decade or two; certainly not longer. This may come in the form of a slow slide leading to a partial breakdown which is simply difficult and a time of austerity, or the sheer weight of our many problems may tilt the U.S. and Europe toward major collapse.

Either way, since the economies of the U.S. and Europe drive much of the world's economy, when either falters it affects the entire planet. At that point societies and economies will start to spiral downward.

Safe Haven

Take another look at the illustration that is at the beginning of this chapter. Add to it the other, additional concerns you are aware of, and then start paying particular attention to news stories and other developments which affect these tipping-point subjects.

Watch closely for the circumstances and timing of developments; those things which increase the stress load on society. Visible cracks in a society will often appear before things start to crumple, so we need to closely watch these areas of weakness that emerge.

There are usually warning signs that pop-up to alert us to infectious change. As the story at the beginning of this book so powerfully reminds us, being fully prepared and ready to respond to these go-signals will likely dictate whether we experience success vs. unnecessary hardship or deadly disaster. Our rapid response to these signals of change can make all the difference in the world.

If things start to slide and a confluence disaster is brewing, this isn't the time to just lock our doors and get out our guns. It's time for us to flee to our 'safe haven' retreat locations. We need to wait there until things settle down. Don't return until it is safe.

Developing Our Own All-Threats Contingency Plan

An effective disaster preparedness plan includes real-world contingency planning. It focuses on the most likely cause-and-effect scenarios, prioritizes preparedness tasks, identifies the resources needed, and designs flexibility and adaptability into the response. Too many people plan for one type of disaster, while failing to adequately consider the universal needs which are part of most disasters. It's these universal needs that need to be tackled first.

Next is the need for a comprehensive approach to your planning. Having lots of food but no method to purify water is deadly, as is having guns without tactical training, or a big garden without the ability to can the fruits and vegetables you harvest. Your Personal Preparedness Plan must be well rounded.

Whether you encounter a long-term loss of electrical power, violent anarchy, a pandemic, drought, or economic collapse, there are common features which are central to all disaster scenarios. These common needs are the place to start or re-start your planning efforts.

Since we now have many weaknesses which might precipitate a national disaster, there are many potential disaster scenarios. Even the unlikely must be considered, but planning starts with likely disasters and preparations which are universal, followed by the specific forms of disaster that require specialized preparations. (For example: a nuclear incident, pandemic, EMP / Geomagnetic Solar Storm, etc.)

Keep in mind that it is often not the disaster itself that brings serious harm. It is the aftermath. It is often the social fallout which turns a serious disaster into a major disaster. It is the public's response to the incident which generally brings the direst consequences.

Do what you can to protect yourself from the direct effects of each source of disaster you deem to be a viable threat. However, as a first step, apply most of your effort to the tasks which relate to self reliance, safety, and independence (no need for outside assistance).

Truth is Often Uncomfortable

Once you discern the truth about the various threats we are facing, there is a tendency to become depressed and fatalistic. It's the devil that prefers death to life, don't follow his example. Don't succumb to these deadly sins. Armed with the truth, you can still maintain rational hope while you develop a comprehensive response.

Don't allow yourself to suffer analysis paralysis, either. You don't need a lot of story-behind-the-story data to build a basic contingency plan. By all means continue with your own investigations, but this three book series contains enough of what you need to get started.

To speed your implementation, Book-2 and -3 contain foundational elements. These practical steps can be used to establish your own plan, which you can then aggressively implement.

As a valued friend once reminded me, *"it's better to do it poorly than not at all."* This may sound odd but it is valid. Even if a perfect plan is beyond your capacity due to cost, time or some other impediment, it is better to do something proactive than nothing at all.

"But He [Jesus] replied to them,
*'When it is evening, you say, it will be fair
weather, for the sky is red.' And in the morning,
'There will be a storm today, for the sky is red
and threatening.' Do you know how to discern
the appearance of the sky, but cannot discern the
signs of the times?"*

Holy Bible
Matthew 16:2-4

Chapter 8

Determining Your Own Response

In addition to connecting the dots of the federal government's preparations, let's look at some of the specific problems we are facing. As these are considered together, we can figure out how we should respond with our own preparations.

At the core, each of us need to develop a plan for a future which includes major changes; a time in which we will also have unprecedented opportunities. Change seems inevitable, but we don't need to let it sweep over us as a surprise.

Moreover, it is still reasonable to hope for a better future for us and our children, but only if we get busy; only if we get ready for the major changes which are coming. We don't need to panic. We need to prepare.

If we empower our hopes with wise counsel, discerning action, plan our steps, keep our eyes on the signs, and use our mind to creatively adapt our plans as necessary, then we will have the opportunity to succeed. At the same time, we need to maintain an attitude which is hopeful and charitable. Then we can thrive in the future.

With God's help and our precautions, we can still have a bright future even if the days themselves become dark. The future may be very different from today, but if we do what we can to prepare, we can be over-comers.

"**The world is exploding all over.** Whether they're cyber threats, which are relatively new, but are just as real and deadly and lethal as anything we've ever dealt with; obviously, what's going on in North Korea, China's behavior in the South China Sea, East China Sea; Russia's actions in Ukraine; North Africa, the Middle East today, every part of that world is troubled under great stress." [88]

- Chuck Hagel

U.S. Secretary of Defense

Threat and Risk Assessment

Experts in each category of risk tell us that a major life-changing problem is on the horizon. The big question seems to be which bubble will burst first, how bad will it get, and how long it will take before things start to get better again. The serious experts agree that something big will happen soon, perhaps next month, next year, or certainly within the next decade.

Yet, they don't all agree on which problem will boil over first. So our response needs to concentrate first on general preparations which are universal to all of these problems. Likewise, these need to be prioritized. We need to accomplish the most important preparations first.

---

[88] Chuck Hagel, United States Secretary of Defense, in an address to a group of Marines in San Diego, California, August 12, 2014. Source: The Weekly Standard, "Defense Secretary: 'The World is Exploding All Over" by Jeryl Bier, 8/13/2014; http://www.weeklystandard.com/blogs/defense-secretary-world-exploding-all-over_802893.html

Preparation, protection and recovery are similar for most major disasters.

Most of our preparedness efforts need to concentrate on the conditions which develop in the aftermath of a disastrous event, not simply protection from the direct effects of the initiating incident. For example, the primary problem of the Katrina hurricane disaster of 2005 was not the 174 MPH (280 km/h) winds, but the shortage of pure water, food, and personal safety problems which grew to epic proportions in the weeks and months after the storm.

Reiterating Important Exceptions

The exception to the universal-preparation rule is four types of world-changing disastrous events. Each of these will require threat-specific protective measures as a first line of defense. These threats include:

1) EMP attack or solar storm (electrical and technology failures);

2) Nuclear attack (contamination as a result of a terrorist incident or war);

3) Biologic attack or accident (airborne pathogens carried by the wind); and,

4) Pandemic (widespread infectious disease, which requires isolation from potentially infected people).

A disaster initiated by one of the above is increasingly possible. This is especially true as we look forward into the next decade or two. By necessity, protective measures for these are far more elaborate and therefore costly. Moreover, preparations for these risks need to be threat specific. For example, protection against a nuclear threat may involve moving your home to a safer location.

If your primary concern is one (or more) of these threats, you will need to incorporate threat-specific preparations into your plan. If you think these are a lower priority, tackle them after the universal preparations have been completed.[89]

Absent specific knowledge of a particular threat, for most people our first task is to prepare for those needs and eventualities which are common to all major disasters. Yet as we plan, it is still worthwhile to identify the threats which our research suggests are the most likely. For example, if for some reason we think the threat of airborne pathogens is a primary concern, then we will want to select our 'safe haven' retreat location according to prevailing winds emanating from a likely target. Conversely, if we think violence and marauding gangs of looters will likely become a major problem, we will locate our 'safe haven' away from urban areas and major roadways.

While most Americans agree that Muslim extremists continue to pose a growing threat, terrorist attacks such as the ones we have suffered in the past, though horrible, are limited in scope.

If you live in a major urban area such as Manhattan or San Francisco, or near a military base or an iconic location such as Washington, DC, then you need to give greater attention to the direct threats of terrorism. However, for most people, traditional terrorist attacks such as homicide bombings, may not be their highest-risk threat. In almost all emergency situations it is the secondary effects, such as public panic and a lack of self reliance, which turns a tragic event into a cataclysmic event.

---

[89] Personally, my analysis suggests that the EMP/solar threat are sufficiently credible to be worth immediate consideration. Since the ramifications are so extreme and the preparations for ordinary civilians so limited, I have included these measures with my basic preparations. The nuclear threat may be several years away, but this is also a viable threat, but distance from a likely target is the best defense. The level of risk posed by the other two may be high, but these preparations are so threat-specific and expensive that they are impractical. As with the nuclear threat, the best defense may be the selection of a safe-haven retreat location based on its proximity to a likely area of contamination, which is away from the path of prevailing winds. For threats 2-4, most other long-term protections are beyond the financial ability of most people.

The Cause of Disaster is Unpredictable

General Martin Dempsey, the most senior military officer in the United States, wrote this in the opening paragraph of the most recent National Military Strategy plan:

> "Today's global security environment is the most unpredictable I have seen in 40-years of service... global disorder has significantly increased while some of our comparative military advantage has begun to erode. We now face multiple, simultaneous security challenges from traditional state actors [nations like China and Russia], and transregional networks of sub-state groups – all taking advantage of rapid technological change. Future conflicts will come more rapidly, last longer, and take place on a much more technically challenging battlefield. They will have increasing implications to the U.S. homeland." [90]

> -- U.S Military, Joint Chiefs of Staff

The potential for a major disaster is increasing every day. In addition to a growing threat of war here in our homeland, we are facing other threats which are also increasing and it seems inevitable that these will eventually gain sufficient momentum to initiate a major disaster.

We observe that the number of antibiotic-resistant viruses is growing, as is the number of diseases which have pandemic potential. Water shortages and drought are affecting areas where water has not historically been a major problem. The apparently irreversible negative effects genetic manipulation seem to be multiplying the disclosure of new health hazards apparently caused

---

[90] Official U.S. Government document, "The National Military Strategy of the United States of America, 2015, pg. 1; Pentagon, U.S. Military, Joint Chiefs of Staff.

http://www.jcs.mil/Portals/36/Documents/Publications/National_Military_Strategy_2015.pdf by modified organisms in our foods is alarming. Our food supply is becoming increasingly vulnerable and on and on goes the list. Moreover, there are many other manmade problems which have us hovering on the brink of disaster. Any of these could suddenly tip the scales, dropping us into a major disaster in a matter of days.

In regard to war, Americans generally feel that they have no enemies. The American people do not want to attack or do harm to other nations. Yet, just because the people of the USA feel benevolent toward others, does not mean this attitude is reciprocal.

Whether the American people want to admit it or not, the U.S. has a number of serious enemies who vehemently hate America and want to see it destroyed. One example is the growing threat of the Madrassas school movement in the Muslim world. Each year these schools crank out hundreds of thousands of graduates who want to kill infidels and look forward to dying in the service of Allah. To them, the U.S. is the Great Satan and they are taught that their god will reward them for the most heinous acts against Americans.

The potential for major terrorist strikes against the U.S. and European nations, which are facilitated by Islamic State or rogue Islamic governments, make a multi-city strike using weapons of mass destruction increasingly likely.

We also face a potential attack initiated by an ideological enemy such as China. We think of them as a trading partner, but in speeches made by Chinese leaders to their own people, they refer to us as their enemy. The Chinese government has already conducted a number of 'practice' cyber attacks against our government, our power grid, and U.S. corporations. It has also stolen personal data of millions of U.S. government employees as well as millions of ordinary Americans. The Chinese malevolence is no longer even hidden. A Chinese cyber attack could send us back to the 1800s tomorrow or they could wait a decade until their next generation of nuclear weapons and Navy is operational.

Similarly, Russia is again growing its nuclear arsenal and developing new intercontinental ballistic missiles, a new generation of mobile missile launchers, and hardened underground manufacturing cities. Again, none of this is secret, but details are rarely reported. The threats to America made by Russia's leaders are similarly ignored by the mainstream media.

The risk assessment contained in the Pentagon report referenced earlier in this chapter, indicates that four countries pose a clear and present danger to the U.S. homeland. These are: Russia, Iran, North Korea, and China.

In addition, as Muslim extremists gain new technologies of mass destruction, the risk of a catastrophic national disaster to the United States and Europe intensifies. These people may not seem sophisticated, but just as with the situation of children playing with matches, eventually they will start a fire.

As we consider the risks of a disaster brought about by irrational people and rogue governments, we need to also recognize that there are other smoldering piles of kindling that are perhaps even more likely to cause a major disaster in the very near future. Such a disaster may be far less severe than nuclear war or an EMP strike, but widespread suffering is nevertheless likely as a result of other manmade disasters which are beginning to combust.

As discussed in the prior chapter, a confluence disaster has become not just possible, but likely. A number of serious problems have the potential to boil over and flow together like a row of colliding dominoes.

There are at least a dozen economic, political and international issues which make our county unstable, as well as security threats to our way of life such as the rise of militant Islam. Plus, experts warn us about natural disasters which are long overdue, Pandora's Box technology threats, environmental problems, medical and health concerns, food supply corruption, and energy risks which are increasingly volatile.

Add to these the many social factors which have weakened the fabric of society; apathy, a distain for morality and virtue, loss of self-reliance, a dumbed-down electorate that is uneducated but feels good about it, impediments such as self-serving leaders, a national spirit of entitlement, political advancement through race baiting, a Darwinian survival-of-the-fittest mentality which fosters a lack of accountability, and government and corporate corruption, and we have ample ingredients for a recipe of disaster. We have proudly made the 7-deadly sins into a to-do list.

As if these problems aren't enough, our culture has been compromised by a distain for the sanctity of human life and the rights of others, the loss of respect for the U.S. Constitution by government officials, lack of trust in the president, congress and the judiciary, and an overarching spirit of lawlessness, above-the-law attitudes and actions by top leaders, and it becomes readily apparent that the next major crisis will quickly get out of control.

Doubtless you can think of other factors which have the potential to either initiate a crisis or exacerbate one. When the time comes, all of these weaknesses will add more fuel to what can easily become a national bonfire.

In America's 10-year economic disaster which started in 1929, known as the Great Depression, the people knew how to be poor. Most city dwellers were only one generation removed from the farm, so they still knew how to grow their own food. Even those living in the city often had vegetable gardens and canned their own food. They took pride in being self-reliant.

Today, the American people don't even know how to prepare food from scratch, so a similar economic meltdown would produce far more disastrous results. If our present condition of moral bankruptcy is combined with financial bankruptcy, we can expect to encounter caustic anger and a violent crime wave beyond anything we can currently imagine.

Prevailing Factors

In regard to disaster preparation, what are the frequently occurring problems which most disaster scenarios have in common? Once we identify these prevailing factors, we can develop a plan that prepares us to face the direct and indirect effects of most emergency situations.

Having personally experienced the aftermath of a number of disasters, I have compiled the below list to help you face the unpleasant reality of what happens after a major disaster. As you reflect on each item below, consider what you can do now to either eliminate the problem or at least mitigate the effects of it. Then add to this list your own concerns and problem-solve those as well.

If you have a viable solution for each of these common problems, your plan will have a solid foundation. Over time, you may be able to prepare better solutions, but don't neglect any of these for even a basic 'starter' disaster preparedness plan.

Solutions to standard, routinely occurring problems such as these, need to be built into every plan:

a) Violence may become widespread, especially in major urban areas. Those cities and regions which have a large number of people receiving government assistance will likely be the most volatile. Even suburban and rural areas near these hotbeds will not be safe.

b) Depending on the government to deliver pure water, whether it be from the faucet or bottled water after a disaster contaminates local sources, is problematic. Since humans can only live for a few days without water, the ability to purify your own source of water is a top priority.

c) Even good people, including good 'church' people, will often become violent when they feel threatened. You may be the target of a violent attack even though you didn't do anything wrong. The assault may be sourced in frustration, or their own guilt for not preparing, but you may still be the target of their violence or irrational acts of retaliation. The failure to accept personal responsibility is common in our society, so it is also common to transfer blame to someone else. Grocery stores and gas stations will become places of violence, because the individual believes they have a "right" to have their needs met. Therefore, it is best to avoid interaction with people who are not part of your inner circle and places where violent people tend to congregate.

d) During an emergency situation, criminals tend to quickly ratchet-up their criminal behavior to the next level. Ordinary people, who have never committed a crime more serious than shoplifting or petty theft, will quickly succumb to looting and burglary. If a food shortage develops, by day-3 of the disaster, ordinary people will resort to theft, robbery, and burglary to survive.

e) Unattended possessions, even on private property, will be considered to have been abandoned by the owner. In the mind of the Robin Hood thief, this makes it acceptable to 'appropriate' (steal) the item. This will include gas in the tank of your vehicles, as well as food or supplies stored inside your house or garage.

Expect items which are locked or bolted down to be pilfered or stolen. Locks and other precautions which work well in 'normal' times may be wholly inadequate during an emergency situation. Expect people to indiscriminately vandalize and steal things they can't possibly use.

f) Unprepared people will exploit their relationships with friends and acquaintances to obtain food and other necessities for their families. Those who are refused assistance will have a tendency to use force and become violent. Those who have food, and have remained in an urban area, will sooner or later be targeted. Long term, even an armed individual will not be able to protect their supplies from inundation.

g) Grocery stores, gas stations, food banks, social service organizations, restaurants, hospitals, churches, and pastors will be targeted as soon as the flow of assistance stops. Grocery stores will be emptied of most food, water, batteries, and other useful goods, within hours. What remains will be looted within 3-5 days. It is therefore essential to have your own *secret* and hidden stockpile of food, fuel and other essential supplies.

h) Sickness will become widespread as a result of poor sanitation, drinking tainted water and ingesting spoiled food. If the disaster lasts more than 2 months, the number of deaths will skyrocket.

i) Infirm elderly and those who are dependent on medication will often become sick within a few days after a disaster strikes. Many of these will die within two weeks of the onset of the disaster. Those who suffer from depression in normal times will often become suicidal when exposed to the uncertainties and hardships of an emergency situation. Those who previously showed no signs of emotional instability or depression may also become suicidal if they feel helpless and hopeless.

j) The frequency of sexual assaults will increase within a week of the onset. Assaults and robbery will become routine and good people will stop intervening.

k) Even pet owners who ordinarily dote on their animals will begin to release them to fend for themselves. Abandoned dogs will forage together as roving packs. Attacks against people will become common, particularly children as they are more vulnerable.

l)   Hospitals will be overwhelmed by people seeking non-medical assistance, as well as by those with minor and major injuries. If the power grid was affected by the disaster, hospitals will be forced to prematurely release most of their patients. Since hospitals typically only have 3-5 days of fuel for their emergency generators, the patient capacity of most hospitals will drop by 90-95% once their HVAC and lights stop working. Where possible, surgery and other emergency medical services will be moved outdoors. Since electric medical equipment such as scans and test equipment will no longer function, diagnosis and care will be rudimentary. Since resupply may be spotty, many hospitals will not be able to continue to deliver advanced medical care. Armed robberies of drugs and supplies will become frequent even after supplies have been depleted. If these situations are not corrected, hospitals will lose medical and support personnel and be functionally relegated to services similar to a doctor's office. Hospitals may remain open, but they will no longer be able to deliver traditional hospital services.

m)   Police and sheriff's deputies will not be able to cope with the demand for services. 9-1-1 systems will be overwhelmed and the public will begin to panic and act irrationally. Within 3 days, law enforcement officers will leave their jobs, going home to protect their own families.

n)   Firefighters will not be able to handle the volume of fires and neighborhoods and commercial districts will burn unchecked. When firefighters are dispatched to fight fires and provide emergency medical care, their stations will be ransacked and vandalized. After experiencing irrational obstruction and armed robberies by those who are looking for drugs and medical supplies, firefighters will give up and go home. However, in the weeks which follow, some of these fire stations will reopen as community centers and medical clinics.

o)   Military bases will initially be locked down and trespassers shot. After several days, military patrols and National Guard troops will seek to restore order. Once it is recognized that these troops are unable to restore order, the President will declare a national emergency and will authorize federal troops to use deadly force to restore order. The president will put into action federal disaster plans authorized by his own presidential Executive Orders, such as EO 13603, the National Defense Resources

Preparedness Act. The inner cities will become so dangerous that they are left to burn, and will become no-man's-land areas that are ruled by gangs. Former residents of these areas will begin to flow into suburban and then rural areas. As suburban areas are inundated by these refugees, the residents of suburbia will flee and try to move into rural areas in advance of the onslaught. As presidential Executive Orders become fully implemented, all essential goods and services will be nationalized, private stockpiles of goods seized, and distributed according to government edict. This will include fuel, and all non-governmental transportation will cease as civilian supplies of gasoline become exhausted. Mobile phones and the Internet will be shut down to impede organized crime and resistance.

p) The U.S. military will take over administration of media outlets and communities. Identification will be required. Travel permits will be needed to cross county lines.

q) Displaced people will be housed in temporary locations such as large retail stores, schools, and sports stadiums. After processing, these refugees will be transported to federal I/R Centers (Internment/Resettlement Centers run by the U.S. Army) on military bases and other federal properties. Many of these people will be transported to I/R Centers in other states.

r) Private homes will be searched using police and military personnel. Food and other supplies will be confiscated, as these items will be needed to feed displaced people. Whereas some supplies will periodically be available from FEMA warehouses, private supplies will be needed due to the sheer volume of displaced people. Water rationing will be implemented. Despite these seizures, if the disaster is widespread or protracted, displaced people will often not have adequate access to food, pure water, and sanitation.

s) If the government thinks the emergency situation will be protracted, those who are capable of delivering essential services, such as medical doctors, law enforcement officers, firefighters, those who operate power plants, etc., will be drafted into federal service. Most of these individuals will be relocated to another part of the country based on need, and also as part of a strategy of control and priority setting, which cannot be maintained if these specialists are allowed to return to their families and communities.

t) Those who find themselves living in Intern-ment/Resettlement Centers (I/R), will be expected to work for the common good of their new community. Allotments of food and other supplies will be influenced by the residents' participa-tion in the Center's service, agricultural, or manufacturing programs.[91]

u) Civilians who 'disappear' into low population rural areas are often ignored unless they do something to draw attention to themselves. However, to be left alone after a relocation directive has been issued, the 'safe haven' will need to be inconspicuous and the residents wholly self-reliant, so the safe haven must be equipped for water and food independence.

For longevity, these safe havens will need to be deemed by the authorities to be inconsequential and irrelevant for appropriation, so they will need to look like the movie set for the film "Deliverance." If the disaster is widespread and serious, maintaining independence will require unobtrusive living for several years, but these bastions will nevertheless provide the greatest opportunity for the rebuilding of a healthy society.[92]

---

[91] The civilian labor program is described in U.S. Army Regulation 210-35, 14-January-2005.

[92] Book-3 in this "Prepared: Ready to Roll" series focuses on selecting a location and preparing a 'safe haven' retreat community.

Planning to 'Disappear' into a Rural Safe-Haven Retreat Location

- Applying Our Skills and Experiences -

Being aware of government planning and the signs-of-the-times is the crucial starting point. Yet, this isn't enough. A wise response also requires the application of our own skills, experiences, and relationships to the task at hand. Without this practical aspect we will flounder in our preparation efforts.

Experience has taught us that we can't depend on government to solve our problems. So, personal plans which include an expectation of helpful government assistance need to be discarded. If we do get help, great, but we can't plan on getting it.

We need to prepare to face the future alone; just you, your family and friends. You don't need to literally be alone, but you will be on your own.

It is imperative for us to become self-reliant and self-sufficient.

Even after the disastrous governmental response to hurricane Katrina in 2005, the authorities still weren't prepared for hurricane Sandy in 2012. In both cases we had warning. Preparations had been made. Nevertheless, the U.S. government, local authorities, and our fellow citizens were not ready to handle the aftermath.

Imagine what will happen when the crisis is not just regional. Consider what will happen if the emergency situation is widespread or national in scope.

Past events are a powerful reminder that we can't depend on government, or others, to solve our personal problems. We have a personal responsibility to prepare for the future, and to be ready to help ourselves and others.

Unlike past disasters which have always been localized, the U.S. Government is currently preparing for a nationwide disaster. The scope of these preparations indicates either specific knowledge, or the general expectation of something which is far beyond anything we have previously encountered, even during war time.

During the wars of World War I and World War II, and during the years of the Cold War nuclear threat, as well as times of emergency like the Cuban missile crisis when the United States came close to launching its own nuclear missiles, the U.S. Government has never engaged in anything which comes close to the current level of preparation. Not even close. The U.S. Government's current level of preparation is unprecedented to the extreme.

The federal government and military vehemently denies this, but the preparations and legal maneuvering through presidential Executive Orders, government agency preparations, the militarization of the police, and activities such as the distribution of thousands of MRAP tanks, speaks more loudly than vacuous denials.

Regardless of what is motivating the U.S. Government, our future welfare is our own responsibility. It's up to us. We must accept our personal responsibility and become wholly self-reliant and self-sufficient for what is coming. This doesn't mean we need to be Lone Rangers when it comes to our preparations. In fact, that would be foolish.

My point is that we cannot depend on the government to solve any aspect of the problems we may face. We need to develop our own cadres of support and mutual assistance. Just as small settlements tamed the Wild West, the wild days ahead will be best faced by small groups of self-reliant, self-sufficient people.

If outside help is available to us, great. But we need to be ready to solve problems on our own—without government assistance. On our own, with family and friends, we need to be ready for the uncertain days which are ahead.

Since we have the ability to recognize the signs of the times, we have the opportunity to get ready for specific types of problems. This is important.

For us as civilians, all of these dangers share the same foundation of preparedness: economic security (our finances and ability to engage in trade for goods and services); self-reliance in regard to essential water, food and food production, provisions and gear, and safe-haven locations and facilities; and, being ready for defense. These are the basics. This is where we must start.

As individuals, we need to embrace each aspect of being ready for uncertain times. Furthermore, we must work toward building a community of family and friends at a safe haven retreat location.[93] Individually and together, we must prepare financially, prepare with provisions, and prepare to defend ourselves and each other.[94]

Are you equipped and ready? Are you self-reliant and self-sufficient? Do you have a plan? Are you ready for an extended period without being able to shop for what you need, without the protection of the police and fire department, and without any government services or assistance?

What are you going to do? Will you delay, effectively putting your head in the sand? Or, will you bemoan our state of affairs and complain to your friends, and wring your hands and fret about it? Will you forward doomsday emails and get more active politically? How are you going to respond?

I'm not suggesting that you shouldn't do these things, but I want to be clear that activities such as this are not part of disaster preparedness. Don't confuse concern and talk with action. And, don't confuse busyness with effective action. The question is, "Will you actually do what it takes to get ready?"

If you identify as a Christian, are you ready to be the hands and feet of Jesus in a future which will be very different from today? If you aren't a Christian but you care about others, are you

---

[93] If you have a retreat location suitable for your 'safe haven' you will probably want to invite family members to be part of your community. This is a natural desire, but if your family isn't enthusiastically on board, this can present some serious problems for sustainability. You can stockpile food and other supplies for them, of course, but there is more to developing a 'safe haven' than just stockpiling goods. Book 3 in this series is can help you overcome this problem and other community-building challenges.

[94] Jesus, in His final instructions to His disciples before His arrest and murder, clearly outlined the three-fold responsibility of each individual to prepare for uncertain times. This injunction can be found in the Bible (Luke 22:36). This is the basis for the 36 READY Preparedness Code which is included in the appendix of this book.

prepared to help others in addition to your own family and friends?

We are facing hard times, but these changes will also usher in a new era filled with many opportunities. For those who are ready, this will be a time to embrace a life filled with meaning and purpose; a life in which there will be a clear distinction between good and evil. It will be a time when the agents of peace and justice will live in stark contrast to those who are self-centered and vile. This will be a time during which you will have the opportunity to make a big difference.

If we are well-rounded with our preparations and ready for what is coming, we will be able to be like a city on a hill that stands as a beacon of hope. If we prepare and ready ourselves, and live like sheepdogs rather than sheep, we will be an asset to our family and community. If we remain hopeful and courageously face these problems, then we will not just survive, we will be able to thrive in service.

Speaking from experience, if you are prepared and ready, you will literally be able to save lives and help people at their time of greatest need. You will be able to do more than talk and vote; you will be able to be a world-changer as you take a stand for liberty and justice. You will be able to engage in many activities which will make a huge difference in the lives of your family members, friends, neighbors, and country. For those who are followers of Jesus Christ, this can lead to a time after which you will be able to hear the words, "well done, my good and faithful servant." [95]

— — — — — — —

---

[95] Mathew 25:14-30

Appendix 1

Author's Postscript

If you have taken off the blinders created by a normalcy bias and are viewing the signs of the times such as the U.S. Government's preparations, you may be experiencing fear. If you aren't at least apprehensive, you haven't been paying attention.

Even if you are a Navy SEAL who has been hardened by adversity and combat, or a U.S. Government employee who anticipates protection through a *Continuity of Government* program, you are probably still sobered by the prospect of widespread suffering.

If you are a 'connected' government leader you recognize that the coming crisis is big. Like a railroad worker watching a runaway passenger train, you understand that it's too big of a problem to painlessly fix. Our only viable option is to encourage personal responsibility and facilitate personal preparedness.

All of us can appreciate the blessing of free will, but we observe that many people continue to foolishly choose to be distracted by the affairs of today. They hit the "snooze" button on the ticking clock and refuse to wake-up and prepare for the future. These are the voluntary victims who will be doubly victimized. First by the disaster itself, and then by the crisis which will inevitably follow. Unfortunately, there is little we can do for these people. It is those who are awake or awakening, that deserve our help.

Even after reading "Prepared: Ready to Roll," many will continue to make poor choices. Many will fail to make preparing a top priority. Like the main character in the fiction story that kicked off this book, they will succumb to procrastination and the failure to make timely and comprehensive preparations. Don't be that person.

Beyond this, you probably have family and friends who are in denial and obstinately refuse to leave their comfort zone. If necessary, patiently suffer their ridicule. If they call you a "prepper" or some other name they hope you will find insulting, I encourage you to remain unruffled, and to periodically send them well-reasoned news articles from sources they will respect.

Don't be a one-issue soapboxer, but let your resolve and consistency show. Don't be discouraged or sidetracked by their negativity. Just do what you can to kindly communicate your concern for them, and be privately busy with your own preparations.

We can only encourage, we can't make people embrace reality, nor can we force them to accept personal responsibility. If we have the resources, we can stockpile provisions for them and include them in our disaster plan, but this is still problematic. During emergency situations, clueless people are often dangerous to others.

Even awake people often confuse diligent news watching, whining emails and research on the coming trials, as effective action. We need to help these friends understand that the time for simple solutions has passed. If you care about them, guide them toward effective action; *comprehensive preparedness.*

Those who are awake but still not preparing are usually confused or overwhelmed. They don't know where to start. Like a fibrillating human heart that is throbbing but not pumping blood, their energy is expended but it is wicked away through ineffectual activities. You may be able to defibrillate them by giving them a copy of this book, and by offering to help them develop a step-by-step action plan.

Personally, according to the information that has been revealed to me, it is highly likely that we will experience a very serious emergency situation in the near future. Those who emerge relatively unscathed will feel shell-shocked but ecstatic. However, according to my information, this will not be the end of our problems. It will only be the first wave, a precursor to a far more serious disaster.

Like a pre-quake preceding a Full-Margin Rupture earthquake, the subsequent event will be far more deadly than the initial catastrophe. So don't relax and become complacent when the turmoil of the first event dissipates. Continue to remain vigilant. Redouble your efforts, and prepare for the next wave of turmoil.

Interestingly, those who do what they can to prepare, also experience less fear. I encourage you to do what you can, and then leave the rest in God's hands.

Fear can be debilitating for anyone, but those without a vibrant relationship with their Creator are more prone to despair. According to my sources, in the coming crisis FEMA anticipates more deaths from suicide than from the direct effects of the disaster.

Those with no Faith and those with a weak or superficial Faith, will have greater difficulty coping. Correcting this deficiency is yet another form of disaster preparation that should be addressed in advance.

Personally, I unapologetically urge you to seek reconciliation with your Creator as part of your disaster preparations. Even if you don't do anything else to prepare for what's coming, at least prepare your soul.

I've lived my life as a warrior not a preacher, so I can't finesse this counsel with flowery prose. All I can do is tell you that my personal relationship with Jesus is what has brought me through many harrowing circumstances. Knowing that to live means a loving and meaningful relationship with Him as Lord of my life, and that physical death is simply a transition to eternity with Him in heaven, is freeing.

Knowing that my future is secure, situations which appear to be hopeless can become hope-filled as I'm able to keep the big picture in mind. I'm not in a hurry to die, but for me, this big-picture knowledge has repeatedly replaced debilitating fear with invigorating peace. I do my part, and then I leave the rest in God's capable hands.

A dozen times I have faced imminent death; situations in which I knew, without a doubt, that I would not survive. Reconciled to death, I experienced a new level of freedom and the resolve to go out with a bang not a whimper. Yet, in spite of my reasoned analysis of those situations, here I am, still alive. Apparently it wasn't my time to die.

Please keep this in mind: When a circumstance appears to be bleak, and we are tempted to lose all hope and give up, we don't know the future. Even when we think we have a clear view into the future, good or bad, our personal future is unknown.

Life is a gift from God. Even when we have confidence that heaven is our future, we should never surrender to death without a fight. To do any less is an affront to God who gave each of us this priceless gift of life.

As we fight, we need to remember that while God doesn't promise to protect us from harm, He does promise to see us through to the other side—if we put our trust in Him. If we are willing to accept it, God has a plan for us.

"For I know the plans I have for you,' **says the Lord.** *"They are plans for good and not for disaster, to give you a [eternal] future and a hope. In those days when you pray, I will listen. If you will look for me wholeheartedly, you will find me."*

Holy Bible

Jeremiah 29:11-13

If your inner spirit resonates with what you have read, don't delay. Get ready for disaster, but even more important, get ready for eternity.[96] Only then will you be fully prepared for what is coming.

---

[96] If you are interested in exploring how to enter into a personal relationship with your Creator who loves you deeply, follow this link: http://www.cru.org/how-to-know-god/would-you-like-to-know-god-person-ally.html Or, find a Holy Bible that has been translated into your language (http://dbs.org/libraries/index.php or inscript.org) and start by reading the *Book of John*, which is in the New Testament portion of the Bible.

* For free online Bible study materials, visit: www.blueletterbible.org

* For an instructional video overview to help you understand the Bible, go to KHouse.org or search YouTube.com for "Dr Chuck Missler, Learn the Bible in 24 Hours".

*"**Be dressed in readiness**, and keep your lamps lit."*

Holy Bible
Luke 12:35a

*"**Be strong and courageous,** and act; do not fear nor be dismayed, for the Lord God, my God, is with you. He will not fail you nor forsake you until all the work for the service of the house of the Lord is finished."*

Holy Bible
1 Chronicles 28:20-21

*"**[When] My people** who are called by My name humble themselves and pray, and seek My face and turn from their wicked ways, then I will hear from heaven, will forgive their sin, and will heal their land."*

Holy Bible
2 Chronicles 7:14

---

* If you identify as a Christian and want to imbed the key principles of your Faith to help you stand tall against adversity, read the book or view the video series, "Believe" (general editor Pastor Randy Frazee). Use this as a beginning point to center yourself in the Bible, and to help you maintain your focus on the basis of truth. (For more on the subject of 'truth,' read: Psalms 119:160; Proverbs 12:19; John 8:32; 14:6; 17:15-21; Romans 1:18-25.)

* For inclusion in your GO-Bag, select a pocket-size New Testament that also includes the Old Testament books of *Psalms* and *Proverbs*.

Appendix 2

About the Author

SIG SWANSTROM is a former police officer and police SWAT team operator who worked in the Los Angeles area. During his years of service he had many deadly-force encounters with armed criminals. He also has first-hand experience with different types of disasters, and has personally experienced both natural disasters such as major earthquakes, as well as terrorist incidents and guerrilla warfare attacks. As a result, his approach is real-world practical.

Today, SIG is the owner of a two highly acclaimed firearm training academies serving civilians and law enforcement. He is also the creator of the internationally popular disaster preparedness blog, 36READY (www.36ReadyBlog.com).

After taking an early retirement from law enforcement, SIG lived in Guatemala with his family for a number of years during that country's bloody civil war. This added to his police experience, giving him additional occasions to be involved in other types of real-world WTSHTF situations.

While living in Guatemala, SIG was on hand for several floods and volcano eruptions, the crash of a commercial airliner in the densely populated capital city, as well as several terrorist and guerrilla attacks. (SIG and his family survived an attack by terrorists who struck their apartment with RPG rockets. As well as two guerrilla attacks on their installation conducted by dozens of insurgents firing automatic weapons and mortars.)

Background: Raised in California and Washington, SIG graduated with a university degree in Criminology. After college, he became a police officer in the State of Washington. A few years later he transferred to the Los Angeles area of California to continue his law enforcement career.

As a police SWAT operator, one ongoing special assignment was to serve as the personal bodyguard for Ronald Reagan. Though SIG did work with Reagan after he became president, SIG's one-on-one time with him was after Reagan was governor of California, but before he officially announced his candidacy for president of the United States. During those years, SIG also worked with General Daniel Shomron (the legendary IDF paratrooper, commando, and commander of the Operation Entebbe rescue mission).

During his career as a police officer, SIG served as a uniformed patrol officer, a Crime Scene Investigator (CSI), detective, and SWAT officer. After joining the SWAT team, SIG received advanced certifications in: special weapons and tactics, close quarters combat, counter sniper, officer survival, bomb and IED threat, weapons of mass destruction (WMD) disaster response, and was trained by the U.S. Secret Service in special protection missions.

During SIG's law enforcement career he was named "Police Officer of the Year", was a "Commendation for Valor" recipient, and received the Mayor's Commendation, U.S. Attorney General's Commendation (Ed Meese), and numerous other awards and citations.

Today, SIG is married to his college sweetheart and lives in Texas. When he is not writing, speaking, or teaching firearm defense and preparedness skills at Texas Republic Firearms Academy (www.TexasRepublicFirearmsAcademy.com) or Camp Barkeley Tactical (www.CampBarkeleyTactical.com), he is busy with church activities or the operations of the Heritage Institute of Texas.

Other Books by SIG SWANSTROM

- God, Guns, and Guts of Firearm Defense: The Bible View

- Family and Personal Protection: Selecting the Best Gun for Self-Defense at Home

Author's Website: www.SIGSWANSTROM.com

Be sure to check the author's website for updates, additional resources, and other important information on the topic of preparedness.

Appendix 3

About Book-2 and -3 in this Series

There is an important distinction between recognizing the need to prepare, and having a clear understanding of what needs to be done. The next two books in this "Prepared: Ready to Roll" series can help you move beyond the need to prepare, to the specifics of how to BE prepared.

PREPARED: Ready to Roll, Book-2

The focus of this book is the "how-to" of advance planning and preparations. It focuses on making sure you are "ready to roll" in an evacuation situation (bug-out), plus it explains why it is so important to have a 'safe haven,' and it gives you the criteria for selecting a safe and viable retreat location.

This book also includes details on bug-out route selection, maps, navigation, and communications. It teaches you the nuts 'n bolts specifics on putting together a GO-Bag (Bug-Out Bag) that fits your needs and your situation (and the needs of your family). It gives you options for water purification, food selection and preparing it for storage, what you need to know about clothing, as well as information on other gear that will help you bug-out successfully.

It also gives you real-world information on selecting firearms for self-defense, practical recommendations on non-lethal defense options, and how to prepare for other safety challenges like medical and dental emergencies. It even includes practical instructions on the often neglected topic of preparing portable but secure personal records to help you get better medical care and speed your recovery after a disaster. Publication Date: December 2015

PREPARED: Ready to Roll, Book-3

The third and last book in this series expands on how to set-up a 'safe haven' retreat location, the selection of participants, and what you need for a viable, healthy community. It also includes details on emergency food options, growing your own food, TransFarming, do-it-yourself long-term food storage, and other practical information for surviving and thriving during a protracted emergency situation.

In this information packed book, you will also find a primer on proactive medical preparations, community health, water purification and storage, cooking, and power options. Plus, essentials on getting news updates during an emergency, options for 2-way radio communication, scanners to listen to local emergency services, and multipurpose radios which can monitor the government's Emergency Broadcast System. It also explains how to set-up a radio equipped with S.A.M.E. technology, which turns itself on, alerting you to an emergency broadcast.

Importantly, Book 3 is not just about gear, it can also prepare you for developments such as increased crime and violence in the aftermath of a disaster. And it also provides factual information on threats such as solar storms and electromagnetic pulse incidents which are largely misunderstood, but for which we also need to prepare since these are growing threats. Publication Date: February 2016

Appendix 4

Alternative News Sources

Drudge Report: www.DrudgeReport.com

Drudge Report is a website which serves as a news consolidator. On one website page, Drudge Report endeavors to list all the significant news stories (in their view). These are listed by article title, and the title also serves as a hyperlink to access the related news story. Since most major news stories are reported by multiple news organizations, Drudge Report posts either the link to the story which broke the news, or the story which contains the most important details.

In addition to headlines, Drudge Report also provides links to the most respected news organizations. For local news, there is place to enter your zip code. Since Drudge Report maintains an extensive archive, and has a search feature to help you scan their archives based on keywords or date, it is a quick way to find information on a particular topic or news incident. For many people, Drudge Report is the first-stop for obtaining a recap of relevant news stories.

News Sources:

There are many excellent sources for news commentary online, and Drudge Report includes the most popular. These are listed in the middle column at the bottom of the main Drudge Report page. However, the following list is different.

This list includes news sources which are known for being on the cutting edge of news reporting. More to the point, these are often the sources of new, breaking news stories. This list includes Conservative, Religious, Liberal and Progressive news sources, and many of these also provide commentary. However, the reason they are included here is their penchant for scooping other news organizations. Like a police officer or reporter who has informants and contacts in different echelons of society, so we, too, need to have sources of information that are outside our own social networks.

I encourage you to first use this list to find sources of news that you find to be the most helpful. Select the top half dozen sites – the ones that are the most helpful to *you*. Accomplish a quick scan, daily. Then, when you are looking for information on a particular topic, use the rest of these sources to help with more in-depth research. These websites are valuable for research, and also to get advanced notice and heads-up developments on hot 'tipping point' topics.

It is up to you to determine the veracity of all of these sources. Moreover, the same website may have stellar information on one news story and yet be in left field on another. Therefore, inclusion in this list is not an endorsement by the author.

Some of these news sources are very quirky, while the moderators of others are extremely annoying, but don't be quick to disregard them. When it comes to news commentary we may appreciate being in sync with the presenter, but we shouldn't demand this from our sources of unreported news and breaking news. We are searching for reliable information, not a club to join.

The key to relevancy is to find news sources which have unusual access to insiders who feed them unreported, reliable information. In this quest, first-hand accounts, personal knowledge, and the credentials of the source are what are important. In-depth interviews with knowledgeable people are often what set these news sources apart from the mainstream news organizations.

For example, in my opinion the host of the TruNews.com radio show / podcast can be offensive, dogmatic and arrogant. Yet, to his credit, he often interviews knowledgeable experts and lets them talk without interruption.

Occasionally these alternative news sources will talk with the same 'expert' who was interviewed by a mainstream news organization. The important difference is that a helpful alternative news source will do an extended interview with the expert which gives them the opportunity to get deeper into the subject. This will always reveal more than the sound-bite interview of the mainstream media, where the expert has little opportunity to talk because the news segment is either short or dominated by the talking-head newscaster.

The 'alternative media' list provided here is solely to help you find new, alternative sources of information which you might find helpful in your quest for the truth. We constantly need to look for new sources of reliable information, additionally so if we are to accomplish story-behind-the-story research.

Many of these websites also offer a free subscription to news updates. This makes it possible to get "breaking" news on a smart phone or via email. When you find a news source that is beneficial, don't miss this opportunity to get important updates via their subscription service.

Further, if you want to maximize commute time, some of these websites, like PrisonPlanet.tv, also have extensive video and audio archives on their own website, as well as on iTunes (audio podcast downloads) and YouTube.com (videos). These can be used to transform wasted time into valuable time.

Popular Alternative News Sources

(Listed in Alphabetical Order)

Alex Jones Channel	www.youtube.com/user/TheAlexJonesChannel/videos
All News Pipeline	allnewspipeline.com
Associated Press Raw News Feed	bigstory.ap.org
Bloomberg Business News	www.bloomberg.com
Breitbart	www.breitbart.com
Coast-to-Coast AM (George Noory)	www.coasttocoastam.com
Daily Caller	dailycaller.com

Daily Coin	thedailycoin.com
DEBKA*file*	www.debka.com
Economy and Markets Daily	harrydent.com
Free Republic	www.freerepublic.com
Freedom Outpost	freedomoutpost.com
Financial Sense	www.financialsesne.com
Guardian (UK, but info on US)	www.theguardian.com/us
Hagmann & Hagmann Report	www.hagmannandhagmann.com
Hal Lindsey Report	www.hallindsey.com
Horowitz Freedom Center	www.horowitzfreedomcenter.org
InfoWars	www.infowars.com *and* www.youtube.com Alex Jones Channel
Intelligence Hub	www.intellihub.com
Hot Air	hotair.com
Huffington Post	www.huffingtonpost.com
Independent Activist Post	www.activistpost.com
Intellihub	www.intellihub.com
Jerusalem Post	www.jpost.com
King World News	kingworldnews.com
Koinonia Institute eNews	www.khouse.org/enews
Liberty Mill	www.thelibertymill.com
Live Leak	www.liveleak.com
Lucianne	lucianne.com
Middle East Media Research	www.memri.org
Mr Conservative	mrconservative.com
Natural News	www.naturalnews.com
Newsmax	www.newsmax.com
Next News Network	nextnewsnetwork.com
NRA Institute for Legislative Action	www.nraila.org
Oath Keepers	oathkeepers.org
Paul Craig Roberts	www.paulcraigroberts.org
PJ Media	pjmedia.com
Pravda (Russia)	english.pravda.ru
Restore the Republic	rtr.org

Reuters News Service	www.reuters.com/news
SGT Report	sgtreport.com
SHTFPlan	www.shtfplan.com
Sky Watch TV	www.skywatchtv.com
Sovereign Man (Simon Black)	www.sovereignman.com
Steve Quayle Q-Alerts	www.stevequayle.com
STRATFOR	www.stratfor.com
Trends Journal (Subscription Required)	trendsresearch.com
TruNews	www.trunews.com
USA Watchdog (Greg Hunter)	usawatchdog.com
Veterans Today	www.veteranstoday.com
Watchman's Cry	watchmanscry.com
Weekend Vigilante (Shelia Zilinsky)	www.weekendvigilante.com
Wikileaks	wikileaks.org
World Affairs Brief (Joel Skousen)	www.worldaffairsbrief.com
World News Dailey (WND)	www.wnd.com
Xinhuanet (China)	www.xinhuanet.com/english
ZeroHedge	www.zerohedge.com

Don't succumb to the natural tendency to get bogged down in stories which relate to your favorite subjects. It's fine to follow sports or stories about entertainers, etc., but don't confuse the time spent on these topics as being useful for decision making, developing awareness, or disaster and emergency situation preparedness.

The information we are looking for will usually be contained in a news story that touches one of society's 'gates of influence.' These are those entry points for change, both good and bad, which redirect the roadways of a culture and pave the way for the type of consequential changes which lead to transformation.

The catalog of 'gates of influence' topics included in Appendix-5 is simply an example, a starting place to help you develop your own list. You might also find it helpful to review the chart which is in chapter 7. Your review of news stories will be quicker if you have your own watch-list of 'hot' and 'influential' topics in mind.

Appendix 5

Gates of Influence on Society and Culture

Look for material changes and new developments in:

- Agriculture, Food and Water
- Arts and Entertainment
  (Also includes sports, athletics and recreation)
- Business / Economics / Trade / Financial Capital
- Church / Religion / Philosophy
- Communications & Transportation
  Includes: Internet, radio, telephone, roads, rail, aviation, and
  other mechanisms which link people to people, and enterprise
  to enterprise.
- Education / Education Delivery
- Energy & High-Demand Natural Resources
- Environment
  Work and living environments, location, weather, and nature.
- Family & Community
- Government & Law
  Includes justice and equal treatment under law, plus regulation.
- Mass Media / Visual Arts
  Includes advertising, movies, television, etc.
- Medicine / Public Health
- Public Safety / National Defense
- Science & Technology

We are living in a time of consequential change. We need to stop whining and get down to business, and this includes developing a greater awareness of the world around us. The time has come.

> "He should not be lulled to repose by the delusion that he does no harm who takes no part in public affairs. He should know that bad men need no better opportunity than when good men look on and do nothing. He should stand to his principles even if leaders go wrong." [97]

In addition to the problems created by external forces, affluence, normalcy bias, and the quest for personal pleasure has weakened us. This must change, and the first step is to change ourselves.

Along with the many attributes of Western society, we have exported run-amok hedonism and deception, and individually we binge on entitlement and self-centeredness. Our national legacy of good deeds has now been overshadowed by 'progressive' leaders and policies which have failed.

We have traded individualism for personal responsibility, and become disagreeable and conflict oriented. Unity is gone along with virtue, and we have few true friends, both as a nation as well as personally.

The needle of our internal compass has been pulled out of position. Our fast paced lives have subtlety caused a deviation from the right path. Since our culture exerts a strong magnetic pull on our lives, we must be intentional about recalibrating our lives. If we fail to do so we will suffer dire consequences in the new tomorrow.

To be effective, preparation for the future must include personal centering. We need to become better informed, and we also need to become more balanced with our priorities.

As we monitor the gates of influence, we need to: Stop. Look. Listen. Similar to what we were taught in elementary school, now

---

[97] "The Medical Bulletin: A Monthly Journal of Medicine and Surgery, Volume 17, page 203. Year: 1895

we need to heed this advice again. We need to look at ourselves and the world around us. We need to reflect, refocus, pay attention, and be active with important tasks.

In Jesus' day, the gates of the city weren't just the doorway to get into a walled urban area; they were also where people met for discussion, counsel, negotiations, and relationship building. This is where they came to discuss the issues of the day. It was a place of commerce, for socializing, and for serious discussions on matters that impacted life.

The same is true for us today, but our modern "gates" can be virtual as well as face-to-face. Either way, we need community and counsel to hone our thinking. We need to have less empty chatter and more meaningful talk. We also need to do more listening, both to those around us, as well as to sources of nontrivial news.

Major change is now inevitable. Our task is not to try and stop the changes which are coming. That is humanly impossible. Our duty is to monitor change closely, and when we can, guide it. Plus, to prepare ourselves and others for these inevitable changes.

There are hazards and blessings to our current circumstance, but blessings will generally only come to those who are taking the time to watch, listen and act proactively. If there was ever a time in which it was reasonable to simply be a good person, to do our job well, or be a good parent, those days are over.

Today we have nefarious and self-centered people exploiting the system for their own agendas, while good people are feeling that it's okay to remain clueless. When good people look to their own affairs and hope for the best, they are living self absorbed and self-centered lives. We can't let good things and busyness get in the way of doing what is best. That is a luxury we can no longer afford.

Our most loving response is *not* to simply do-no-harm. It is to serve in these gates of influence with intentionality, and then utilize the opportunities we are given to exert a positive influence, and to be a conduit of truth. At the very least, we can be news mavens who help others understand the times in which we are living and the changes which are upon us—and how to respond. We shouldn't be a news junkie, but rather a proactive news source.

We shouldn't live life alone, or in cloistered isolation with a few family members or friends. We need the marketplace of ideas if we are going to wisely prepare for the future.

Like new ideas, sound strategy is honed through joint effort. Though some strategies emerge at the time of a "ah ha" moment, a sharp understanding more often comes from "iron sharpening iron."[98] We can't afford to avoid controversy. When two like objects generate friction and heat, this has the capacity to produce two well-honed sharp edges. We need to have that edge.

Importantly, the Proverb doesn't say "file sharpens iron." We're not talking about interactions which produce incendiary sparks and abrasive attitudes, nor should we endure insipid dullness. Rather, we need lively value-added relationships which enrich each other and build unity.

Ultimately, success isn't our responsibility, but faithfulness is. As President Roosevelt[99] famously chimed,

> "Far better it is to dare mighty things – to win glorious triumphs, even though checkered by failure, than to take rank with those poor souls who neither enjoy much, nor suffer much, because they live in the gray twilight that knows not victory nor defeat."

> "It is not the critic who counts, not the man who points out how the strong man stumbled, or where the doer of deeds could have done them better. The credit belongs to the man who is actually in the arena; whose face is marred by dust and sweat and blood; who strives valiantly; who errs and comes short again and again; who knows the great enthusiasms, the great devotions, and spends himself in a worthy cause; who, at best, knows in the end the triumph of high achievement; and who, at the worst, if he fails, at least fails while daring greatly, so that his place shall never be with those cold and timid souls who know neither victory nor defeat."

---

[98] Proverbs 27:17

[99] Theodore "Teddy" Roosevelt, 26th President of the United States.

15-30 Minutes of news gathering is a good start. If we don't allow ourselves to get sidetracked by off-topic news stories, a quick review of the Drudge Report and a couple favorite alternative news sites is far better than nothing. We can't let the perceived size of the information-gathering task dissuade us. It is essential for us to daily keep our ears tuned to noteworthy developments and change.

Early Warning is Essential. If you find yourself unable to regularly look for important news developments, go to Plan-B. You probably have several friends who are news junkies, or at least well informed, ask them to send you email or text messages on important news updates. Ask them to call you if something momentous is happening. You don't want to be caught unawares. Some 24/7 conduit for early-warning is essential.

Appendix 6

The 36-READY Preparedness Code

**Don't be a victim. You have the choice
to be prepared and ready.**

3-Core Aspects of *Preparedness*

To be ready, we need to be prepared:

1. Financially (finances, money and means of exchange); prepared with...

2. Provisions (GO-Bag; basic necessities such as water, food, and gear); and prepared for...

3. Defense (in Jesus day it was a sword, the modern equivalent is a self-defense firearm).

6-Vital Activities Required for *Readiness*

Those who commit to being prepared and ready, pledge to…

1. Plan for emergencies, be savvy to circumstances, and vigilant in their surroundings. And to acquire…

2. Practical training to be ready for plausible real-world challenges, as well as to…

3. Prepare body, mind, spirit, and family for healthy living today and for future times of adversity. To assemble…

4. Provisions and cache gear, water and food; essential supplies for today and the days ahead; GO-Bags, firearms and ammunition, cash and means of trade. And to undertake…

5. Painstaking logistics while being systematic in their maintenance and management of the many different facets of readiness. Plus, they commit to engage in regular…

6. Practice; both personal and family/group exercises.

3-Core Aspects, 6-Vital Activities = 36 READY.

This is aptly summed up by Jesus in his statement to his disciples, which He made just prior to His arrest, the day before He was murdered:

> **Then Jesus asked them,** *"When I sent you out to preach the Good News and you did not have money, a traveler's bag [provisions/gear], or extra clothing, did you need anything?"*
>
> *"No," they replied.*
>
> *"But now," He said, "take your money and a traveler's bag [provisions / gear]. And if you don't have a sword, sell your cloak [coat/jacket] and buy one!"*
>
> Holy Bible, Luke 22:35-36

Whether you acknowledge Jesus as God or only regard Him as the premiere example of a man of peace, this injunction to His followers is a surprise to many.[100] Jesus wasn't just being pragmatic; He understood that there can be no peace without standing up for justice. He knew that an essential aspect of justice is ordinary people, who are ready to apply appropriate force against evil. As the sword of Jesus' day exemplified, this includes the use of deadly force.

To live up to the 36-READY Code involves more than being armed and more than having essential resources and stockpiles of supplies. It also involves contemplating various scenarios in advance—and then planning and preparing for them. It's about being ready…

36 READY.

---

[100] For more on this topic, read *"God, Guns, and Guts: The Bible View,"* by SIG Swanstrom, Oxbridge Press, 2013.

Appendix 7

Verses and Quotations
Used in this Book

Chapter 1

"A prudent person foresees danger and takes precautions. The simpleton goes blindly on and suffers the consequences."

Holy Bible
Proverbs 22:3

"Take a lesson from the ants, you slacker. Learn from their ways and become wise! Though they have no prince or governor or ruler to make them work, they labor hard all summer, gathering food for the winter.'

'But you lazy slacker, how long will you sleep?
When will you wake up?'

"A little extra sleep, a little more slumber [ignoring that which is important], a little folding of the hands to rest [relax and contemplate]— then poverty will pounce on you like a bandit; scarcity will attack you like an armed robber."

Holy Bible
Proverbs 6:6-11

Chapter 2

"When people are saying, 'Everything is peaceful and secure,' then disaster will fall on them as suddenly as a pregnant woman's labor pains begin. And there will be no escape."

Holy Bible
1 Thessalonians 5:3

Chapter 3

"Let no one deceive you with empty words"

Holy Bible
Ephesians 5:6a

Chapter 4

Investigation Principle #1

"There is a principle which is a bar against all information which is proof against all argument, and which cannot fail to keep man in everlasting ignorance. That principle is contempt [condemnation] before investigation."

-- William Paley (1743-1805)

"He who gives an answer before he hears, It is folly and shame to him."

"The first to plead his case SEEMS right, until another comes and examines him."

Holy Bible
Proverbs 18:13, 17

Chapter 5

"When the people fear the government, there is tyranny; when the government fears the people, there is liberty."

> \- Thomas Jefferson
> 3rd U.S. President
> Principal author of the
> Declaration of Independence

"The 10 most dangerous words in the English language are, 'Hi, I'm from the government and I'm here to help.'" [101]

> \- Ronald Reagan
> 40th U.S. President

"Man is not free unless government is limited. There's a clear cause and effect here that is as neat and predictable as a law of physics: As government expands, liberty contracts." [102]

> \- Ronald Reagan

"They conceive mischief and bring forth iniquity, and their mind prepares deception."

> Holy Bible
> Job 15:35

---

[101] Remarks to Future Farmers of America, July 28, 1988.

[102] Presidential Farewell Address, Washington, D.C., January 11, 1989

"See to it that no one takes you captive through philosophy and devoid-of-truth deception, according to the tradition of men, according to the elementary principles of the world rather than according to Christ."

Holy Bible
Colossians 2:8

"... we have made falsehood our refuge, and we have concealed ourselves with deception."

Holy Bible
Isaiah 28:15b

"He [Satan] will use every kind of evil deception to fool those on their way to destruction, because they refuse to love and accept the truth that would save them."

Holy Bible
2 Thessalonians 2:10

"They speak falsehood to one another; with flattering lips and with a double heart they speak."

Holy Bible
Psalm 12:2

"Through knowledge the righteous are rescued."

Holy Bible
Proverbs 11:9b

Chapter 6

"Eternal vigilance is the price of liberty."

- Thomas Jefferson [103]
Third President of the United States
Principal author of the
Declaration of Independence

"And you will know the truth, and the truth will make you free."

Holy Bible
John 8:32

Chapter 7

"But He [Jesus] replied to them, 'When it is evening, you say, it will be fair weather, for the sky is red. And in the morning, 'There will be a storm today, for the sky is red and threatening.' Do you know how to discern the appearance of the sky, but cannot discern the signs of the times?"

Holy Bible
Matthew 16:2-4

---

[103] Variations of this statement are attributed to a number of the Founding Fathers of the United States, but Thomas Jefferson is often cited as the one who popularized this truism. Source: "The Union," *Pennsylvania Inquirer* and Daily Courier, January 4, 1838, Issue 4, column B.

Chapter 8

"The world is exploding all over. Whether they're cyber threats, which are relatively new, but are just as real and deadly and lethal as anything we've ever dealt with; obviously, what's going on in North Korea, China's behavior in the South China Sea, East China Sea; Russia's actions in Ukraine; North Africa, the Middle East today, every part of that world is troubled under great stress." [104]

- Chuck Hagel
U.S. Secretary of Defense

"Today's global security environment is the most unpredictable I have seen in 40-years of service... global disorder has significantly increased while some of our comparative military advantage has begun to erode. We now face multiple, simultaneous security challenges from traditional state actors [nations like China and Russia], and transregional networks of sub-state groups – all taking advantage of rapid technological change. Future conflicts will come more rapidly, last longer, and take place on a much more technically challenging battlefield. They will have increasing implications to the U.S. homeland." [105]

- Joint Chiefs of Staff
U.S. Military

---

[104] Chuck Hagel, United States Secretary of Defense, in an address to a group of Marines in San Diego, California, August 12, 2014. Source: The Weekly Standard, "Defense Secretary: 'The World is Exploding All Over" by Jeryl Bier, 8/13/2014; http://www.weeklystandard.com/blogs/defense-secretary-world-exploding-all-over_802893.html

[105] Source: Official U.S. Government document, "The National Military Strategy of the United States of America, 2015, pg. 1; Pentagon, U.S. Military, Authors: Joint Chiefs of Staff.
http://www.jcs.mil/Portals/36/Documents/Publications/National_Military_Strategy_2015.pdf

A-1

"For I know the plans I have for you,' says the Lord. "They are plans for good and not for disaster, to give you a [eternal] future and a hope. In those days when you pray, I will listen. If you will look for me wholeheartedly, you will find me."

Holy Bible

Jeremiah 29:11-13

"Be dressed in readiness, and keep your lamps lit."

Jesus

Holy Bible

Luke 12:35a

"Be strong and courageous, and act; do not fear nor be dismayed, for the Lord God, my God, is with you. He will not fail you nor forsake you until all the work for the service of the house of the Lord is finished."

Holy Bible

1 Chronicles 28:20-21

"[When] My people who are called by My name humble themselves and pray, and seek My face and turn from their wicked ways, then I will hear from heaven, will forgive their sin, and will heal their land."

Holy Bible

2 Chronicles 7:14

A-5

"He should not be lulled to repose by the delusion that he does no harm who takes no part in public affairs. He should know that bad men need no better opportunity than when good men look on and do nothing. He should stand to his principles even if leaders go wrong." [106]

-- Medical Journal, 1895

"Far better it is to dare mighty things – to win glorious triumphs, even though checkered by failure, than to take rank with those poor souls who neither enjoy much, nor suffer much, because they live in the gray twilight that knows not victory nor defeat."

"It is not the critic who counts, not the man who points out how the strong man stumbled, or where the doer of deeds could have done them better. The credit belongs to the man who is actually in the arena; whose face is marred by dust and sweat and blood; who strives valiantly; who errs and comes short again and again; who knows the great enthusiasms, the great devotions, and spends himself in a worthy cause; who, at best, knows in the end the triumph of high achievement; and who, at the worst, if he fails, at least fails while daring greatly, so that his place shall never be with those cold and timid souls who know neither victory nor defeat."

- President Theodore Roosevelt
26th President of the United States

---

[106] "The Medical Bulletin: A Monthly Journal of Medicine and Surgery, Volume 17, page 203. Year: 1895

A-6

Then Jesus asked them, *"When I sent you out to preach the Good News and you did not have money, a traveler's bag [provisions/gear], or extra clothing, did you need anything?"*

"No," they replied.

"But now," He said, "take your money and a traveler's bag [provisions / gear]. And if you don't have a sword, sell your cloak [coat/jacket] and buy one!"

Holy Bible
Luke 22:35-36

More Sage Preparedness Counsel from the Bible

"Woe to him who builds his house without righteousness, and his upper rooms without justice."

Jeremiah 22:13a

"Never abandon a friend—either yours or your father's. When disaster strikes, you won't have to ask your brother for assistance. It's better to go to a neighbor than to a brother who lives far away."

Proverbs 27:10

"When people are saying, 'Everything is peaceful and secure,' then disaster will fall on them as suddenly as a pregnant woman's labor pains begin. And there will be no escape."

1 Thessalonians 5:3

"The instruction of the wise is like a life-giving fountain; those who accept it avoid the snares of death."

Proverbs 13:14

"Prepare yourself and be ready, you and all your companies that are gathered about you; and be a guard for them."

Ezekiel 38:7

"The LORD is our refuge and strength, a very present help in trouble. Therefore we will not fear,"

Psalms 46:1

"I will save you that you may become a blessing. Do not fear; let your hands be strong."

Zechariah 8:13

"Beware of false prophets who come disguised as harmless sheep but are really vicious wolves."

Matthew 7:15

"The LORD abhors a man of bloodshed and deceit."

Psalm 5:6b

[The wicked,] **"his mouth is full of curses and deceit and oppression;** under his tongue is mischief and wickedness."

Psalm 10:7

"The acquisition of treasures by a lying tongue is a fleeting vapor, the pursuit of death. The violence of the wicked will drag them away, because they refuse to act with justice."

Proverbs 21:5-6

"Woe to him who builds his house without righteousness and his upper rooms without justice."

Jeremiah 22:13a

"The LORD is our refuge and strength, a very present help in trouble. Therefore we will not fear, though the earth should change and though the mountains slip into the heart of the sea; though its waters roar and foam, though the mountains quake at its swelling pride."

Psalms 46:1-3

"And He [Jesus] said to them, "But now, whoever has a money belt is to take it along, likewise also a bag [of provisions], and whoever has no sword is to sell his coat and buy one."

Luke 22:36

Appendix 8

Presidential Executive Order 13603

The following is the actual text, the legal transcript, of what is referred to as the National Defense Resources Preparedness Act which came into force after President Barack Obama signed it on March 16, 2012.

It is important to understand that even if this frightening Act is subsequently suspended, there are dozens of other Executive Orders (EO) which establish the same authorities and actions. This particular Act, EO 13603, is a compilation designed to unify and harmonize the other Orders. These other Executive Orders will remain in effect even under a different president, until each one is individually cancelled.

There are inherently insidious aspects of the unconstitutional Executive Order process. For example, provisions which are similar to those contained in this Act can be buried within some other Executive Order, an administrative directive which seemingly has nothing to do with disaster preparedness. Or, an EO can be established which on the surface, seems entirely reasonable.

A good example of this is President Roosevelt's EO 9066 which he signed in the early days of World War II. This EO had the innocuous and reasonable-sounding title, "Authorizing the Secretary of War to Prescribe Military Areas." [107] However, its

---

[107] A transcript of President Roosevelt's Executive Order 9066 is available online, at this U.S. Government website:

intended purpose was far from reasonable. It became the basis on which American citizens of Japanese ancestry were arrested. It was the authority used to put innocent, patriotic Americans into internment camps for the duration of the war.

Without evidence, without trial, a presidential Executive Order was used to forcibly incarcerate 127,000 people. Based solely on the authority of that EO, the Constitutional Rights of these people were suspended, all by the fiat of a U.S. President. How did this shameful crime happen?[108] Public fear equals public support.

For those who are willing to learn from history, the words of the following Executive Order are chilling. Moreover, why did President Obama write this unpopular Order, and why has Congress let it stand? In their minds, they must think there is a good chance that these provisions will be needed in the future.

---

http://www.ourdocuments.gov/print_friendly.php?flash=true&page=transcript&doc=74&title=Transcript+of+Executive+Order+9066%3A++Resulting+in+the+Relocation+of+Japanese+(1942)

[108] In Germany during WWII, if the Jews had fought back against the Nazis, many would still have died but they would have died with dignity. In the U.S., if the Americans of Japanese descent had fought back, it would have been used to prove that President Roosevelt had made the right decision. We need to remember that the best response is not reactionary, it's strategic.

EO 13603

The White House
Office of the Press Secretary
For Immediate Release
March 16, 2012

Executive Order -- National Defense Resources Preparedness

EXECUTIVE ORDER
NATIONAL DEFENSE RESOURCES PREPAREDNESS

By the authority vested in me as President by the Constitution and the laws of the United States of America, including the Defense Production Act of 1950, as amended (50 U.S.C. App. 2061 *et seq.*), and section 301 of title 3, United States Code, and as Commander in Chief of the Armed Forces of the United States, it is hereby ordered as follows:

PART I - PURPOSE, POLICY, AND IMPLEMENTATION

Section 101. Purpose. This order delegates authorities and addresses national defense resource policies and programs under the Defense Production Act of 1950, as amended (the "Act").

Sec. 102. Policy. The United States must have an industrial and technological base capable of meeting national defense requirements and capable of contributing to the technological superiority of its national defense equipment in peacetime and in times of national emergency. The domestic industrial and technological base is the foundation for national defense preparedness. The authorities provided in the Act shall be used to strengthen this base and to ensure it is capable of responding to the national defense needs of the United States.

Sec. 103. General Functions. Executive departments and agencies (agencies) responsible for plans and programs relating to national defense (as defined in section 801(j) of this order), or for resources and services needed to support such plans and programs, shall:

(a) identify requirements for the full spectrum of emergencies, including essential military and civilian demand;

(b) assess on an ongoing basis the capability of the domestic industrial and technological base to satisfy requirements in peacetime and times of national emergency, specifically evaluating the availability of the most critical resource and production sources, including subcontractors and suppliers, materials, skilled labor, and professional and technical personnel;

(c) be prepared, in the event of a potential threat to the security of the United States, to take actions necessary to ensure the availability of adequate resources and production capability, including services and critical technology, for national defense requirements;

(d) improve the efficiency and responsiveness of the domestic industrial base to support national defense requirements; and

(e) foster cooperation between the defense and commercial sectors for research and development and for acquisition of materials, services, components, and equipment to enhance industrial base efficiency and responsiveness.

Sec. 104. Implementation. (a) The National Security Council and Homeland Security Council, in conjunction with the National Economic Council, shall serve as the integrated policymaking forum for consideration and formulation of national defense resource preparedness policy and shall make recommendations to the President on the use of authorities under the Act.

(b) The Secretary of Homeland Security shall:

(1) advise the President on issues of national defense resource preparedness and on the use of the authorities and functions delegated by this order;

(2) provide for the central coordination of the plans and programs incident to authorities and functions delegated under this order, and provide guidance to agencies assigned functions under this order, developed in consultation with such agencies; and

(3) report to the President periodically concerning all program activities conducted pursuant to this order.

(c) The Defense Production Act Committee, described in section 701 of this order, shall:

(1) in a manner consistent with section 2(b) of the Act, 50 U.S.C. App. 2062(b), advise the President through the Assistant to the President and National Security Advisor, the Assistant to the President for Homeland Security and Counterterrorism, and the Assistant to the President for Economic Policy on the effective use of the authorities under the Act; and

(2) prepare and coordinate an annual report to the Congress pursuant to section 722(d) of the Act, 50 U.S.C. App. 2171(d).

(d) The Secretary of Commerce, in cooperation with the Secretary of Defense, the Secretary of Homeland Security, and other agencies, shall:

(1) analyze potential effects of national emergencies on actual production capability, taking into account the entire production system, including shortages of resources, and develop recommended preparedness measures to strengthen capabilities for production increases in national emergencies; and

(2) perform industry analyses to assess capabilities of the industrial base to support the national defense, and develop policy recommendations to improve the international competitiveness of specific domestic industries and their abilities to meet national defense program needs.

PART II - PRIORITIES AND ALLOCATIONS

Sec. 201. Priorities and Allocations Authorities. (a) The authority of the President conferred by section 101 of the Act, 50 U.S.C. App. 2071, to require acceptance and priority performance of contracts or orders (other than contracts of employment) to promote the national defense over performance of any other contracts or orders, and to allocate materials, services, and facilities as deemed necessary or appropriate to promote the national defense, is delegated to the following agency heads:

(1) the Secretary of Agriculture with respect to food resources, food resource facilities, livestock resources, veterinary resources, plant health resources, and the domestic distribution of farm equipment and commercial fertilizer;

(2) the Secretary of Energy with respect to all forms of energy;

(3) the Secretary of Health and Human Services with respect to health resources;

(4) the Secretary of Transportation with respect to all forms of civil transportation;

(5) the Secretary of Defense with respect to water resources; and

(6) the Secretary of Commerce with respect to all other materials, services, and facilities, including construction materials.

(b) The Secretary of each agency delegated authority under subsection (a) of this section (resource departments) shall plan for and issue regulations to prioritize and allocate resources and establish standards and procedures by which the authority shall be used to promote the national defense, under both emergency and non-emergency conditions. Each Secretary shall authorize the heads of other agencies, as appropriate, to place priority ratings on contracts and orders for materials, services, and facilities needed in support of programs approved under section 202 of this order.

(c) Each resource department shall act, as necessary and appropriate, upon requests for special priorities assistance, as defined by section 801(l) of this order, in a time frame consistent with the urgency of the need at hand. In situations where there are competing program requirements for limited resources, the resource department shall consult with the Secretary who made the required determination under section 202 of this order. Such Secretary shall coordinate with and identify for the resource department which program requirements to prioritize on the basis of operational urgency. In situations involving more than one Secretary making such a required determination under section 202 of this order, the Secretaries shall coordinate with and identify for the resource department which program requirements should receive priority on the basis of operational urgency.

(d) If agreement cannot be reached between two such Secretaries, then the issue shall be referred to the President through the Assistant to the President and National Security Advisor and the Assistant to the President for Homeland Security and Counterterrorism.

(e) The Secretary of each resource department, when necessary, shall make the finding required under section 101(b) of the Act, 50 U.S.C. App. 2071(b). This finding shall be submitted for the President's approval through the Assistant to the President and National Security Advisor and the Assistant to the President for Homeland Security and Counterterrorism. Upon such approval, the Secretary of the resource department that made the finding may use the authority of section 101(a) of the Act, 50 U.S.C. App. 2071(a), to control the general distribution of any material (including applicable services) in the civilian market.

Sec. 202. Determinations. Except as provided in section 201(e) of this order, the authority delegated by section 201 of this order may be used only to support programs that have been determined in writing as necessary or appropriate to promote the national defense:

(a) by the Secretary of Defense with respect to military production and construction, military assistance to foreign nations, military use of civil transportation, stockpiles managed by the Department of Defense, space, and directly related activities;

(b) by the Secretary of Energy with respect to energy production and construction, distribution and use, and directly related activities; and

(c) by the Secretary of Homeland Security with respect to all other national defense programs, including civil defense and continuity of Government.

Sec. 203. Maximizing Domestic Energy Supplies. The authorities of the President under section 101(c)(1) (2) of the Act, 50 U.S.C. App. 2071(c)(1) (2), are delegated to the Secretary of Commerce, with the exception that the authority to make findings that materials (including equipment), services, and facilities are critical and essential, as described in section 101(c)(2)(A) of the Act, 50 U.S.C. App. 2071(c)(2)(A), is delegated to the Secretary of Energy.

Sec. 204. Chemical and Biological Warfare. The authority of the President conferred by section 104(b) of the Act, 50 U.S.C. App. 2074(b), is delegated to the Secretary of Defense. This authority may not be further delegated by the Secretary.

PART III - EXPANSION OF PRODUCTIVE CAPACITY AND SUPPLY

Sec. 301. Loan Guarantees. (a) To reduce current or projected shortfalls of resources, critical technology items, or materials essential for the national defense, the head of each agency engaged in procurement for the national defense, as defined in section 801(h) of this order, is authorized pursuant to section 301 of the Act, 50 U.S.C. App. 2091, to guarantee loans by private institutions.

(b) Each guaranteeing agency is designated and authorized to: (1) act as fiscal agent in the making of its own guarantee contracts and in otherwise carrying out the purposes of section 301 of the Act; and (2) contract with any Federal Reserve Bank to assist the agency in serving as fiscal agent.

(c) Terms and conditions of guarantees under this authority shall be determined in consultation with the Secretary of the Treasury and the Director of the Office of Management and Budget (OMB). The guaranteeing agency is authorized, following such consultation, to prescribe: (1) either specifically or by maximum limits or otherwise, rates of interest, guarantee and commitment fees, and other charges which may be made in connection with such guarantee contracts; and (2) regulations governing the forms and procedures (which shall be uniform to the extent practicable) to be utilized in connection therewith.

Sec. 302. Loans. To reduce current or projected shortfalls of resources, critical technology items, or materials essential for the national defense, the head of each agency engaged in procurement for the national defense is delegated the authority of the President under section 302 of the Act, 50 U.S.C. App. 2092, to make loans there under. Terms and conditions of loans under this authority shall be determined in consultation with the Secretary of the Treasury and the Director of OMB.

Sec. 303. Additional Authorities. (a) To create, maintain, protect, expand, or restore domestic industrial base capabilities essential for the national defense, the head of each agency engaged in procurement for the national defense is delegated the authority of the President under section 303 of the Act, 50 U.S.C. App. 2093, to make provision for purchases of, or commitments to purchase, an industrial resource or a critical technology item for Government use or resale, and to make provision for the development of production capabilities, and for the increased use of emerging technologies in security program applications, and to enable rapid transition of emerging technologies.

(b) Materials acquired under section 303 of the Act, 50 U.S.C. App. 2093, that exceed the needs of the programs under the Act may be transferred to the National Defense Stockpile, if, in the judgment of the Secretary of Defense as the National Defense Stockpile Manager, such transfers are in the public interest.

Sec. 304. Subsidy Payments. To ensure the supply of raw or nonprocessed materials from high cost sources, or to ensure maximum production or supply in any area at stable prices of any materials in light of a temporary increase in transportation cost, the head of each agency engaged in procurement for the national defense is delegated the authority of the President under section 303(c) of the Act, 50 U.S.C. App. 2093(c), to make subsidy payments, after consultation with the Secretary of the Treasury and the Director of OMB.

Sec. 305. Determinations and Findings. (a) Pursuant to budget authority provided by an appropriations act in advance for credit assistance under section 301 or 302 of the Act, 50 U.S.C. App. 2091, 2092, and consistent with the Federal Credit Reform Act of 1990, as amended (FCRA), 2 U.S.C. 661 *et seq.*, the head of each agency engaged in procurement for the national defense is delegated the authority to make the determinations set forth in sections 301(a)(2) and 302(b)(2) of the Act, in consultation with the Secretary making the required determination under section 202 of this order; provided, that such determinations shall be made after due consideration of the provisions of OMB Circular A 129 and the credit subsidy score for the relevant loan or loan guarantee as approved by OMB pursuant to FCRA.

(b) Other than any determination by the President under section 303(a)(7)(b) of the Act, the head of each agency engaged in procurement for the national defense is delegated the authority to make the required determinations, judgments, certifications, findings, and notifications defined under section 303 of the Act, 50 U.S.C. App. 2093, in consultation with the Secretary making the required determination under section 202 of this order.

Sec. 306. Strategic and Critical Materials. The Secretary of Defense, and the Secretary of the Interior in consultation with the Secretary of Defense as the National Defense Stockpile Manager, are each delegated the authority of the President under section 303(a)(1)(B) of the Act, 50 U.S.C. App. 2093(a)(1)(B), to encourage the exploration, development, and mining of strategic and critical materials and other materials.

Sec. 307. Substitutes. The head of each agency engaged in procurement for the national defense is delegated the authority of the President under section 303(g) of the Act, 50 U.S.C. App. 2093(g), to make provision for the development of substitutes for strategic and critical materials, critical components, critical technology items, and other resources to aid the national defense.

Sec. 308. Government-Owned Equipment. The head of each agency engaged in procurement for the national defense is delegated the authority of the President under section 303(e) of the Act, 50 U.S.C. App. 2093(e), to:

(a) procure and install additional equipment, facilities, processes, or improvements to plants, factories, and other industrial facilities owned by the Federal Government and to procure and install Government owned equipment in plants, factories, or other industrial facilities owned by private persons;

(b) provide for the modification or expansion of privately owned facilities, including the modification or improvement of production processes, when taking actions under sections 301, 302, or 303 of the Act, 50 U.S.C. App. 2091, 2092, 2093; and

(c) sell or otherwise transfer equipment owned by the Federal Government and installed under section 303(e) of the Act, 50 U.S.C. App. 2093(e), to the owners of such plants, factories, or other industrial facilities.

Sec. 309. Defense Production Act Fund. The Secretary of Defense is designated the Defense Production Act Fund Manager, in accordance with section 304(f) of the Act, 50 U.S.C. App. 2094(f), and shall carry out the duties specified in section 304 of the Act, in consultation with the agency heads having approved, and appropriated funds for, projects under title III of the Act.

Sec. 310. Critical Items. The head of each agency engaged in procurement for the national defense is delegated the authority of the President under section 107(b)(1) of the Act, 50 U.S.C. App. 2077(b)(1), to take appropriate action to ensure that critical components, critical technology items, essential materials, and industrial resources are available from reliable sources when needed to meet defense requirements during peacetime, graduated mobilization, and national emergency. Appropriate action may include restricting contract solicitations to reliable sources, restricting contract solicitations to domestic sources (pursuant to statutory authority), stockpiling critical components, and developing substitutes for critical components or critical technology items.

Sec. 311. Strengthening Domestic Capability. The head of each agency engaged in procurement for the national defense is delegated the authority of the President under section 107(a) of the Act, 50 U.S.C. App. 2077(a), to utilize the authority of title III of the Act or any other provision of law to provide appropriate incentives to develop, maintain, modernize, restore, and expand the productive capacities of domestic sources for critical components, critical technology items, materials, and industrial resources essential for the execution of the national security strategy of the United States.

Sec. 312. Modernization of Equipment. The head of each agency engaged in procurement for the national defense, in accordance with section 108(b) of the Act, 50 U.S.C. App. 2078(b), may utilize the authority of title III of the Act to guarantee the purchase or lease of advance manufacturing equipment, and any related services with respect to any such equipment for purposes of the Act. In considering title III projects, the head of each agency engaged in procurement for the national defense shall provide a strong preference for proposals submitted by a small business supplier or subcontractor in accordance with section 108(b)(2) of the Act, 50 U.S.C. App. 2078(b)(2).

PART IV - VOLUNTARY AGREEMENTS AND ADVISORY COMMITTEES

Sec. 401. Delegations. The authority of the President under sections 708(c) and (d) of the Act, 50 U.S.C. App. 2158(c), (d), is delegated to the heads of agencies otherwise delegated authority under this order. The status of the use of such delegations shall be furnished to the Secretary of Homeland Security.

Sec. 402. Advisory Committees. The authority of the President under section 708(d) of the Act, 50 U.S.C. App. 2158(d), and delegated in section 401 of this order (relating to establishment of advisory committees) shall be exercised only after consultation with, and in accordance with, guidelines and procedures established by the Administrator of General Services.

Sec. 403. Regulations. The Secretary of Homeland Security, after approval of the Attorney General, and after consultation by the Attorney General with the Chairman of the Federal Trade Commission, shall promulgate rules pursuant to section 708(e) of the Act, 50 U.S.C. App. 2158(e), incorporating standards and procedures by which voluntary agreements and plans of action may be developed and carried out. Such rules may be adopted by other agencies to fulfill the rulemaking requirement of section 708(e) of the Act, 50 U.S.C. App. 2158(e).

PART V - EMPLOYMENT OF PERSONNEL

Sec. 501. National Defense Executive Reserve. (a) In accordance with section 710(e) of the Act, 50 U.S.C. App. 2160(e), there is established in the executive branch a National Defense Executive Reserve (NDER) composed of persons of recognized expertise from various segments of the private sector and from Government (except full time Federal employees) for training for employment in executive positions in the Federal Government in the event of a national defense emergency.

(b) The Secretary of Homeland Security shall issue necessary guidance for the NDER program, including appropriate guidance for establishment, recruitment, training, monitoring, and activation of NDER units and shall be responsible for the overall coordination of the NDER program. The authority of the President under section 710(e) of the Act, 50 U.S.C. App. 2160(e), to determine periods of national defense emergency is delegated to the Secretary of Homeland Security.

(c) The head of any agency may implement section 501(a) of this order with respect to NDER operations in such agency.

(d) The head of each agency with an NDER unit may exercise the authority under section 703 of the Act, 50 U.S.C. App. 2153, to employ civilian personnel when activating all or a part of its NDER unit. The exercise of this authority shall be subject to the provisions of sections 501(e) and (f) of this order and shall not be redelegated.

(e) The head of an agency may activate an NDER unit, in whole or in part, upon the written determination of the Secretary of Homeland Security that an emergency affecting the national defense exists and that the activation of the unit is necessary to carry out the emergency program functions of the agency.

(f) Prior to activating the NDER unit, the head of the agency shall notify, in writing, the Assistant to the President for Homeland Security and Counterterrorism of the impending activation.

Sec. 502. Consultants. The head of each agency otherwise delegated functions under this order is delegated the authority of the President under sections 710(b) and (c) of the Act, 50 U.S.C. App. 2160(b), (c), to employ persons of outstanding experience and ability without compensation and to employ experts, consultants, or organizations. The authority delegated by this section may not be redelegated.

PART VI - LABOR REQUIREMENTS

Sec. 601. Secretary of Labor. (a) The Secretary of Labor, in coordination with the Secretary of Defense and the heads of other agencies, as deemed appropriate by the Secretary of Labor, shall:

(1) collect and maintain data necessary to make a continuing appraisal of the Nation's workforce needs for purposes of national defense;

(2) upon request by the Director of Selective Service, and in coordination with the Secretary of Defense, assist the Director of Selective Service in development of policies regulating the induction and deferment of persons for duty in the armed services;

(3) upon request from the head of an agency with authority under this order, consult with that agency with respect to: (i) the effect of contemplated actions on labor demand and utilization; (ii) the relation of labor demand to materials and facilities requirements; and (iii) such other matters as will assist in making the exercise of priority and allocations functions consistent with effective utilization and distribution of labor;

(4) upon request from the head of an agency with authority under this order: (i) formulate plans, programs, and policies for meeting the labor requirements of actions to be taken for national defense purposes; and (ii) estimate training needs to help address national defense requirements and promote necessary and appropriate training programs; and

(5) develop and implement an effective labor management relations policy to support the activities and programs under this order, with the cooperation of other agencies as deemed appropriate by the Secretary of Labor, including the National Labor Relations Board, the Federal Labor Relations Authority, the National Mediation Board, and the Federal Mediation and Conciliation Service.

(b) All agencies shall cooperate with the Secretary of Labor, upon request, for the purposes of this section, to the extent permitted by law.

PART VII - DEFENSE PRODUCTION ACT COMMITTEE

Sec. 701. The Defense Production Act Committee. (a) The Defense Production Act Committee (Committee) shall be composed of the following members, in accordance with section 722(b) of the Act, 50 U.S.C. App. 2171(b):

(1) The Secretary of State;

(2) The Secretary of the Treasury;

(3) The Secretary of Defense;

(4) The Attorney General;

(5) The Secretary of the Interior;

(6) The Secretary of Agriculture;

(7) The Secretary of Commerce;

(8) The Secretary of Labor;

(9) The Secretary of Health and Human Services;

(10) The Secretary of Transportation;

(11) The Secretary of Energy;

(12) The Secretary of Homeland Security;

(13) The Director of National Intelligence;

(14) The Director of the Central Intelligence Agency;

(15) The Chair of the Council of Economic Advisers;

(16) The Administrator of the National Aeronautics and Space Administration; and

(17) The Administrator of General Services.

(b) The Director of OMB and the Director of the Office of Science and Technology Policy shall be invited to participate in all

Committee meetings and activities in an advisory role. The Chairperson, as designated by the President pursuant to section 722 of the Act, 50 U.S.C. App. 2171, may invite the heads of other agencies or offices to participate in Committee meetings and activities in an advisory role, as appropriate.

Sec. 702. Offsets. The Secretary of Commerce shall prepare and submit to the Congress the annual report required by section 723 of the Act, 50 U.S.C. App. 2172, in consultation with the Secretaries of State, the Treasury, Defense, and Labor, the United States Trade Representative, the Director of National Intelligence, and the heads of other agencies as appropriate. The heads of agencies shall provide the Secretary of Commerce with such information as may be necessary for the effective performance of this function.

PART VIII - GENERAL PROVISIONS

Sec. 801. Definitions. In addition to the definitions in section 702 of the Act, 50 U.S.C. App. 2152, the following definitions apply throughout this order:

(a) "Civil transportation" includes movement of persons and property by all modes of transportation in interstate, intrastate, or foreign commerce within the United States, its territories and possessions, and the District of Columbia, and related public storage and warehousing, ports, services, equipment and facilities, such as transportation carrier shop and repair facilities. "Civil transportation" also shall include direction, control, and coordination of civil transportation capacity regardless of ownership. "Civil transportation" shall not include transportation owned or controlled by the Department of Defense, use of petroleum and gas pipelines, and coal slurry pipelines used only to supply energy production facilities directly.

(b) "Energy" means all forms of energy including petroleum, gas (both natural and manufactured), electricity, solid fuels (including all forms of coal, coke, coal chemicals, coal liquification, and coal gasification), solar, wind, other types of renewable energy, atomic energy, and the production, conservation, use, control, and distribution (including pipelines) of all of these forms of energy.

(c) "Farm equipment" means equipment, machinery, and repair parts manufactured for use on farms in connection with the production or preparation for market use of food resources.

(d) "Fertilizer" means any product or combination of products that contain one or more of the elements nitrogen, phosphorus, and potassium for use as a plant nutrient.

(e) "Food resources" means all commodities and products, (simple, mixed, or compound), or complements to such commodities or products, that are capable of being ingested by either human beings or animals, irrespective of other uses to which such commodities or products may be put, at all stages of processing from the raw commodity to the products thereof in vendible form for human or animal consumption. "Food resources" also means potable water packaged in commercially marketable containers, all starches, sugars, vegetable and animal or marine fats and oils, seed, cotton, hemp, and flax fiber, but does not mean any such material after it loses its identity as an agricultural commodity or agricultural product.

(f) "Food resource facilities" means plants, machinery, vehicles (including on farm), and other facilities required for the production, processing, distribution, and storage (including cold storage) of food resources, and for the domestic distribution of farm equipment and fertilizer (excluding transportation thereof).

(g) "Functions" include powers, duties, authority, responsibilities, and discretion.

(h) "Head of each agency engaged in procurement for the national defense" means the heads of the Departments of State, Justice, the Interior, and Homeland Security, the Office of the Director of National Intelligence, the Central Intelligence Agency, the National Aeronautics and Space Administration, the General Services Administration, and all other agencies with authority delegated under section 201 of this order.

(i) "Health resources" means drugs, biological products, medical devices, materials, facilities, health supplies, services and equipment required to diagnose, mitigate or prevent the impairment of, improve, treat, cure, or restore the physical or mental health conditions of the population.

(j) "National defense" means programs for military and energy production or construction, military or critical infrastructure assistance to any foreign nation, homeland security, stockpiling, space, and any directly related activity. Such term includes emergency preparedness activities conducted pursuant to title VI of the Robert T. Stafford Disaster Relief and Emergency

Assistance Act, 42 U.S.C. 5195 *et seq.*, and critical infrastructure protection and restoration.

(k) "Offsets" means compensation practices required as a condition of purchase in either government to government or commercial sales of defense articles and/or defense services as defined by the Arms Export Control Act, 22 U.S.C. 2751 *et seq.*, and the International Traffic in Arms Regulations, 22 C.F.R. 120.1 130.17.

(l) "Special priorities assistance" means action by resource departments to assist with expediting deliveries, placing rated orders, locating suppliers, resolving production or delivery conflicts between various rated orders, addressing problems that arise in the fulfillment of a rated order or other action authorized by a delegated agency, and determining the validity of rated orders.

(m) "Strategic and critical materials" means materials (including energy) that (1) would be needed to supply the military, industrial, and essential civilian needs of the United States during a national emergency, and (2) are not found or produced in the United States in sufficient quantities to meet such need and are vulnerable to the termination or reduction of the availability of the material.

(n) "Water resources" means all usable water, from all sources, within the jurisdiction of the United States, that can be managed, controlled, and allocated to meet emergency requirements, except "water resources" does not include usable water that qualifies as "food resources."

Sec. 802. General. (a) Except as otherwise provided in section 802(c) of this order, the authorities vested in the President by title VII of the Act, 50 U.S.C. App. 2151 *et seq.*, are delegated to the head of each agency in carrying out the delegated authorities under the Act and this order, by the Secretary of Labor in carrying out part VI of this order, and by the Secretary of the Treasury in exercising the functions assigned in Executive Order 11858, as amended.

(b) The authorities that may be exercised and performed pursuant to section 802(a) of this order shall include:

(1) the power to redelegate authorities, and to authorize the successive redelegation of authorities to agencies, officers, and employees of the Government; and

(2) the power of subpoena under section 705 of the Act, 50 U.S.C. App. 2155, with respect to (i) authorities delegated in parts II, III, and section 702 of this order, and (ii) the functions assigned to the Secretary of the Treasury in Executive Order 11858, as amended, provided that the subpoena power referenced in subsections (i) and (ii) shall be utilized only after the scope and purpose of the investigation, inspection, or inquiry to which the subpoena relates have been defined either by the appropriate officer identified in section 802(a) of this order or by such other person or persons as the officer shall designate.

(c) Excluded from the authorities delegated by section 802(a) of this order are authorities delegated by parts IV and V of this order, authorities in section 721 and 722 of the Act, 50 U.S.C. App. 2170 2171, and the authority with respect to fixing compensation under section 703 of the Act, 50 U.S.C. App. 2153.

Sec. 803. Authority. (a) Executive Order 12919 of June 3, 1994, and sections 401(3) (4) of Executive Order 12656 of November 18, 1988, are revoked. All other previously issued orders, regulations, rulings, certificates, directives, and other actions relating to any function affected by this order shall remain in effect except as they are inconsistent with this order or are subsequently amended or revoked under proper authority. Nothing in this order shall affect the validity or force of anything done under previous delegations or other assignment of authority under the Act.

(b) Nothing in this order shall affect the authorities assigned under Executive Order 11858 of May 7, 1975, as amended, except as provided in section 802 of this order.

(c) Nothing in this order shall affect the authorities assigned under Executive Order 12472 of April 3, 1984, as amended.

Sec. 804. General Provisions. (a) Nothing in this order shall be construed to impair or otherwise affect functions of the Director of OMB relating to budgetary, administrative, or legislative proposals.

(b) This order shall be implemented consistent with applicable law and subject to the availability of appropriations.

(c) This order is not intended to, and does not, create any right or benefit, substantive or procedural, enforceable at law or in equity by any party against the United States, its departments, agencies, or entities, its officers, employees, or agents, or any other person.

BARACK OBAMA
THE WHITE HOUSE
March 16, 2012.

Source: www.WhiteHouse.gov
Official Copy Available:
Federal Register / Vol. 77, No. 56 / Thursday, March 22, 2012 / Presidential Documents
Presidential Executive Order: 13603
http://www.gpo.gov/fdsys/pkg/FR-2012-03-22/pdf/2012-7019.pdf

Appendix 9

U.S. Constitution
and Bill of Rights

The Constitution and Bill of Rights are the basis on which all other international, federal, state and local laws, government regulations, and presidential Executive Orders are legitimized or cancelled out. This is the supreme law of the land for the United States of America, which is a sovereign nation. No person, government official, agency, court (including the Supreme Court) or Congress, other nation or United Nations, can supersede what is stipulated in these foundational documents except by successful completion of the revision process which is articulated in the Constitution.

The U.S. Constitution and Bill of Rights are not 'living documents.' Moreover, these principles are not subject to modern or 'progressive' interpretation, nor suspension for expediency, war, or a State of Emergency.

When additional clarity is needed to understand a passage contained in one of these documents, it must be based entirely on the original meaning of the words and phrases that were penned by the nation's Founding Fathers. The original meaning of each provision in these two documents is easily determined by other historic documents of the Founding period.

Topics not covered in these documents cannot be appropriated by the federal government. These remain exclusively in the jurisdiction of individuals and their state and local governments.

Constitution of the United States of America

– – – – – – –

WE THE PEOPLE of the United States, in Order to form a more perfect Union, establish Justice, insure domestic Tranquility, provide for the common defence, promote the general Welfare, and secure the Blessings of Liberty to ourselves and our Posterity, do ordain and establish this Constitution for the United States of America.

Article. I.
Section. 1.

All legislative Powers herein granted shall be vested in a Congress of the United States, which shall consist of a Senate and House of Representatives.

Section. 2.

The House of Representatives shall be composed of Members chosen every second Year by the People of the several States, and the Electors in each State shall have the Qualifications requisite for Electors of the most numerous Branch of the State Legislature.

No Person shall be a Representative who shall not have attained to the Age of twenty five Years, and been seven Years a Citizen of the United States, and who shall not, when elected, be an Inhabitant of that State in which he shall be chosen.

Representatives and direct Taxes shall be apportioned among the several States which may be included within this Union, according to their respective Numbers, which shall be determined by adding to the whole Number of free Persons, including those bound to Service for a Term of Years, and excluding Indians not taxed, three fifths of all other Persons. The actual Enumeration shall be made within three Years after the first Meeting of the Congress of the United States, and within every subsequent Term of ten Years, in such Manner as they shall by Law direct. The Number of Representatives shall not exceed one for every thirty Thousand, but each State shall have at Least one Representative; and until such enumeration shall be made, the State of New Hampshire shall be entitled to chuse three, Massachusetts eight, Rhode-Island and Providence Plantations one, Connecticut five, New-York six, New Jersey four, Pennsylvania eight, Delaware one, Maryland six, Virginia ten, North Carolina five, South Carolina five, and Georgia three.

When vacancies happen in the Representation from any State, the Executive Authority thereof shall issue Writs of Election to fill such Vacancies.

The House of Representatives shall chuse their Speaker and other Officers; and shall have the sole Power of Impeachment.

Section. 3.

The Senate of the United States shall be composed of two Senators from each State, **chosen by the Legislature** thereof for six Years; and each Senator shall have one Vote.

Immediately after they shall be assembled in Consequence of the first Election, they shall be divided as equally as may be into three Classes. The Seats of the Senators of the first Class shall be vacated at the Expiration of the second Year, of the second Class at the Expiration of the fourth Year, and of the third Class at the

Expiration of the sixth Year, so that one third may be chosen every second Year; **and if Vacancies happen by Resignation, or otherwise, during the Recess of the Legislature of any State, the Executive thereof may make temporary Appointments until the next Meeting of the Legislature, which shall then fill such Vacancies**.

No Person shall be a Senator who shall not have attained to the Age of thirty Years, and been nine Years a Citizen of the United States, and who shall not, when elected, be an Inhabitant of that State for which he shall be chosen.

The Vice President of the United States shall be President of the Senate, but shall have no Vote, unless they be equally divided.

The Senate shall chuse their other Officers, and also a President pro tempore, in the Absence of the Vice President, or when he shall exercise the Office of President of the United States.

The Senate shall have the sole Power to try all Impeachments. When sitting for that Purpose, they shall be on Oath or Affirmation. When the President of the United States is tried, the Chief Justice shall preside: And no Person shall be convicted without the Concurrence of two thirds of the Members present.

Judgment in Cases of Impeachment shall not extend further than to removal from Office, and disqualification to hold and enjoy any Office of honor, Trust or Profit under the United States: but the Party convicted shall nevertheless be liable and subject to Indictment, Trial, Judgment and Punishment, according to Law.

Section. 4.

The Times, Places and Manner of holding Elections for Senators and Representatives, shall be prescribed in each State by the Legislature thereof; but the Congress may at any time by Law make or alter such Regulations, except as to the Places of chusing Senators.

The Congress shall assemble at least once in every Year, and such Meeting shall **be on the first Monday in December**, unless they shall by Law appoint a different Day.

Section. 5.

Each House shall be the Judge of the Elections, Returns and Qualifications of its own Members, and a Majority of each shall constitute a Quorum to do Business; but a smaller Number may adjourn from day to day, and may be authorized to compel the Attendance of absent Members, in such Manner, and under such Penalties as each House may provide.

Each House may determine the Rules of its Proceedings, punish its Members for disorderly Behaviour, and, with the Concurrence of two thirds, expel a Member.

Each House shall keep a Journal of its Proceedings, and from time to time publish the same, excepting such Parts as may in their Judgment require Secrecy; and the Yeas and Nays of the Members of either House on any question shall, at the Desire of one fifth of those Present, be entered on the Journal.

Neither House, during the Session of Congress, shall, without the Consent of the other, adjourn for more than three days, nor to any other Place than that in which the two Houses shall be sitting.

Section. 6.

The Senators and Representatives shall receive a Compensation for their Services, to be ascertained by Law, and paid out of the Treasury of the United States. They shall in all Cases, except Treason, Felony and Breach of the Peace, be privileged from Arrest during their Attendance at the Session of their respective Houses, and in going to and returning from the same; and for any Speech or Debate in either House, they shall not be questioned in any other Place.

No Senator or Representative shall, during the Time for which he was elected, be appointed to any civil Office under the Authority of the United States, which shall have been created, or the Emoluments whereof shall have been encreased during such time; and no Person holding any Office under the United States, shall be a Member of either House during his Continuance in Office.

Section. 7.

All Bills for raising Revenue shall originate in the House of Representatives; but the Senate may propose or concur with Amendments as on other Bills.

Every Bill which shall have passed the House of Representatives and the Senate, shall, before it become a Law, be presented to the President of the United States: If he approve he shall sign it, but if not he shall return it, with his Objections to that House in which it shall have originated, who shall enter the Objections at large on their Journal, and proceed to reconsider it. If after such Reconsideration two thirds of that House shall agree to pass the Bill, it shall be sent, together with the Objections, to the other House, by which it shall likewise be reconsidered, and if approved by two thirds of that House, it shall become a Law. But in all such Cases the Votes of both Houses shall be determined by yeas and Nays, and the Names of the Persons voting for and against the Bill shall be entered on the Journal of each House respectively. If any Bill shall not be returned by the President within ten Days (Sundays excepted) after it shall have been presented to him, the Same shall be a Law, in like Manner as if he had signed it, unless the Congress by their Adjournment prevent its Return, in which Case it shall not be a Law.

Every Order, Resolution, or Vote to which the Concurrence of the Senate and House of Representatives may be necessary (except on a question of Adjournment) shall be presented to the President of the United States; and before the Same shall take Effect, shall be approved by him, or being disapproved by him, shall be repassed by two thirds of the Senate and House of Representatives, according to the Rules and Limitations prescribed in the Case of a Bill.

Section. 8.

The Congress shall have Power To lay and collect Taxes, Duties, Imposts and Excises, to pay the Debts and provide for the common Defence and general Welfare of the United States; but all Duties, Imposts and Excises shall be uniform throughout the United States;

To borrow Money on the credit of the United States;

To regulate Commerce with foreign Nations, and among the several States, and with the Indian Tribes;

To establish an uniform Rule of Naturalization, and uniform Laws on the subject of Bankruptcies throughout the United States;

To coin Money, regulate the Value thereof, and of foreign Coin, and fix the Standard of Weights and Measures;

To provide for the Punishment of counterfeiting the Securities and current Coin of the United States;

To establish Post Offices and post Roads;

To promote the Progress of Science and useful Arts, by securing for limited Times to Authors and Inventors the exclusive Right to their respective Writings and Discoveries;

To constitute Tribunals inferior to the supreme Court;

To define and punish Piracies and Felonies committed on the high Seas, and Offences against the Law of Nations;

To declare War, grant Letters of Marque and Reprisal, and make Rules concerning Captures on Land and Water;

To raise and support Armies, but no Appropriation of Money to that Use shall be for a longer Term than two Years;

To provide and maintain a Navy;

To make Rules for the Government and Regulation of the land and naval Forces;

To provide for calling forth the Militia to execute the Laws of the Union, suppress Insurrections and repel Invasions;

To provide for organizing, arming, and disciplining, the Militia, and for governing such Part of them as may be employed in the Service of the United States, reserving to the States respectively, the Appointment of the Officers, and the Authority of training the Militia according to the discipline prescribed by Congress;

To exercise exclusive Legislation in all Cases whatsoever, over such District (not exceeding ten Miles square) as may, by Cession of particular States, and the Acceptance of Congress, become the Seat of the Government of the United States, and to exercise like Authority over all Places purchased by the Consent of the Legislature of the State in which the Same shall be, for the Erection of Forts, Magazines, Arsenals, dock-Yards, and other needful Buildings;--And

To make all Laws which shall be necessary and proper for carrying into Execution the foregoing Powers, and all other Powers vested by this Constitution in the Government of the United States, or in any Department or Officer thereof.

Section. 9.

The Migration or Importation of such Persons as any of the States now existing shall think proper to admit, shall not be prohibited by the Congress prior to the Year one thousand eight hundred and eight, but a Tax or duty may be imposed on such Importation, not exceeding ten dollars for each Person.

The Privilege of the Writ of Habeas Corpus shall not be suspended, unless when in Cases of Rebellion or Invasion the public Safety may require it.

No Bill of Attainder or ex post facto Law shall be passed.

No Capitation, or other direct, Tax shall be laid, **unless in Proportion to the Census or enumeration herein before directed to be taken.**

No Tax or Duty shall be laid on Articles exported from any State.

No Preference shall be given by any Regulation of Commerce or Revenue to the Ports of one State over those of another; nor shall Vessels bound to, or from, one State, be obliged to enter, clear, or pay Duties in another.

No Money shall be drawn from the Treasury, but in Consequence of Appropriations made by Law; and a regular Statement and Account of the Receipts and Expenditures of all public Money shall be published from time to time.

No Title of Nobility shall be granted by the United States: And no Person holding any Office of Profit or Trust under them, shall, without the Consent of the Congress, accept of any present, Emolument, Office, or Title, of any kind whatever, from any King, Prince, or foreign State.

Section. 10.

No State shall enter into any Treaty, Alliance, or Confederation; grant Letters of Marque and Reprisal; coin Money; emit Bills of Credit; make any Thing but gold and silver Coin a Tender in Payment of Debts; pass any Bill of Attainder, ex post facto Law, or Law impairing the Obligation of Contracts, or grant any Title of Nobility.

No State shall, without the Consent of the Congress, lay any Imposts or Duties on Imports or Exports, except what may be absolutely necessary for executing it's inspection Laws: and the net Produce of all Duties and Imposts, laid by any State on Imports or Exports, shall be for the Use of the Treasury of the United States; and all such Laws shall be subject to the Revision and Controul of the Congress.

No State shall, without the Consent of Congress, lay any Duty of Tonnage, keep Troops, or Ships of War in time of Peace, enter into any Agreement or Compact with another State, or with a foreign Power, or engage in War, unless actually invaded, or in such imminent Danger as will not admit of delay.

Article. II.
Section. 1.

The executive Power shall be vested in a President of the United States of America. He shall hold his Office during the Term of four Years, and, together with the Vice President, chosen for the same Term, be elected, as follows:

Each State shall appoint, in such Manner as the Legislature thereof may direct, a Number of Electors, equal to the whole Number of Senators and Representatives to which the State may be entitled in the Congress: but no Senator or Representative, or Person holding an Office of Trust or Profit under the United States, shall be appointed an Elector.

The Electors shall meet in their respective States, and vote by Ballot for two Persons, of whom one at least shall not be an Inhabitant of the same State with themselves. And they shall make a List of all the Persons voted for, and of the Number of Votes for each; which List they shall sign and certify, and transmit sealed to the Seat of the Government of the United States, directed to the President of the Senate. The President of the Senate shall, in the Presence of the Senate and House of Representatives, open all the Certificates, and the Votes shall then be counted. The Person having the greatest Number of Votes shall be the President, if such Number be a Majority of the whole Number of Electors appointed; and if there be more than one who have such Majority, and have an equal Number of Votes, then the House of Representatives shall immediately chuse by Ballot one of them for President; and if no Person have a Majority, then from the five highest on the List the said House shall in like Manner chuse the President. But in chusing the President, the Votes shall be taken by States, the Representation from each State having one Vote; A quorum for this purpose shall consist of a Member or Members from two thirds of the States, and a Majority of all the States shall be necessary to a Choice. In every Case, after the Choice of the President, the Person having the greatest Number of

Votes of the Electors shall be the Vice President. But if there should remain two or more who have equal Votes, the Senate shall chuse from them by Ballot the Vice President.

The Congress may determine the Time of chusing the Electors, and the Day on which they shall give their Votes; which Day shall be the same throughout the United States.

No Person except a natural born Citizen, or a Citizen of the United States, at the time of the Adoption of this Constitution, shall be eligible to the Office of President; neither shall any Person be eligible to that Office who shall not have attained to the Age of thirty five Years, and been fourteen Years a Resident within the United States.

In Case of the Removal of the President from Office, or of his Death, Resignation, or Inability to discharge the Powers and Duties of the said Office, the Same shall devolve on the Vice President, and the Congress may by Law provide for the Case of Removal, Death, Resignation or Inability, both of the President and Vice President, declaring what Officer shall then act as President, and such Officer shall act accordingly, until the Disability be removed, or a President shall be elected

The President shall, at stated Times, receive for his Services, a Compensation, which shall neither be increased nor diminished during the Period for which he shall have been elected, and he shall not receive within that Period any other Emolument from the United States, or any of them.

Before he enter on the Execution of his Office, he shall take the following Oath or Affirmation:--"I do solemnly swear (or affirm) that I will faithfully execute the Office of President of the United States, and will to the best of my Ability, preserve, protect and defend the Constitution of the United States."

Section. 2.

The President shall be Commander in Chief of the Army and Navy of the United States, and of the Militia of the several States, when called into the actual Service of the United States; he may require the Opinion, in writing, of the principal Officer in each of the executive Departments, upon any Subject relating to the Duties of their respective Offices, and he shall have Power to grant Reprieves and Pardons for Offences against the United States, except in Cases of Impeachment.

He shall have Power, by and with the Advice and Consent of the Senate, to make Treaties, provided two thirds of the Senators present concur; and he shall nominate, and by and with the Advice and Consent of the Senate, shall appoint Ambassadors, other public Ministers and Consuls, Judges of the supreme Court, and all other Officers of the United States, whose Appointments are not herein otherwise provided for, and which shall be established by Law: but the Congress may by Law vest the Appointment of such inferior Officers, as they think proper, in the President alone, in the Courts of Law, or in the Heads of Departments.

The President shall have Power to fill up all Vacancies that may happen during the Recess of the Senate, by granting Commissions which shall expire at the End of their next Session.

Section. 3.

He shall from time to time give to the Congress Information of the State of the Union, and recommend to their Consideration such Measures as he shall judge necessary and expedient; he may, on extraordinary Occasions, convene both Houses, or either of them, and in Case of Disagreement between them, with Respect to the Time of Adjournment, he may adjourn them to such Time as he shall think proper; he shall receive Ambassadors and other public Ministers; he shall take Care that the Laws be faithfully executed, and shall Commission all the Officers of the United States.

Section. 4.

The President, Vice President and all civil Officers of the United States, shall be removed from Office on Impeachment for, and Conviction of, Treason, Bribery, or other high Crimes and Misdemeanors.

Article III.
Section. 1.

The judicial Power of the United States shall be vested in one supreme Court, and in such inferior Courts as the Congress may from time to time ordain and establish. The Judges, both of the supreme and inferior Courts, shall hold their Offices during good Behaviour, and shall, at stated Times, receive for their Services a Compensation, which shall not be diminished during their Continuance in Office.

Section. 2.

The judicial Power shall extend to all Cases, in Law and Equity, arising under this Constitution, the Laws of the United States, and Treaties made, or which shall be made, under their Authority;--to all Cases affecting Ambassadors, other public Ministers and Consuls;--to all Cases of admiralty and maritime Jurisdiction;--to Controversies to which the United States shall be a Party;--to Controversies between two or more States;--**between a State and Citizens of another State**,--between Citizens of different States,--between Citizens of the same State claiming Lands under Grants of different States, and between a State, or the Citizens thereof, and foreign States, Citizens or Subjects.

In all Cases affecting Ambassadors, other public Ministers and Consuls, and those in which a State shall be Party, the supreme Court shall have original Jurisdiction. In all the other Cases before mentioned, the supreme Court shall have appellate Jurisdiction, both as to Law and Fact, with such Exceptions, and under such Regulations as the Congress shall make.

The Trial of all Crimes, except in Cases of Impeachment, shall be by Jury; and such Trial shall be held in the State where the said Crimes shall have been committed; but when not committed within any State, the Trial shall be at such Place or Places as the Congress may by Law have directed.

Section. 3.

Treason against the United States, shall consist only in levying War against them, or in adhering to their Enemies, giving them Aid and Comfort. No Person shall be convicted of Treason unless on the Testimony of two Witnesses to the same overt Act, or on Confession in open Court.

The Congress shall have Power to declare the Punishment of Treason, but no Attainder of Treason shall work Corruption of Blood, or Forfeiture except during the Life of the Person attainted.

Article. IV.
Section. 1.

Full Faith and Credit shall be given in each State to the public Acts, Records, and judicial Proceedings of every other State. And the Congress may by general Laws prescribe the Manner in which such Acts, Records and Proceedings shall be proved, and the Effect thereof.

Section. 2.

The Citizens of each State shall be entitled to all Privileges and Immunities of Citizens in the several States.

A Person charged in any State with Treason, Felony, or other Crime, who shall flee from Justice, and be found in another State, shall on Demand of the executive Authority of the State from which he fled, be delivered up, to be removed to the State having Jurisdiction of the Crime.

No Person held to Service or Labour in one State, under the Laws thereof, escaping into another, shall, in Consequence of any Law or Regulation therein, be discharged from such Service or Labour, but shall be delivered up on Claim of the Party to whom such Service or Labour may be due.

Section. 3.

New States may be admitted by the Congress into this Union; but no new State shall be formed or erected within the Jurisdiction of any other State; nor any State be formed by the Junction of two or more States, or Parts of States, without the Consent of the Legislatures of the States concerned as well as of the Congress.

The Congress shall have Power to dispose of and make all needful Rules and Regulations respecting the Territory or other Property belonging to the United States; and nothing in this Constitution shall be so construed as to Prejudice any Claims of the United States, or of any particular State.

Section. 4.

The United States shall guarantee to every State in this Union a Republican Form of Government, and shall protect each of them against Invasion; and on Application of the Legislature, or of the Executive (when the Legislature cannot be convened), against domestic Violence.

Article. V.

The Congress, whenever two thirds of both Houses shall deem it necessary, shall propose Amendments to this Constitution, or, on the Application of the Legislatures of two thirds of the several States, shall call a Convention for proposing Amendments, which, in either Case, shall be valid to all Intents and Purposes, as Part of this Constitution, when ratified by the Legislatures of three fourths of the several States, or by Conventions in three fourths thereof, as the one or the other Mode of Ratification may be proposed by the Congress; Provided that no Amendment which may be made prior to the Year One thousand eight hundred and eight shall in any Manner affect the first and fourth Clauses in the Ninth Section of the first Article; and that no State, without its Consent, shall be deprived of its equal Suffrage in the Senate.

Article. VI.

All Debts contracted and Engagements entered into, before the Adoption of this Constitution, shall be as valid against the United States under this Constitution, as under the Confederation.

This Constitution, and the Laws of the United States which shall be made in Pursuance thereof; and all Treaties made, or which shall be made, under the Authority of the United States, shall be the supreme Law of the Land; and the Judges in every State shall be bound thereby, any Thing in the Constitution or Laws of any State to the Contrary notwithstanding.

The Senators and Representatives before mentioned, and the Members of the several State Legislatures, and all executive and judicial Officers, both of the United States and of the several States, shall be bound by Oath or Affirmation, to support this Constitution; but no religious Test shall ever be required as a Qualification to any Office or public Trust under the United States.

Article. VII.

The Ratification of the Conventions of nine States, shall be sufficient for the Establishment of this Constitution between the States so ratifying the Same.

The Word, "the," being interlined between the seventh and eighth Lines of the first Page, the Word "Thirty" being partly written on an Erazure in the fifteenth Line of the first Page, The Words "is tried" being interlined between the thirty second and thirty third Lines of the first Page and the Word "the" being interlined between the forty third and forty fourth Lines of the second Page.

Attest William Jackson Secretary

done in Convention by the Unanimous Consent of the States present the Seventeenth Day of September in the Year of our Lord one thousand seven hundred and Eighty seven and of the Independance of the United States of America the Twelfth In witness whereof We have hereunto subscribed our Names,

Go. Washington
Presidt and deputy from Virginia

Delaware
Geo: Read
Gunning Bedford jun
John Dickinson
Richard Bassett
Jaco: Broom

Maryland
James McHenry
Dan of St Thos. Jenifer
Danl. Carroll

Virginia
John Blair
James Madison Jr.

North Carolina
Wm. Blount
Richd. Dobbs Spaight
Hu Williamson

South Carolina
J. Rutledge
Charles Cotesworth Pinckney
Charles Pinckney
Pierce Butler

Georgia
William Few
Abr Baldwin

New Hampshire
John Langdon
Nicholas Gilman

Massachusetts
Nathaniel Gorham
Rufus King

Connecticut
Wm. Saml. Johnson
Roger Sherman

New York
Alexander Hamilton

New Jersey
Wil: Livingston
David Brearley
Wm. Paterson
Jona: Dayton

Pennsylvania
B Franklin
Thomas Mifflin
Robt. Morris
Geo. Clymer
Thos. FitzSimons
Jared Ingersoll
James Wilson
Gouv Morris

Official Transcript obtained from the U.S. National Archives

Spelling and grammar is as used in the original document.

The Bill of Rights was added by the nation's Founding Fathers to provide additional clarity to the U.S. Constitution.

Bill of Rights of the United States of America

— — — — — — —

Congress of the United States

begun and held at the City of New-York, on Wednesday the fourth of March, one thousand seven hundred and eighty nine.

THE Conventions of a number of the States, having at the time of their adopting the Constitution, expressed a desire, in order to prevent misconstruction or abuse of its powers, that further declaratory and restrictive clauses should be added: And as extending the ground of public confidence in the Government, will best ensure the beneficent ends of its institution.

RESOLVED by the Senate and House of Representatives of the United States of America, in Congress assembled, two thirds of both Houses concurring, that the following Articles be proposed to the Legislatures of the several States, as amendments to the Constitution of the United States, all, or any of which Articles, when ratified by three fourths of the said Legislatures, to be valid to all intents and purposes, as part of the said Constitution; viz.

ARTICLES in addition to, and Amendment of the Constitution of the United States of America, proposed by Congress, and ratified by the Legislatures of the several States, pursuant to the fifth Article of the original Constitution.

Amendment I

Congress shall make no law respecting an establishment of religion, or prohibiting the free exercise thereof; or abridging the freedom of speech, or of the press; or the right of the people peaceably to assemble, and to petition the Government for a redress of grievances.

Amendment II

A well regulated Militia, being necessary to the security of a free State, the right of the people to keep and bear Arms, shall not be infringed.

Amendment III

No Soldier shall, in time of peace be quartered in any house, without the consent of the Owner, nor in time of war, but in a manner to be prescribed by law.

Amendment IV

The right of the people to be secure in their persons, houses, papers, and effects, against unreasonable searches and seizures, shall not be violated, and no Warrants shall issue, but upon probable cause, supported by Oath or affirmation, and particularly describing the place to be searched, and the persons or things to be seized.

Amendment V

No person shall be held to answer for a capital, or otherwise infamous crime, unless on a presentment or indictment of a Grand Jury, except in cases arising in the land or naval forces, or in the Militia, when in actual service in time of War or public danger; nor shall any person be subject for the same offence to be twice put in jeopardy of life or limb; nor shall be compelled in any criminal case to be a witness against himself, nor be deprived of life, liberty, or property, without due process of law; nor shall private property be taken for public use, without just compensation.

Amendment VI

In all criminal prosecutions, the accused shall enjoy the right to a speedy and public trial, by an impartial jury of the State and district wherein the crime shall have been committed, which district shall have been previously ascertained by law, and to be informed of the nature and cause of the accusation; to be confronted with the witnesses against him; to have compulsory process for obtaining witnesses in his favor, and to have the Assistance of Counsel for his defence.

Amendment VII

In Suits at common law, where the value in controversy shall exceed twenty dollars, the right of trial by jury shall be preserved, and no fact tried by a jury, shall be otherwise re-examined in any Court of the United States, than according to the rules of the common law.

Amendment VIII

Excessive bail shall not be required, nor excessive fines imposed, nor cruel and unusual punishments inflicted.

Amendment IX

The enumeration in the Constitution, of certain rights, shall not be construed to deny or disparage others retained by the people.

Amendment X

The powers not delegated to the United States by the Constitution, nor prohibited by it to the States, are reserved to the States respectively, or to the people.

– – – – – – –

To read the amendments to the Constitution which were enacted after the Bill of Rights was ratified, follow this link to Amendments 11-27:

http://www.archives.gov/exhibits/charters/constitution_amendmen ts_11-27.html

The preceding documents represent the unaltered, official transcript of the U.S. Constitution and the Bill of Rights as obtained from the U.S. National Archives in Washington, D.C.

Made in the USA
Lexington, KY
17 January 2017